THE SCHEME

THE SCHEME

How the Right Wing Used Dark Money to Capture the Supreme Court

Senator Sheldon Whitehouse

with Jennifer Mueller

THE
NEW
PRESS

NEW YORK
LONDON

Published in the United States by The New Press, New York, 2022
Distributed by Two Rivers Distribution

ISBN 978-1-62097-738-5 (hc)
ISBN 978-1-62097-777-4 (ebook)
CIP data is available

The New Press publishes books that promote and enrich public discussion and
understanding of the issues vital to our democracy and to a more equitable world.
These books are made possible by the enthusiasm of our readers; the support
of a committed group of donors, large and small; the collaboration of our many
partners in the independent media and the not-for-profit sector; booksellers, who
often hand-sell New Press books; librarians; and above all by our authors.

www.thenewpress.com

Composition by dix!
This book was set in Electra

*This book is dedicated to the small brave band of writers, researchers,
and scientists who investigate and report on the poisonous creep
of secret influence into America's democracy. They include Jane Mayer,
Naomi Oreskes, Nancy MacLean, Michael Mann, Bob Brulle,
Riley Dunlap, Justin Farrell, and Lisa Graves, among others.*

*Their warnings have received too little attention,
but history will note their work.*
—S.W.

For Ana, Christopher, Thomas, and Julia
—J.M.

Justice removed, then, what are kingdoms but great bands of robbers?

—SAINT AUGUSTINE

Contents

Part V: Method

Part VI: A Susceptible Victim: The Compromised Court

Part VII: Payday: The Captured Court

Part VIII: Rebuttal

Part IX: Closing Argument

THE SCHEME

Introduction

A judiciary independent of the Nation . . . can turn its guns on
those it was meant to defend.

—THOMAS JEFFERSON

THERE IS A SCHEME AFOOT.

If that sounds dramatic, it should. Because it involves a decades-
long effort by a handful of corporate oligarchs to subvert American democracy by capturing the Supreme Court and making it their Court,
not our Court. It's happening right under our noses. And it puts at
risk one of our most cherished American principles: equal justice under law.

The Scheme has penetrated deeply into all of our federal courts,
but its prize is the Supreme Court. The buck stops, as they say, with
the Supreme Court: there is no higher authority that can be appealed
to once it has issued a constitutional decision, all roads of review
lead to the Court, and escalating gridlock and dysfunction in Congress hamper legislative correction when the Court undoes or rewrites
a law. Despite all this power, remarkably, no Supreme Court justice,
conservative or liberal, is bound by the judicial code of ethics that
constrains all other federal judges.

Because its actions are essentially unreviewable and its members
serve for life without having to answer to the public, the Supreme
Court has the power to overturn precedent, ignore evidence, and
reshape the law, immunized from electoral consequence. In case

after case, this is exactly what the Court under Chief Justice John Roberts has done. In literally dozens of partisan decisions that ignore both precedent and principle, the Roberts Court has advanced a far-right agenda that is deeply out of touch with the will of most Americans—unleashing massive amounts of dark money, impeding citizens from voting, allowing corporations to dodge lawsuits and liability, undermining civil rights, and denying individuals access to juries.

The path to this point was not politics as usual. Set aside Mitch McConnell's unconscionable refusal even to hold a hearing for Merrick Garland, President Obama's nominee to fill the seat vacated by Justice Scalia's death. Set aside the troubling non-investigation by the FBI into the allegations about Brett Kavanaugh. Set aside the unseemly and unprecedented rush to fill Justice Ginsburg's seat while voting in the 2020 election was under way across the country. Those actions were viscerally enraging, but they're not as sinister as the millions of dollars of dark money that flowed into campaigns and political coffers to secure the confirmations of Neil Gorsuch, Brett Kavanaugh, and Amy Coney Barrett. They're not as dangerous as President Trump's public "insourcing" of a private organization, the Federalist Society— also funded by dark money—to name, vet, and approve his judicial nominees. And they're not as alarming as the millions—likely billions—of dollars in dark money that corporate oligarchs have spent for decades to cook up and push fringe legal theories that undermine even the federal government itself.

A handful of Republican Supreme Court justices opened the floodgates to this dark money, and the donors who got them there have been rewarded handsomely. A single anonymous donor spent more than $17 million in both the Gorsuch and the Kavanaugh confirmation battles to secure the nominee's ascension to the Court (and in a sign of how broken our disclosure system is, we will likely never know who the donor is or what business he or she had before the Court—nor do we yet know what money was spent on the Barrett confirmation). All told, researchers have tracked at least $580 million spent by people who don't want you to know who they are, but who are hell-bent on remaking the federal courts. Over half a billion dollars is a massive investment.* Who was paying, and what did they think they were getting for their money?

This is the Scheme: a decades-long, behind-the-scenes manipulation of our political and justice systems to capture our courts—especially the Supreme Court—as a way to control the future of our democracy.

The trail left behind by the Scheme can be viewed the way a prosecutor considers evidence of a crime. Was there a motive? Were the means available to do the deed? Was there a plan, and a method to execute the plan? Were there efforts at secrecy and subterfuge? At the end of the day, were there proceeds of the crime, and who ended up benefiting from those proceeds?

I didn't set out looking for a scheme. In the beginning, I was simply trying to understand an apparent paradox: why, as science established ever more conclusively that climate change presents a clear and present danger to our way of life, did Republican senators increasingly deny the data and refuse to support commonsense policies to limit fossil fuel emissions? After all, not long ago Republicans prided themselves on being the party of facts and figures, the party whose president established the Environmental Protection Agency in 1970.

I came to the Senate in 2007. In those first years, climate change was a bipartisan concern. At least three strong bipartisan climate bills were kicking around in the Senate, and John McCain (who was to become a dear friend) had a strong climate platform in his 2008 Republican presidential campaign.

Then in January 2010 all that bipartisanship stopped, as if a switch had been turned off. Climate progress died. The sudden shift came immediately after a bare majority of Republican-appointed justices set loose unlimited political spending in the Supreme Court's disastrous *Citizens United* decision.

Before joining the Senate, I'd spent decades as an attorney,

---

*The *Washington Post* first estimated the number at $250 million dollars; in my Judiciary subcommittee hearing, Center for Media and Democracy's Lisa Graves raised the estimate to $400 million; on March 22, 2022, upon further research, Graves raised the estimate to $580 million.[1]

including as Rhode Island's U.S. attorney and attorney general. I'd been around politics a while—investigating political crimes, working in political campaigns, negotiating political deals, understanding political institutions and their norms and rules, and seeing human behavior in the political ecosystem. I'd learned that when I saw people acting in a way that didn't make sense, I should look offstage to see who was pulling their strings.

So to understand this paradox, I began to "follow the money." I discovered a network of trade associations, think tanks, front groups, and political organizations acting in concert to deny climate change. It was hard to discern the true sources of funding for this apparatus, in part because my Republican colleagues blocked laws and regulations that would reveal the donors—and in part because an increasingly complicit Supreme Court let dark money flow. But year after year, researchers and investigative reporters painstakingly dug through paper records to connect the dots.

A picture began to emerge. Supposedly independent organizations were revealed to have overlapping directors, staff, and even locations. The web of groups appeared to be funded and directed by a small group of radical right-wing billionaires. And it had purposes beyond just climate denial.

I don't say "radical" lightly. I don't know how else to describe a philosophy that elevates a corporation's "freedom" to pollute over the freedom of everyone else to breathe clean air and drink clean water, that seeks to replace trial by jury with a private process funded by the very corporations whose actions are being challenged (guess how often the little guy wins), or that actively works to squelch public participation in the world's greatest democracy.

I first reported on what I had learned in my book *Captured*, which I finished just weeks after the 2016 election. This current book isn't about Donald Trump, but let's just say nothing that happened in our agencies or in Congress during the Trump years should have surprised anyone who'd been watching dark money operate in Washington. The only thing surprising was how much worse things got, and how quickly, and how badly we had overlooked the aim of all these machinations to install reliable, reactionary policy agents on the Supreme Court.

In the Senate, not much happened on the legislative front during the Trump years. Even though the House sent us hundreds of bills, most of them bipartisan, Senate Majority Leader Mitch McConnell sent them to his legislative graveyard. His goal was not legislating. His single focus was to appoint as many judges to the federal bench as possible, even if that meant violating Senate norms and confirming nominees rated "unqualified" by the nonpartisan American Bar Association.

By the time President Trump left office, the Senate had confirmed 234 judges to lifetime appointments—more than a quarter of the federal judiciary and nearly a third of the active federal appellate bench. The trophies included three seats on the U.S. Supreme Court—for Justices Neil Gorsuch, Brett Kavanaugh, and Amy Coney Barrett— shifting what had been a balanced 4–4 conservative–liberal Court (after Justice Scalia's death) to an activist 6–3 Court, likely for most of our lifetimes. Veteran *Washington Post* reporter Ruth Marcus explained the impact of this shift at the start of the Court's 2021 term:

A five-justice majority is inherently fragile. It necessitates compromise and discourages overreach. Five justices tend to proceed with baby steps.

A six-justice majority is a different animal. A six-justice majority, such as the one now firmly in control, is the judicial equivalent of the monarchy's "heir and a spare." The pathways to victory are enlarged. The overall impact is far greater than the single-digit difference suggests.

On the current court, each conservative justice enjoys the prospect of being able to corral four colleagues, if not all five, in support of his or her beliefs, point of view or pet projects, whether that is outlawing affirmative action, ending constitutional protection for abortion, exalting religious liberty over all other rights or restraining the power of government agencies.

A six-justice majority is emboldened rather than hesitant; so, too, are the conservative advocates who appear before it. Such a court doesn't need to trim its sails, hedge its language, or abide by legal niceties if it seems more convenient to dispense with them.[2]

As I watched Senate rules and norms bent and broken in the rush to appoint Trump judges—and especially to rig the Supreme Court—I realized that the Supreme Court wasn't just a target of the Scheme; it was enabling the Scheme. There was a feedback loop between the Scheme and the Court. And my heart sank to realize that if the right-wing corporate oligarchs succeeded in capturing the Court, the results could forever damage our American republic, its integrity, and its principle of majority rule. They weren't just in it to win cases; they were out to change America.

This is a serious charge, and I do not make it lightly. I make the same request of you that lawyers make to men and women of the jury: that you set aside your preconceived notions, consider the evidence, and draw reasonable inferences. Decide for yourself if my alarm is justified. Look at the patterns of behavior, including well-documented previous efforts by corporate powers to "capture" regulatory agencies. Look at hard black-and-white facts and figures measuring the tsunami of dark money that gushes into our politics and flows around the Court. Look at what my Senate colleagues and I have witnessed firsthand over the last several years. Some of the evidence is what in court we would call "rebuttal," because it refutes the explanation that what's going on at the Court is just a difference of opinion over legal doctrines or principles, or that both sides are playing the same game.

Think of me as a prosecutor presenting my case. Or, if *Law & Order* isn't your thing, consider me your field biologist, bringing you a report from my political ecosystem. A hunter can read things in the woods that a city kid doesn't notice happening, and a city kid can read what's going down on the streets where a hunter from the woods would be clueless.

The classic film *The Usual Suspects* features the memorable line "The greatest trick the devil ever pulled was convincing the world that he didn't exist." The Scheme would love you to think it doesn't exist. But I have found clues and made deductions; I invite you to examine them with me. (If there was a silver lining to President Trump's election, it was that it threw the Scheme into high gear, churning up a lot of nasty stuff—including considerable evidence of its existence.) Sometimes a clue will be no more than weird and inexplicable behavior, or a hypocritical reversal, or an action against apparent interest, or something conspicuously hidden. Sometimes there's a surprising admission, and sometimes you can follow the money. The story became clear to me as I put the pieces together. My goal here is to help you connect the dots, so you too can see what I see.

Because of the secrecy of the Scheme, much of the evidence I will provide is what a court would consider "circumstantial." Here is what federal courts tell juries about circumstantial evidence: "Circumstantial evidence is the proof of a series of facts that tend to show whether the defendant is guilty or not guilty."[3] Juries deduce what is logical to believe from those facts. Juries are told: "The law makes no distinction between the weight to be given either direct or circumstantial evidence. You should decide how much weight to give to any evidence." Circumstantial evidence is valid evidence. Indeed, courts also instruct juries that they may draw reasonable inferences. An example often used in jury instructions is someone coming in from outside closing up a wet umbrella. As a juror, you are entitled to infer that it's raining out, even if you can't see rain falling. It's the reasonable inference.

As you consider what I have seen and what I have learned, consider also that the law allows a judge, when someone hides evidence, to instruct the jury that they may assume the worst about the hidden evidence. A jury may assume that the party hiding the evidence failed to produce it because the evidence was inculpatory, harmful to that party's case. As you consider the rivers and streams of dark money flowing, ask yourself why the donors seek anonymity, and why the front groups need to hide their donors. In baseball, ties go to the runner; in politics, secrecy should cut against anonymous donors and their dark-money organizations.

Let me tell you what this is not about.

This is not about abstract arguments over arcane legal doctrines or principles. In fact, the "Roberts Five" (now Six) have repeatedly abandoned "conservative" legal principles to reach politically desirable outcomes.

It's not about hypothetical harms. The results of the Scheme's success have real-world impacts in the lives of regular people, of workers and consumers, making it harder both to vindicate their rights and to trust a system increasingly rigged against them by shadowy forces.

Nor is it about electoral politics. Yes, I'm a Democrat and speak in political terms, but the Scheme to harness the judiciary is not truly about Republicans versus Democrats. This is rather about deep-pocketed, anti-democratic, *private* forces out to rewrite the laws and the Constitution to their *private* advantage. They know that a captured Court can interpret laws and the Constitution favorably to them, and do so without electoral consequences. Yes, there are Republicans who are willing henchmen in this Scheme, but they are agents, not principals. To find the principals, you have to look for the big donors behind the curtains. I certainly hope that the Grand Old Party can find a way to escape the destructive influence of these secretive donors, but I confess I doubt it. The lure of unlimited political dark money is too attractive.

And this is not a jeremiad against corporations (though I do not doubt that behind a lot of this dark-money smoke and mirrors is likely corporate-powered, and particularly fossil fuel–powered). The corporate form may well be the greatest wealth-generating invention in human history. Economically, it is without peer in the way it allocates risk, aggregates capital, and focuses economic effort. Many corporations, in both the public and the private sectors, are a blessing and a boon to their employees and their communities. They are engines of economic advancement.

But corporate power creeping into our politics is different, and corporate power creeping in secretly is . . . well, creepy. Corporations are different—in purpose, life span, and interests—from us individual human citizens granted rights under our Constitution and Bill of Rights. America is a country of "We, the People," not corporations. Our Founders foresaw no role for corporations in the political body they were creating, and corporate political influence in American democracy comes at our peril.

To understand how dark-money forces have remade our courts and weakened our democracy, look no further than the Supreme Court's current membership. All six of the conservative majority are affiliated with the Federalist Society, a dark-money group that played an oversized role in indoctrinating, grooming, auditioning, and selecting justices for the Court and in shaping what they do there. Five of those six were confirmed to lifetime appointments on our highest court by such a scant Senate majority that the senators approving their confirmation represented fewer Americans than the senators who opposed their confirmation. These justices embody minority rule.

The results haven't just been a disaster for democracy. They have hollowed out the independence of our once-vaunted court system. I have filed more than a dozen "friend of the court" briefs in the Supreme Court in recent years, trying to alert the justices to the dark-money forces that are funding coordinated litigation efforts and creating procedural "fast lanes" around regular litigation procedures. I have flagged the risk to the Court itself if it continues to place its thumb on the scales of justice for the benefit of powerful interests. I have reminded the justices of the "elemental tension" in history between those powerful interests and regular, normal people.* The influencers are a class that occupies itself with favor-seeking from government and wants rules of engagement that make government amenable to its influence; regular, ordinary people mostly just want a government that can and will resist that special-interest influence.

This tension is not new. A hundred years ago, the "influencers" seeking to manipulate the political process represented mills and railroads. A thousand years ago, they were feudal barons and greedy courtiers. Today they are major players in the financial, pharmaceutical, insurance, technology, and fossil fuel industries. The players may have changed, but the game's the same. And no player today is more pernicious than the fossil fuel industry (more on that later). Now, as

---

*I have invoked this phrase in brief after brief that I have filed with the Court. Here is how colleagues and I expressed the point in our brief in *Cedar Point Nursery*, an anti-union case:

. We remind the Court again of the elemental tension we live with in politics and government between two classes of citizens. One is an insider influencer class that occupies itself with rent-seeking from government, and desires rules of political engagement that make government more and more amenable to its power and influence. The second class is the general population, which has an abiding institutional interest in a government with the capacity to resist that special-interest influence. This is a centuries-old tension.[4]

always, the last thing the big influencers want is a robust, functioning government that actually honors the will of the people. Instead, they want power, and they want it without public accountability.

Sadly, research confirms that they have been wildly successful. According to a recent study by professors at Princeton and Northwestern Universities, "the preferences of the average American appear to have only a minuscule, near-zero, statistically non-significant impact upon public policy."[5] And polling shows that regular working people now see their democracy failing to work for them. People on both the right and the left "generally agree that people like them, working people, the poor, and small businesses don't have enough power in Washington, and that political lobbyists, Wall Street, large businesses, and the wealthy have too much influence."[6] By a margin of seven to one, they believe that the Supreme Court will back big business over an individual, rather than vice versa.[7] The win rate of corporate interests before the Roberts Court confirms their intuitions.

My goals in this book are to create a historical record of what's gone haywire, to issue a wake-up call about the sordid role of dark money in our courts and our democracy, and to make the case that the situation merits alarm and correction. Truly, our present Supreme Court is The Court That Dark Money Built. The forces behind that dark money built it for a reason.

PART I

Behind the Scheme

CHAPTER ONE

Climate Denial, Regulatory Capture, and Covert Ops

Evil isn't an army that besieges a city from outside the walls. It is a native of the city. It is the mutiny of the garrison, the poison in the water, the ashes in the bread.

—CHARLES MORGAN

CLIMATE DENIAL

The unlimited money unleashed into politics by the *Citizens United* decision in 2010 powered up the influence of the fossil fuel industry, which went to work hiding its political mischief behind an array of phony front groups and co-opted trade associations. The fossil fuel industry had unlimited political money to spend, a massive motive to spend it, and plenty of screens to hide behind.

The timing of *Citizens United* was especially bad because we Democrats had let a key moment pass in 2009—an episode that broke my heart. In June 2009, Speaker Pelosi passed her cap-and-trade climate bill in the House. We had sixty Democrats then in the Senate, as well as several Republican senators who'd cosponsored big climate bills. And the heartbreaker was: Harry Reid, then the Senate majority leader, told me we'd do nothing on climate. He said the Obama White House had no appetite for a climate fight; they'd had enough conflict over health care, and he'd been told to stand down. We never even passed a tiny little shell of a climate bill to try to get into conference with the House and see what could emerge. We just walked off the field. Pelosi and her House members who had voted on the legislation were left exposed. Consistent with what Harry told me, the White House went dark on climate change, for years afterward rarely even putting the two words in the same sentence. Climate was not revived as an issue until President Obama returned to it in a speech at Georgetown University four years later, in June 2013. By then it was too late.

I remember that the weather for that speech was mercilessly hot. The sun beat down into an airless stone college quadrangle. Jackets were off, and men were sweating through their shirts. People packed into what little corners of shade they could find. Out in the middle of the quadrangle, in the beating sun, shaking hands with students and well-wishers, unperturbed in a bright blue jacket without a bead of sweat, was Speaker Pelosi. She seemed superhuman, as well as super-forgiving.

In a roundabout way, our walk-away from climate in 2009 helped me to uncover the Scheme. It led me to start a series of speeches on climate from the Senate Floor that I called my "Time to Wake Up" speeches. It never crossed my mind that I'd end up doing over 280 of them.[1] I just wanted to be damned sure that no week went by on the Senate Floor without someone at least talking about climate change. Now the Smithsonian wants my battered "Time to Wake Up" poster as the most-used-ever Senate Floor graphic. That's a bitter-tasting historical accomplishment.

I really got into the details in those climate speeches, both about the threat to Earth's natural systems posed by climate change and about what I at first saw as irrational obstruction from my Republican colleagues. After all, there's no reason climate should be a "red" or "blue" issue—we all represent people who have lost their homes to floods, fires, or hurricanes; who have seen crops, herds, or fisheries suffer; who have had their air and water polluted. How had we gone so quickly from regular, bipartisan Senate work on climate change to gridlock?

As I dug deeper, the parts fell into place. *Citizens United* had allowed the fossil fuel industry to use its massive money advantage to strike at this bipartisan progress, and it struck hard. Once the Supreme Court gave it the green light, the fossil fuel industry set its political forces to work instantly, targeting pro-climate-action candidates, particularly Republicans. Congressman Bob Inglis, for instance, was run out of the Republican Party over his climate heresy, crushed in a primary; being "Inglissed" became a word. A lurking climate denial apparatus, funded with anonymous money, shifted into high gear. Outside spending in 2010's congressional races increased by more than $200 million over the previous midterm elections—a nearly 450 percent increase.[2]

My climate speeches became less about polar bears, pteropods, and science, and more about the fossil fuel industry's dark-money front groups, which at any given time numbered sixty or more. I got my education in the dark arts of climate denial. I realized that dark money was the other side of the climate denial coin. On several occasions, I rounded up Senate colleagues to speak in chorus about the "Web of Denial" that dark money funded to block climate action. I came to know the brave band of scientists who track this climate denial operation. I studied, and I learned.

There was a lot of pain and anguish behind those climate speeches, and some anger, too. At the end of the day, I don't know whether my long and often solitary effort accomplished a thing to advance the cause of climate legislation. I was up against the biggest political manipulation and disinformation campaign in modern history. My effort was probably a failure, a lost cause. I couldn't *not* do it, however; I had to try, even if I was only beating my head against a wall. It was frustrating and maddening, and in the end perhaps in vain, but it accomplished one thing: it gave me an education into the massive dark-money apparatus set up by the fossil fuel industry.

So when the decision-making of the Supreme Court began to smell bad, when its decisions seemed increasingly outcome-oriented rather than reasoned in accordance with long-standing judicial principles, I had the instinct to look for dark money and phony front groups. Sure enough, not only did I find them, I found many of the same front groups and donor conduits that I knew from climate denial. They turned up, for instance, when the EPA issued its first-ever plan to limit carbon emissions from power plants and five conservative justices (then including Justice Scalia) blocked the law while it was still under review in the lower courts, before it had even reached them. This was a procedural eyebrow-raiser of a ruling without precedent in U.S.

history, one that I reckon saved the fossil fuel industry $100 billion per year (assuming it would have cost them about one-sixth of their annual federal pollution subsidy).[3]

To put that number in perspective, consider testimony offered before my Judiciary subcommittee that the Scheme to capture the Court had cost at least $400 million—a number later raised by the Center for Media and Democracy to $580 million.[4] It's easy to do the math. For simplicity, let's use the $400 million from the hearing testimony. If you spend $400 million and get a $100 billion annual payback, you make your Court-capture investment back 1,000 times in four years. And that doesn't count all the other helpful decisions a captured Court could provide. Capturing the Supreme Court is a lucrative scheme.

REGULATORY CAPTURE

The Scheme to capture the Court has its roots in "regulatory capture." Decades of research shows that when you regulate an industry, some actors in that industry don't take it well. They don't like oversight, much less oversight that is based on observable facts, that is informed by knowledgeable input and public comment, and that is implemented by career experts who know the industry well. A classic response by regulated entities has been to try to "capture" the agency meant to be overseeing them.

A straight-up bribe could land you in prison, so capture is a longer and subtler game. This is a game with tactics. First and foremost, you try to control who gets appointed to the agency, and stack it with friends of industry. Put people in charge who will decide things your way. You can more or less take the agency over this way.

You can also make sure that friendly members get cushy, well-paid, low-effort jobs when they leave the agency (the proverbial "revolving door"), and that the ones who are not sufficiently friendly get a cold shoulder. That sends a message. You can launch lobbyists at Congress to threaten the agency, putting its funding at risk or challenging its powers. You can bury the agency in paper blizzards of data, or burn its resources with endless litigation. You can develop pet theories that steer the agency toward the outcomes you seek. And you can promote a culture of chumminess so regulators forget they are supposed to be the referees and instead begin to see themselves as the pals of the regulated industry. This is what many people think happened with the SEC in the years leading up to the Great Recession, and what had happened at the Minerals Management Service prior to the massive explosion of BP's drilling rig in the Gulf of Mexico.

Capture is a well-documented phenomenon. Hundreds of academic articles in dozens of academic journals have been written on regulatory capture, sometimes called "agency capture."[5] Big industries capturing agencies of government is a well-known and well-chronicled practice.

For decades, this sordid practice was focused on regulatory agencies. It would have been indecent to think of our courts of justice, let alone our Supreme Court, as just another agency to be captured. But once someone had that idea, once that Rubicon of indecency was crossed, once powerful forces turned their arsenal on the Court, little stood between the Court and those weapons of capture. Once the decision was made to capture it, the Court fell with almost no resistance at all. Regulatory capture became Court capture.

COVERT OPS

In the same way that ordinary decency kept regulatory capture efforts away from the Supreme Court, until it didn't, ordinary decency kept covert ops tactics overseas against foreign targets, until it didn't. Regulatory capture and covert operations became the methodology of the Scheme.

Intelligence agencies around the world use covert operations to meddle secretly in other countries' affairs. The United States has used covert operations to disrupt our foreign adversaries, and the Soviet Union, and now Russia, have been particularly adept at deploying these techniques in satellite nations and within their self-proclaimed sphere of influence. Russia has recently begun targeting us with "information warfare" as well.

There is a tradecraft to deploying that malign influence in other nations and disrupting what might otherwise be a functioning political and social system. The techniques of covert disinformation and manipulation will be familiar to anyone who's a fan of spy novels: agents who pretend to be something other than they really are, hidden funding sources, co-opted local organizations, front groups that obscure who's behind the covert op, false propaganda launched to drive division and spread disinformation. Players in this shadow world persist at falsehoods even when caught lying. Truth isn't the point in covert operations; *dis*information is deployed purposefully to drive social discontent, with the purpose secretly to control elements of the society.

Covert ops are a good model for understanding a key element of court capture: it has to be clandestine. David Robarge, the chief historian of the Central Intelligence Agency, has explained that covert intelligence actions are usually not secretive in their impact—"the whole point . . . is to make things different . . . you want people to notice."[6] The trick is in hiding the hand that is pulling the strings and driving the operation.

To run its climate denial "op," the fossil fuel industry borrowed heavily from the covert ops playbook. And the Scheme borrowed heavily from fossil fuel's climate denial operation. Both operations secretly control things, hide their identities, and can lie with impunity. Staying covert often means evading the laws that require financial transparency and disclosure—laws that are wildly popular across the American political spectrum. An elected official who wants to stay in office long can't very well repeal those laws. But an unelected, unaccountable set of Supreme Court justices can.

In fact, they already have.

CHAPTER TWO

Of Courts and Corporations

[The American system] has had the advantage of relegating questions not only intricate and delicate, but peculiarly liable to excite political passions, to the cool, dry atmosphere of judicial determination.

—JAMES BRYCE

If you want the power to impose unpopular ideas on an unwilling public, courts make an alluring target. After all, federal courts have power. They decide how and when laws should be applied. They decide who is allowed to sue, and on what grounds, and how the case proceeds. They decide when an agency has acted improperly in denying a permit, enforcing a law, or issuing a regulation. They decide whether laws are constitutional. They decide winners and losers in lawsuits, and they set the rules of litigation. Sometimes hundreds of millions of dollars can be at stake; sometimes an entire business model. Federal judges don't have to respect popular opinion. They are appointed for life, removable only by impeachment. "The power thus put in their hands is great," wrote Justice Benjamin Cardozo, "and subject, like all power, to abuse."[1]

So if you're someone used to getting your way, it's worth your time and effort—and millions, perhaps billions, of your dollars—to try to re-orient courts to your liking.

But the Framers of the Constitution didn't make it easy. They understood human nature. They were acutely aware that, in the words of James Madison, "In framing a government which is to be administered by men over men, the great difficulty lies in this: you must first enable the government to control the governed; and in the next place oblige it to control itself."[2] They built into the Constitution failsafes designed to ensure that democracy could survive the inevitable temptations of tyranny and corruption. The Framers worried that a government that served the few rather than the many could ultimately undermine the public's trust, compromising the government they had worked so hard to establish.[3] They were determined that their unprecedented experiment in self-governance should succeed. So they used what they knew of human nature to make American democracy, in twenty-first-century parlance, hack-proof.

They took particular care with the judiciary, with its unrivaled power to act outside democratic control. The Constitution's Article III gives judges a lifetime appointment. They don't need to audition for a future employer or worry about where the next paycheck is coming from if they issue an unpopular ruling. Nor do they have voters to worry about appeasing. They can focus on justice for the parties before them.

Litigants can't ordinarily pick their judge. Selection is usually random, so someone trying to woo or threaten a judge has no guarantee that judge will be assigned to her case. This protection is even stronger with juries. Juries are constituted for one particular case, and only after it is filed, so there's no way to cozy up to jurors beforehand. And tampering with a judge or a jury is a crime.

Another guardrail is appeal, an entirely separate process, and one where judges' jobs change. At trial, judges determine what evidence can be used to decide the case, parties present their evidence and arguments, and judges determine what the facts are and assign culpability. On appeal, judges decide only whether the trial court properly applied the law to the evidence before it. Appellate courts are tasked with reviewing the case as presented in the courts below, not relitigating it, which means that they don't get to engage in their own fact-finding or re-question witnesses.

Even with those safeguards, judicial power remains formidable, and its apex is the Supreme Court of the United States—in lawyer-speak, SCOTUS. All appellate roads lead ultimately to the Supreme

Court. Nine justices sit together on every case, with just five required
to get a majority. As one commentator noted, "if any five agree, they
can go galloping off anywhere they choose."[4] The justices review only
a few cases each year—recently, fewer than one hundred—but those
cases have the potential to change the American social, political, and
economic landscape dramatically.[5]

The decision of the Supreme Court is final. This may seem so
commonplace that it doesn't bear mention, but in fact it is one of the
signs of the strength of our system—and of the public's support for
our common constitutional enterprise. With the mere stroke of a pen,
without fielding an army or flexing a budget, a Court ruling becomes
binding law, obeyed even by those who adamantly disagree. The only
way around this is for Congress to change the law, or for the agency to
rewrite the regulation at issue. If the Court decides an issue of constitutional interpretation, the only escape from the power of its edict is to
amend the Constitution. Court rulings cannot be vetoed, and justices
cannot be voted out of office for an unpopular opinion.

This power in a democracy to override the will of the majority and
simply declare what the law is requires constraint, much of it self-
restraint. As a trio of Republican-appointed justices wrote a generation
ago, "The Court must take care to speak and act in ways that allow
people to accept its decisions on the terms the Court claims for them,
as grounded truly in principle, not as compromises with social and political pressures having, as such, no bearing on the principled choices
that the Court is obliged to make."[6]

One particular constraint under the Constitution is that courts cannot make pronouncements willy-nilly on any law they choose. As Justice Amy Coney Barrett explained to my colleague Lindsey Graham
in her confirmation hearing, "Judges can't just wake up one day and
say, 'I have an agenda. I like guns. I hate guns. I like abortion. I hate
abortion,' and walk in like a royal queen and impose their will on the
world."[7]* Instead, they can rule only on an active dispute that "winds
its way up" to them from the lower courts—a "case or controversy"

---

* It seems ironic now, looking back at her testimony, that once she got on the Court
she would so quickly help destroy abortion rights American women have enjoyed for
half a century.

in the language of the Constitution—brought by parties who actually have something at stake in the outcome. In lawyer-speak, parties must have "standing."

Another constraint is that their decisions must be based on evidence that is vetted in the trial courts. Again, appeals courts are not supposed to go off searching for or making up their own facts, but instead they must decide each case based on their review of the facts that were presented in the trial court below. This rule about appellate fact-finding enforces the "case or controversy" requirement by tethering the appellate court to the actual facts of the actual "case or controversy" before it, rather than letting it indulge in hypotheticals or advisory opinions. We constrain our courts not "to innovate at pleasure," as former Justice Benjamin Cardozo memorably put it a century ago, explaining that a judge "is not a knight-errant, roaming at will in pursuit of his own ideal of beauty or of goodness."[8] The Founders sought to ensure that courts would "have neither force nor will but merely judgment," and not "endanger" the "general liberty of the People" with profligate decision-making.[9]

Another constraint is that once the Supreme Court has decided a question, that decision has the force of precedent. New cases should not provide an invitation for "do-overs" once the law has been settled. Trial courts must follow the precedent established by their circuit courts, and all must follow the precedent established by the Supreme Court, including, ordinarily, the Court itself.* Respect for precedent enforces the view that the law is bigger than individual policy preferences, and it allows public and private parties outside the court a degree of predictability—something to rely on as they establish conforming laws and policies. Respect for precedent, known as "*stare decisis*," is what Cardozo called "the everyday working rule of our law."[10]

The greatest safeguard against judicial mischief is a right of the people that limits the role of a judge altogether, a right that James Madison called "as essential to secure the liberty of the people as any

---

* Federal courts are organized into "circuits" based on geography, with each trial, or district, court organized under a specific appellate, or circuit, court. For example, in my home state of Rhode Island, you would file your case initially in the U.S. District Court for the District of Rhode Island, and if you didn't like the result, you'd file your appeal in the First Circuit.

one of the pre-existent rights of nature."[11] That right is enshrined in our Bill of Rights as the Seventh Amendment to the Constitution: the right to a trial by jury in civil cases. (The right to trial by jury in criminal cases is provided by both Article III Section 2 and the Sixth Amendment.)

It is difficult to overstate how important juries were to our country's Founders. Juries were an English tradition, first established in the twelfth century by Henry II, when the king's emissaries rode out to hear disputes in towns and villages throughout the country. Perhaps Henry thought that a jury of one's peers would mete out justice in a manner that better comported with local norms and traditions. Perhaps he understood the value of "preserv[ing] in the hands of the people that share which they ought to have in the administration of public justice," as famed legal scholar William Blackstone later wrote in his *Commentaries*.[12] Perhaps the king suspected that a group of local men (yes, for a long time it was solely men), chosen from the general populace just before trial, would be less susceptible to, in Blackstone's words again, "the encroachments of the more powerful and wealthy citizens."[13]

Whatever Henry's motivations, civil juries endured through centuries. America's colonists quickly established juries in the New World, and when the British crown interfered with the "Benefits of Trial by Jury," Thomas Jefferson listed this outrage in the Declaration of Independence as a *casus belli* of the Revolution.

The original draft of the Constitution failed to include an explicit guarantee of civil trial by jury. Public reaction was explosive, and the Seventh Amendment resulted. The Founders disagreed on many particulars as they debated these documents, but as Alexander Hamilton wryly noted, "The friends and adversaries of the plan of the convention, if they agree in nothing else, concur at least in the value they set upon the trial by jury; or if there is any difference between them it consists in this: the former regard it as a valuable safeguard to liberty; the latter represent it as the very palladium of free government."[14]

Against all these protections, a systematic, wholesale takeover of courts—to turn them from safe havens for justice to robed tribunals of an anti-democratic elite—seemed unimaginable. (Alas, we'll return later to the slow strangulation of the civil jury by the captured Court, to the Court's fact-finding "knight-errantry," and to its repeated demolition of precedent that stood in its way.) The Founders did not intend a partisan conveyor belt to run through the Senate's "advise and consent" function. They had no intent to unleash a flood of dark big-donor and corporate money into the country's elections. And they did not intend courts as an anti-majoritarian back door for billionaire anti-government donors frustrated that the public hates their ideology.

Courts were special. Courts were different. Courts were sacrosanct.

So when the Scheme was launched to capture the Supreme Court, this was not something to be done overnight. It would be a work of decades, requiring an infrastructure to groom and deploy justices who would be loyal to the forces that secured their appointment. It would require the weakening of these various constraints on courts. It would take government allies in the White House and Senate to ensure that the chosen candidates were appointed and confirmed. It would take public relations campaigns to propagandize the public and to legitimize fringe legal theories.

In short, it would take coordination. It would take time. And it would take money. A lot of money.

Corporate power lurks behind the Scheme to capture the Court, whether through the corporations directly, through billionaire fortunes created by corporations, or through entities established or co-opted to work the will of the corporations and billionaires—through "those that wield," in Teddy Roosevelt's words, "the fortunes amassed through corporate organization."[15]

We have all become used to corporations having immense, even controlling, power in our democracy. Corporate power today dominates my workplace, the Congress. But the Constitution offers no reason that corporations should have any role at all in our politics. The Framers did their best to guard their novel experiment against forces that could corrupt the levers of power and frustrate their efforts at popular self-governance. But they failed to anticipate the role that corporations would claim—and be granted—in American political life.

In the Framers' defense, at the time the Constitution was ratified, corporations were usually chartered for what we think of today as an infrastructure project, like building a road or a canal. State legislatures had the power to revoke their charters if they exceeded their mandate or harmed the local community. When the purpose of the corporation was achieved—the road completed, the canal constructed, the debts paid—the corporation would dissolve.

But things changed. In time, corporate charters permitted a company to operate for any purpose and in perpetuity—and corporate power exploded.

At first, federal courts were wary. As early as 1853, the Supreme Court saw that "to subject the state governments to the combined capital of wealthy corporations [could] produce universal corruption," and warned of "the power and influence" of "the combined wealth wielded by corporations in almost every State."[16] This concern about corporate power and influence was true to Blackstone's warning about "the encroachments of the more powerful and wealthy citizens," now including corporate citizens, and true to the role of courts and juries to protect against these encroachments.[17] (In the Founding Era, Blackstone's *Commentaries* were more likely to be on a lawyer's shelf than any other book except the Bible, so Blackstone is a trustworthy window into the views of our Founders.)

As corporate influence continued to grow, so did popular concern. In 1888, President Grover Cleveland alerted Congress in his State of the Union Address: "Corporations, which should be carefully restrained creatures of law and the servants of people, are fast becoming the people's masters."[18] Nearly two decades later, President Teddy Roosevelt's own address to Congress warned that "[t]he fortunes amassed through corporate organization are now so large, and vest such power in those that wield them, as to make it a matter of necessity to give to the sovereign—that is, to the Government, which represents the people as a whole—some effective power of supervision over their corporate use."[19] A few years later, Roosevelt sounded the alarm again: "[T]he United States must effectively control the mighty commercial forces[.] . . . The absence of effective State, and especially, national, restraint upon unfair money-getting has tended to create a small class of enormously wealthy and economically powerful men, whose chief object is to hold and increase their power."[20]

In 1901, the Great Dissenter, Justice Harlan, warned of a "kind of slavery sought to be fastened on the American people; namely, the slavery that would result from aggregations of capital in the hands of a few individuals and corporations controlling, for their own profit and advantage exclusively, the entire business of the country."[21] Thirty years later, Justice Brandeis spoke of the "insidious menace inherent in large aggregations of capital, particularly when held by corporations."[22] That was then.

As we consider "those that wield" corporate power now in our democracy, remember this: corporate political power was created not by the Constitution but by the Supreme Court, it was created recently, and it was created by Republican appointees to the Court. Remember too that an "influencer class," out to use its power and wealth to gain more power and wealth, is always with us. In that ancient contest between the elite influencer class and the general population that has been its prey since biblical times, the influencers want the Court.

PART II

Motive

CHAPTER THREE

Of Social Gains and Election Losses

[O]ne cannot by fair dealing, and without injury to others, satisfy the nobles, but you can satisfy the people, for their object is more righteous than that of the nobles, the latter wishing to oppress, whilst the former only desire not to be oppressed.

—NICCOLO MACHIAVELLI

WHERE THERE'S A SCHEME, THERE'S USUALLY A MOTIVE. In this case, there were several. The corporate establishment was upset about the upheavals of the 1960s and '70s and the price tag of conforming to rules about consumer safety, union rights, and reducing pollution. A separate, persistent arch-conservative fringe was generally irate about things in America. This fringe could trace its lineage back to pre–Civil War secessionists who believed that "liberty" should mean they had the right to own slaves; the corporatists can be traced back to New Deal opponents who balked at laws that reined in their "laissez-faire" capitalism. These groups' repeated efforts to influence America through regular democratic methods had calamitously failed. That failure rankled.

The 1960s brought powerful upheavals, as a country that had so bravely fought for freedom overseas recognized the mismatch between rhetoric and reality back home. Some of these upheavals were cultural (or countercultural), like Woodstock and the hippie movement. Some were social and political, determined to spread the Founders' egalitarian vision more widely. In 1963, Dr. Martin Luther King Jr. led the civil rights March on Washington, where he gave his famous "I Have a Dream" speech, and in 1965 police beat peaceful protesters—including my future colleague John Lewis—as they crossed the Edmund Pettus Bridge in Alabama. In 1968, women's rights protesters converged in Atlantic City to protest the Miss America pageant, decrying it as sexist. In 1969, gay Americans launched protests for gay rights, including the Stonewall Riots. The environmental movement burst into prominence after Ohio's Cuyahoga River burst into flames in 1969.

By the late 1960s, executives faced a public increasingly adamant that corporations should be held accountable for poorly designed, unsafe products. Consumer activists like Ralph Nader had the radical idea that a reasonable response to highway carnage was requiring car companies to sell cars that had seat belts and that didn't explode. Inspired by Rachel Carson's book *Silent Spring*, which had revealed the dangers of commercial pesticides like DDT, environmental activists protested chemical companies. Public health groups sounded the alarm on consumer products like tobacco and lead paint, as well as the health threats of pollution billowing out of corporate smokestacks and chemicals leaching into our drinking water.

As went the country, so went Washington. My Senate predecessors tentatively sported longer hair and ventured into decidedly new policy territory. Through the 1960s and '70s, Congress passed laws to open and expand the American Dream's pathways of opportunity. Congress sent President Johnson the Civil Rights Act of 1964, which prohibited employers and businesses from discriminating on the basis of race, color, religion, sex, or national origin; and the Fair Housing Act, which banned discriminatory practices in selling and renting houses. Congress also passed the Voting Rights Act, one of the most transformative pieces of legislation in our history. Congress wasn't able to amend the Constitution with an Equal Rights Amendment, but it did pass Title IX in 1972, banning discrimination on the basis of sex in education. The next year, it passed Section 504, banning discrimination in education on the basis of disability.

Washington wasn't just transforming the civil rights landscape. It's hard to believe in today's hyper-polarized world, but the National

Traffic and Motor Vehicle Safety Act passed Congress with a unanimous vote. The National Environmental Policy Act, which has served as a model for environmental legislation in countries around the world, passed the Senate unanimously and attracted just fifteen "no" votes in the House. It was signed into law by President Nixon, a Republican, who also signed the Clean Water Act and the Clean Air Act and launched the Environmental Protection Agency.

The Court had a role in these societal changes. The Supreme Court in 1954 had announced its unanimous decision in *Brown v. Board of Education*, ruling that racial segregation of children in public schools was unconstitutional. In subsequent years, federal courts enforced this ruling through injunctions, consent decrees, and their contempt power. In 1964, the Court upheld key portions of the Civil Rights Act, holding that hotels could no longer refuse accommodations to people of color.[1] And in 1967, in the landmark case *Loving v. Virginia*, it struck down as unconstitutional laws that barred people of different races from marrying.

Under Chief Justice Earl Warren—a Republican, by the way—the Supreme Court became a bastion of the Founders' democratic ideals. In 1962 and 1963, the Supreme Court issued a series of decisions upholding the principle of one person, one vote for legislative apportionment—the idea that at both the state and federal levels, legislative districts must contain roughly the same number of people (with the exception of the Senate, an exemption that is written into the Constitution).[2] In 1966, it threw out state poll taxes—an insidious tactic used to keep poor and minority Americans from voting in state and local elections.[3] (The practice had already been barred in federal elections by the passage in 1964 of the Twenty-Fourth Amendment to the U.S. Constitution.)

In 1961, the Court announced that evidence obtained unconstitutionally could not be used against a criminal defendant;[4] and a few years later it ruled that the prosecution must turn exculpatory material over to the defense.[5] In 1963, a unanimous Court held that the Sixth Amendment's guarantee of the right to counsel applied to state criminal defendants as well as those in federal court.[6] Justice Black explained that "fair trials before impartial tribunals in which every defendant stands equal before the law . . . cannot be realized if the poor man charged with crime has to face his accusers without a lawyer to assist him."[7] In 1966, the Court held in *Miranda v. Arizona* that the Constitution's right to avoid self-incrimination ("taking the Fifth") required that an arrested American be told "prior to any questioning that he has the right to remain silent, that anything he says can be used against him in a court of law, that he has the right to the presence of an attorney, and that if he cannot afford an attorney one will be appointed for him prior to any questioning if he so desires."

After Earl Warren retired in 1969, Chief Justice Warren Burger—another Republican—continued many of these trends. In both *New York Times v. Sullivan* in 1964 and *New York Times v. U.S.* in 1972 (the Pentagon Papers case), the Court recognized the importance of a free and independent press to keep citizens informed in a representative democracy. In *Griswold v. Connecticut*, it struck down a state law that had barred married couples from using contraception; eight years later it extended that ruling to all Americans. In *University of California Regents v. Bakke*, the Court gave the green light to affirmative action programs. And, of course, in *Roe v. Wade* the Court held, 7–2, that the Constitution bars states from denying women abortion in the early weeks of their pregnancy.

Most Americans saw these decisions as logical stepping-stones toward our "more perfect union." It is inconceivable today, for example, that a public school would bar any student on the basis of their race, that a state would ban interracial marriage or the purchase of birth control, or that legislative districts could be structured to hold wildly different numbers of voters.

But for some, these actions by the Court came as grave threats to the natural order. A campaign of "massive resistance" erupted across the South against *Brown*, for example, triggering the decision by President Eisenhower (another Republican) to send the Army's 101st Airborne Division to Little Rock to enforce a desegregation decree. *Roe v. Wade* sparked a counter-movement that would force Presidents Nixon, Reagan, Bush, and Trump all to recant earlier support for abortion rights. Polluters were infuriated by new environmental laws, manufacturers were infuriated by judgments against them for unsafe products, all-male boardrooms huffed at the prospect of women's equality, anti-war protests rocked the country, and Black neighborhoods burned in many cities in what were called "race riots." All this upheaval set off panic in segments of American society. Conservative anxiety about social upheaval converged with corporate resentment at new regulation. The focus of much of that ire was the Supreme Court.

At the same time, a persistent, odd strain lurked along the American fringe, chronicled in Richard Hofstadter's Pulitzer Prize–winning 1964 essay, "The Paranoid Style in American Politics." This fringe united around a shifting stream of resentments—against Catholics and Jews, against immigrants, against Blacks, against the government itself. These arch-conservative forces shared a defiant anti-government ideology and the stinging resentment of humiliating political defeats, such as Barry Goldwater's landslide loss in the 1964 presidential election. Clearly, the American public wasn't buying what the far right was selling. But among the far-right fringe were heirs to fabulous dynastic wealth, hailing from powerful industrial and banking families, with money to throw at their project.

One of these rich malcontents, David Koch, ran for vice president on the 1980 Libertarian ticket. His platform was radical. And by "radical," I mean it included getting rid of Social Security, the Post Office, public schools, Medicare, and even federal air traffic control. The Koch Libertarian Party campaign was crushed at the polls. David Koch, who passed away in 2019, and his brother Charles Koch were heirs to an oil refinery and manufacturing business that they grew into a massive fossil fuel empire. They were not accustomed to defeat, let alone humiliating defeat (the Libertarians got around 1 percent of the vote in that 1980 election). So they didn't go home and sulk. Made confident by the arrogance of wealth, driven by extremist ideology, and spurred by the resentment of political rejection, the Koch brothers had ample motive. Combine that with experience in the devious ways of the international business world, corporate skills of long-term planning and patient execution, and unlimited resources to indulge themselves, and the Koch brothers were uniquely positioned to amplify this long-standing, latent extremist fringe, and direct it in secret, over decades if need be.

The Kochs spent literally billions of dollars over the following decades, most of it anonymously, in an effort to restructure America into a system of raw capitalism unfettered by government—a system that would lavishly benefit wealthy polluters and leave the rest of America a dog-eat-dog economic jungle.

But the defeats kept coming. After David Koch's loss, arch-conservatives tried to hitch their wagon to Ronald Reagan's popularity, to get the Reagan administration to impose their fringe ideas. In her book *Democracy in Chains*, Nancy MacLean recounts this saga:

> [Reagan budget director David A. Stockman] had come to his work in the White House as an avid libertarian. . . . [H]e believed that "the politicians were wrecking American capitalism. They were turning democratic government into a lavish give-away auction" and "saddling" those who created wealth with "punitive taxation and demoralizing and wasteful regulation."
>
> But something went terribly awry in the heady rush of the first year. The budget director, it turned out, had failed to make clear to the president and his political advisers—much less to the American people—that the colossal Kemp-Roth tax cut, as it came to be known, would necessitate tearing up the social contract on a scale never attempted in a democracy. To this day, it is unclear how such a consequential misunderstanding occurred.[8]

However it occurred, the public was outraged and inundated representatives with phone calls. Reagan quickly had to backpedal; Stockman had to repent and disclosed that he had been "taken to the woodshed" by Reagan for trying to impose such unpopular, even "ruthless" ideas[9]—ideas that would hurt many, many Americans, including, as Stockman would later recall, "Social Security recipients, veterans, farmers, educators, state and local officials, [and] the housing industry."[10]

The right-wing fringe did not give up their quest to blow the system up. In MacLean's words, they thought that Reagan "had proved to be too much of a pragmatist."[11] They internalized the lesson that instead of advocating directly for their unpopular end goals, as David Koch and Barry Goldwater had done with their disastrous candidacies, they "needed to engage in a kind of crab walk, even if it required advancing misleading claims in order to take terrain bit by bit."[12] In other words, the campaign went underground, into a world of lies and front groups.

The right wing looked more and more to the courts to overcome its rejection by voters. Pat Buchanan, then President Reagan's communications director, argued that conservative judicial appointments "could do more to advance the social agenda—school prayer, anti-pornography, anti-busing, right-to-life, and quotas in employment—than anything Congress can accomplish in 20 years."[13] The right wing's plan to capture the Court became its path around rejection by democracy.

Another provocation came when the Senate, on a bipartisan basis, rejected the Supreme Court nomination of Robert Bork, a favored nominee of the far right whose defeat created a new impetus for right-wing ambitions. As Supreme Court reporter Linda Greenhouse wrote, "Following Judge Bork's defeat, conservatives didn't waste time licking their wounds. They got busy building the infrastructure necessary to accomplish their thwarted goals."[14]

There was motive galore to capture the Court. The motive was rooted in the corporate angst at the upheaval of the 1960s and the social and regulatory changes that ensued, and it was rooted in the repeated defeats, resentments, and frustrations of the far-right fringe and its billionaire backers. The Court could give grumpy billionaires a chance for power after voters rejected their views. The Court could check unwelcome social change and efforts to hold corporations accountable for the true costs of their activities. The Court did not have to answer to voters. There was every motive to pursue the Court-capture Scheme.

PART III

Means

CHAPTER FOUR

The Plan: The Powell Memo

The independence of the judges once destroyed, the Constitution is gone, it is a dead letter; it is a vapor which the breath of faction in a moment may dissipate.

—ALEXANDER HAMILTON

AS IT TURNED OUT, THEY DIDN'T JUST HAVE motive for the Scheme; they also had a plan. The plan was outlined in a now-infamous thirty-four-page memo written in 1971 at the request of the U.S. Chamber of Commerce, an organization that over the next fifty years would become, in the words of its president, the "biggest gorilla" in Washington.[1] The memo, titled "Attack on American Free Enterprise System," was written by attorney Lewis Powell, and was delivered to the Chamber just months before the author would become Justice Powell of the U.S. Supreme Court.[2]

Powell hailed from Richmond, Virginia, where he gained a reputation as an incisive lawyer willing to make tough decisions. He displayed the courtly manners of the southern elite, moving comfortably in the social, political, and business worlds of the state capital. He served as president of the American Bar Association, played a leading role in the development of Colonial Williamsburg, and for nearly a decade was the chairman of the Richmond School Board. He served on corporate boards, including the board of Philip Morris, the enormous tobacco company, and he represented tobacco companies in his corporate practice. One could imagine how someone with Powell's background would have felt rocked by the upheavals that exposed the country to a racial reckoning and challenged the white, male social and economic hierarchies he had surmounted.

What the U.S. Chamber of Commerce wanted was a secret report, a strategic plan to reassert corporate power in the policy and political arena. In Powell's obituary decades later, the *Washington Post* described him as "a lawyer's lawyer, recoiling from extremes and searching out the middle ground."[3] But in his 1971 memo, Powell pulled no punches and sought no middle ground. This is how he began: "No thoughtful person can question that the American economic system is under broad attack."[4] By this, he meant "the 'free enterprise system,' 'capitalism,' and the 'profit system.'" He added, without explanation, that the "American political system of democracy under the rule of law is also under attack, often by the same individuals and organizations who seek to undermine the enterprise system"—no one could accuse him of painting with a narrow brush.[5]

The tone of the report was apocalyptic. It was rife with battle terms like "attack," "frontal assault," "rifle shots," and "guerrilla warfare."[6] "The overriding first need," he wrote, "is for businessmen to recognize that the ultimate issue may be *survival*" (the emphasis was in the original).[7] Powell warned that progressive voices for reform were "far more numerous, better financed, and increasingly welcomed and encouraged by other elements of society," including "perfectly respectable elements of society" like "the college campus, the pulpit, the media, the intellectual and literary journals, the arts and sciences, and [. . .] politicians."[8] Powell name-checked liberal activists such as Ralph Nader, whom he said there should be "no hesitation to attack," as well as *The Greening of America* author Charles Reich and left-wing attorney William Kunstler, who defended the Chicago Seven (later played by Mark Rylance in the 2020 Aaron Sorkin film *The Trial of the Chicago 7*).[9]

Powell longed for a fight. He decried corporate "compromise" and "appeasement" and complained that most businessmen had "shown little stomach for hard-nosed contest with their critics, and little skill in effective intellectual and philosophical debate."[10] He framed his memo as a rallying cry: "The time has come—indeed, it is long overdue—for the wisdom, ingenuity and resources of American business to be marshaled against those who would destroy it."[11] This was necessary, he said, "[i]f our system is to survive."[12]

A crisis of this magnitude called for a plan of equal scope, and Powell was ready with one. In Powell's view, "few elements of American society today have as little influence in government as the American businessman, the corporation, or even the millions of corporate stockholders."[13] The reason? That pesky democracy: "Politicians reflect what they believe to be majority views of their constituents. It is thus evident that most politicians are making the judgment that the public has little sympathy of the businessman or his viewpoint."[14]

To combat this, Powell recommended a propaganda effort staffed with scholars and speakers to proselytize in the media, on college campuses, and in scholarly journals and trade magazines; even to "evaluate social science textbooks, especially in economics, political science, and sociology," to correct information that may be "superficial, biased, and unfair."[15] If campus invitations weren't forthcoming, the Chamber should "aggressively" insist on "'equal time.'"[16] It was "essential," Powell explained, "to exert whatever degree of pressure—publicly and privately—may be necessary to assure opportunities to speak."[17]

Another Powell target was the national television networks, including TV news programs. "National television networks should be monitored in the same way that textbooks should be kept under constant surveillance," he wrote.[18] Powell recommended that American companies flood the airwaves with 10 percent of their total advertising budgets.[19] "It is time for American business—which has demonstrated the greatest capacity in all history to produce and to influence consumer decisions—to apply its great talents vigorously to the preservation of the system itself."[20] Sit with that a moment.

In addition to the propaganda campaign, Powell recommended a parallel corporate political effort, to cultivate power and stem "stampedes by politicians to support any legislation related to 'consumerism' or to the 'environment'" (Powell put both words in derogatory quote marks in the original).[21] Political power, he said, should be used "aggressively and with determination—without embarrassment and without the reluctance which has been so characteristic of American business."[22]

Then came a section of the secret report titled "Neglected

Opportunity in the Courts."[23] Powell recommended that corporations start "exploiting judicial action" by building a "highly competent staff of lawyers" who could be deployed "to appear as counsel *amicus* in the Supreme Court" and who could help select "the cases in which to participate, or the suits to institute."[24] This was, for Powell, an "area of vast opportunity," that "merits the necessary effort," as "the judiciary may be the most important instrument for social, economic and political change."[25]

The role of the Chamber to drive that "social, economic and political change" through the judiciary, he envisioned, would be "vital":

> Strength lies in organization, in careful long-range planning and implementation, in consistency of action over an indefinite period of years, in the scale of financing available only through joint effort, and in the political power available only through united action and national organizations.[26]

Powell also envisioned the value of an intermediary organization to hide the corporate forces behind it, citing "the quite understandable reluctance on the part of any one corporation to get too far out in front and to make itself too visible a target."[27]

Powell's approach to media foreshadows the rise of the right-wing mediaverse, including most notably Fox News; his expectations for the Chamber foreshadow "the gorilla" that organization became, with unbridled corporate funding unleashed by *Citizens United* and other Court decisions; and his targeting of the Court foreshadows the Scheme to take over the American judiciary. Powell warned that this would be "a long road," and "not for the faint hearted."[28] But, he exhorted, "[i]n the final analysis, the payoff—short of revolution—is what government does."[29] He concluded his memo with the same bombast with which he started: "business and the enterprise system are in deep trouble, and the hour is late."[30]

The secret Powell manifesto was dated August 23, 1971. Two months later, President Nixon nominated Lewis Powell to the U.S. Supreme Court to replace Hugo Black, an FDR appointee, former U.S. senator, and one of the longest-serving members of the Supreme Court. The report was not disclosed to the Senate during Powell's confirmation hearings. Strangely, even his authorized biographer gave it no mention, although it is arguably one of the most consequential pieces of writing Powell ever produced. Justice Powell's nomination was confirmed in the Senate by a vote of 89–1. He was sworn in as Justice Powell on January 7, 1972, less than six months after he delivered his secret report to the Chamber.

They had a motive; they had a plan; and now they had a man on the Court.

CHAPTER FIVE

Building the Influence Machine: Campaign Finance Cases

By gnawing through a dike, even a rat may drown a nation.

—EDMUND BURKE

ON THE U.S. SUPREME COURT, JUSTICE LEWIS POWELL was often out of step with the radical right wing. Powell voted with the majority in *Roe v. Wade*, for example; he authored the Court's opinion in *Bakke* upholding affirmative action; and he was part of the Court's unanimous decision ordering President Nixon to obey a federal district court subpoena during the Watergate scandal.[1] But in one area of law Justice Powell kept faith with Attorney Powell's strategic advice to the Chamber of Commerce: he carved a pathway for corporate political power.

On the Court, Justice Powell laid the legal groundwork for exactly the kind of corporate influence campaigns Attorney Powell had recommended. In three landmark campaign finance rulings, Justice Powell helped launch what has become today's massive dark-money, pro-corporate influence operation. In doing so, he also became a living exemplar of what a "man on the Court" could do for the corporate right wing.

Campaign finance regulations are essential in a democracy. The Founders, recall, feared corruption. Few things undermine governmental legitimacy like corruption, or even the appearance of corruption. Nothing corrupts like money. Yet the Court's Republicans have been steadily expanding the power of corporate money in politics, led first by Justice Powell.

For much of the twentieth century, campaign finance laws focused on direct contributions to candidates, donations that raised the specter of "quid pro quo" bribery. Reporting requirements and contribution limits kept that danger at bay. But big interests seek influence, and money buys influence, so they got creative. As Justices O'Connor and Stevens would write in 2003, "money, like water, will always find an outlet."[2] Constant vigilance is required by lawmakers and regulators to anticipate where it might flow next and head it off.

In recent decades, money goes less to candidates, or even to political parties, and more and more to big political influence groups. Technically, these big "outside" groups are required to be "independent," but that's a laugh. A super PAC lobbing unlimited money into an election can be run by former staff and campaign veterans of the candidate. The candidate can even post ad footage on his or her campaign website for the super PAC to run. "Independence" is a joke.

Worse, the "independent" expenditures are now often secret—the public has no idea who is doing the talking. Yes, a super PAC has to disclose its donors, but nothing prevents its donor from being a front group masking the real donor.* Obviously, knowing who's talking is important information to allow citizens to discharge their democratic duties. As First Circuit Judge Bruce Selya (a Rhode Islander and a Republican) recently wrote in a First Circuit case, it is essential "that the electorate can understand who is speaking and, thus, to give proper weight to different speakers and messages when deciding how to vote."[3] If there's a bill in Congress that affects environmental regulations and an ad comes on TV telling viewers how to think about it, shouldn't the viewers know if it's being paid for by ExxonMobil?

---

* In 2020, I led a Democratic senators' brief in support of Representative Ted Lieu's case on the super PAC debacle. We provided examples of various practices that "allow super PACs to dodge pre-election disclosure, depriving voters of information when it is most actionable: when they cast their ballot." For example, " 'Pop-Up' Super PACs flout disclosure by materializing just prior to an election, rapidly spending, and then disclosing donors only after the election. Or Super PACs can claim to spend on credit and not disclose their donors until after Election Day. Sometimes, disclosure comes not merely too late, but never, because the mere threat or promise of an unlimited contribution achieves its goal with no reportable contribution—or because contributions are often routed through complex webs of front groups to obscure the linkage." No surprise: the Supreme Court did nothing.[4]

In the dirty work of politics, hiding the messenger has many advantages. Politicians and their allies can smear at will the candidate they disfavor, without tarnishing the candidate they do favor by association with the attack ads. The candidate benefiting from the ad never has to say he or she "approves this message." The phony name of the front group can add its own signaling, so dark-money groups use names like "Moms for Liberty," or "Keep Dallas Safe." *

Most important, front groups can lie. Lying by candidates can blow back on the candidate, so it has natural bounds. Lying by a disposable front group that will be flushed away as soon as the election is over has no such natural bound. The same reasoning works for corporations. The front group running the ad is as disposable as toilet paper. When the dirty work is done, it gets flushed. The lie is injected into public discourse with no actual individual or corporation accountable for it. Small wonder that since unlimited dark money has been set

---

* A case in point is astroturf groups like Parents Defending Education, which appeared out of nowhere to stoke fears of "critical race theory" in early 2021. PDE and "networked" organizations No Left Turn in Education and Moms for Liberty claimed to be simple grassroots organizations reflecting a national movement of concerned parents. Political scientist Maurice Cunningham looked at the "network map" PDE provided on its website. "Wow—it looks like PDE is blanketing the nation," he wrote. "But it's fake":

> PDE provides links to the Facebook or websites of their "members" so we can see that most of these groups were formed in March or February 2021, rarely earlier. It's a set up. Grassroots means folks joining together on the local level in a collective effort to improve their community. Here are some of the membership numbers for No Left Turn in Education affiliates: Alabama, 7; Arkansas, 3; Delaware, 6; Iowa, 2; Idaho, 4; Indiana, 8; Michigan (Betsy DeVos's home state), 13; Mississippi, 3; Montana, 2; North Dakota, 2; Massachusetts, 17. Well, you get the idea. And my favorite, Hawaii: 1. And Moms for Liberty? Arizona, 17; Wright Co, Minnesota, 8; Corpus Christi Nueces, Texas, 70. Both groups have a handful of states with dozens of members and even over a hundred, but almost all of these operations are tied in with the creation of PDE.[5]

In Diane Ravitch's education blog, Cunningham reported that the "concerned moms" who represent these groups on Fox News (another tell; how many legitimate grassroots groups go straight from launch to Fox News?) have deep ties to right-wing politics and Koch-backed groups. So does PDE's law firm, Consovoy McMullen. "William Consovoy also represents Donald Trump and clerked for Justice Clarence Thomas," Cunningham reported. Put more bluntly: "The firm is conservative legal royalty. PDE did not hire it after an especially successful bake sale."[6]

loose in our politics, voters have been drowned in what journalist Joe Hagan memorably called a "tsunami of slime."[7] The total cost of the 2020 election cycle was $14.4 billion, more than twice what was spent just four years earlier,[8] and much of it was negative. That's a hell of a tsunami.

A quick sidebar from my personal experience: the "air war" of paid advertising in a campaign is less a debate than a contest between competing megaphones. The winning megaphone is the one that garners more airtime, has a consistent and simple message, and most effectively hooks the message into popular concerns. If your opponent is lying about you over his megaphone, and you divert your megaphone to responding to those lies, you have likely made a big mistake. You are now talking about the race on your opponent's terms. You are now "off message."

This was a hard lesson for me, because as a lawyer my deepest instinct is to counterattack and rebut a lie. As a person, I resent people lying about me and yearn to correct the record. When I first ran for the Senate, my opponent suggested I had ducked bringing a political prosecution. I'd actually spent years preparing the case. I desperately wanted to talk about the undercover operation, the cooperating witnesses, the special Department of Justice approvals—all the work I'd put into building the prosecution I'd supposedly avoided. But I had to learn to grit my teeth, ignore it, and "stay on message"; the election wasn't about that case. The result in elections is that lies often go uncorrected.

The worst case for voters is an election in which every megaphone is lying, each trying to drown out the other, as the voter flails for truth in the "tsunami of slime." That worst case is now our political status quo, thanks to a handful of Republican Supreme Court justices. Our road to this sorry state started with three cases effectively decided by Justice Powell.

When Justice Powell joined the Court, the campaign finance scandal was President Nixon's deal with the dairy industry: he overrode a decision within his own administration and increased dairy price supports; they funneled him $2 million in campaign funds—a super deal for the dairy industry, which received $100 million worth of support, a fifty-to-one payday. Congress's response was to strengthen FECA, the

Federal Election Campaign Act. This law limited the contributions that campaigns could receive, capped the amounts they could spend, and required disclosure of any donations over $100 (quaint times, when seen from our present era of unlimited dark money).* When that law was challenged, in a case called *Buckley v. Valeo*, Justice Powell took his first shot at crafting the path for corporate political power that Attorney Powell had advocated.

The *Buckley* decision was a mess. The Court's ruling, concurrences, and dissent, produced with what one observer called "extraordinary" speed, sprawled across more than 200 pages, 138 in the majority opinion alone.[9] The majority opinion was not signed by any single justice—unusual for an opinion of that length and complexity—and different justices joined and dissented from different portions. Just three of the nine justices agreed with the entirety of the majority opinion; one of them was Powell.

Some of the logic you could (sort of) follow. The decision upheld the law's limits on the amounts candidates could receive but knocked out limitations on the amount candidates could spend, and it overturned limits on what wealthy candidates could give to their own campaigns (reasoning that spending one's own money on one's own campaign wasn't corrupting). What was remarkable in *Buckley*—and very much a departure from the real world as those of us in the political realm experience it—was the Court's treatment of so-called independent expenditures, funds spent by an "outside" group (not a political party, politician, or PAC) to influence an election. The Court got rid of FECA's limits on so-called independent expenditures, reasoning that the language in the statute was too vague to enforce, but if it were less vague it would be too easy to circumvent and therefore ineffectual at addressing corruption. So, best to get rid of "independent" spending limits altogether. (I told you it was a mess.)

FECA had also required disclosure of the donors behind these so-called independent political ads. *Buckley* knocked that out too,

---

* Speaking of "quaint," as late as 1982, when Senator John Stennis, then chairman of the Armed Services Committee, "was asked by a colleague to hold a fund-raiser at which defense contractors would be present, Stennis balked. Said Stennis: 'Would that be proper? I hold life and death over these companies. I don't think it would be proper for me to take money from them.'"[10]

inventing a rule that Congress could require disclosure only of ads that were "expressly" political; and then, in a late-added footnote, providing a helpful list of the magic words to avoid in your ads if you wanted to dodge disclosure, including "vote for," "vote against," "elect," and "defeat." In effect, the Powell decision gave corporate spenders a verbal roadmap to avoid disclosure. Attorney Powell had wanted "American business—which has demonstrated the greatest capacity in all history to produce and to influence consumer decisions—to apply its great talents vigorously"; Justice Powell opened the pathway for the vigorous, and anonymous, application of those influence talents.[11]

We all know what happened next. Put eager candidates and greedy funders together, and trouble will follow. An entire cottage industry sprang up making campaign ads that dodged FECA's rules, ads that special interests could fund without disclosure. It turned out that ads were actually *more* persuasive when they *didn't* use the magic words, and that negative ads were far more effective when an outside group, not the candidate, ran them.[12] It was a bonanza for corporate power.

The problem is this was all nonsense. The supposed "independence" of the groups was a fiction. The difference between "issue ads" and political ads was a fiction. What was real was that corporate money could flow anonymously into races. This would not be the last time the Court would make amateurish errors or mischaracterizations about the political battleground to help corporate money flow.

Two years after *Buckley*, Justice Powell had an opportunity to give corporate political spending an even more direct boost, this time in a 5–4 majority opinion that he authored. Along with more than thirty other states, Massachusetts had a law on its books that restricted corporations from spending money on statewide ballot referenda. The First National Bank of Boston sued, arguing that corporations have First and Fourteenth Amendment rights to influence popular referendum elections. In *First National Bank of Boston v. Bellotti*, Powell swung a 5–4 Supreme Court to say they did.

Remember that the Constitution provides absolutely no political role for corporations. A corporation is meant to be no more than a collection of individuals who have pooled their capital for a profit-seeking—not political—purpose. The *Bellotti* majority leapt over this fundamental problem with a clever logical somersault, saying that if corporations had something to say relevant to public debate, the public had a right to hear it. This "right to hear" trick perpetuated the Republican justices' recurring stratagem of conflating corporations with people and money with speech—to the great advantage of corporate money.

Corporations are of course not people—unlike a corporation's executives and shareholders and employees and customers, all of whom are free to represent its interests in politics. Nothing prevented the First National Bank president from marshaling his voice, his wallet, his friends, and any willing employees or customers on behalf of the bank. But that was not enough for Justice Powell. His secret report to the Chamber had urged corporate interests "to press vigorously in all political arenas," and to show no "reluctance to penalize politically" anyone who gets in their way.[13] To press and penalize thusly, it was important that corporations be able to spend corporate money to influence elections. And so it was.

The last case in Justice Powell's hat trick for corporate influence came in 1986, in a case called *Federal Election Commission v. Massachusetts Citizens for Life*. This decision did two big things. First, it reached past the state referendum elections at issue in *Bellotti* to allow corporate contributions in regular political election contests. In federal elections, corporations and unions that wanted to run ads directly supporting or opposing a candidate or political party still had to use a PAC, which had to be funded by reported, limited donations specifically contributed for political purposes (typically from employees or union members), and whose own spending was also reported and limited. *Massachusetts Citizens for Life* allowed unrestricted dollars from certain nonprofit organizations to be spent on political election ads, no PAC needed—a foreshadowing of what was to come in *Citizens United*.

Massachusetts Citizens for Life opened a new gateway for political spending via those nonprofits. By allowing unlimited spending by some types of nonprofits, the decision effectively set them up to act as political intermediaries for big donors' dollars. Remember Attorney Powell's concern for "the quite understandable reluctance on the part of any one corporation to get too far out in front and to make itself too visible a target"? Nonprofit intermediaries could now provide that service. It was a two-fer. Corporate money could flow in all elections, and it could flow through an anonymizing nonprofit entity. No surprise; such nonprofits proliferated.

In 2021, I spoke about Justice Powell and his secret memo on the Floor of the Senate. I traced how, as a Supreme Court justice, Powell made good on the secret strategy he had laid before the Chamber of Commerce in 1971: how he opened a lane for unlimited money into politics, enabling what his secret report had called "the scale of financing available only through joint effort"; how he bulldozed aside bars on corporate spending and politics so corporations could deploy, just as his report had urged, "whatever degree of pressure—publicly and privately—may be necessary"; and how he allowed advocacy organizations to spend their treasuries in politics, opening the way for the "organization," "joint effort," and "united action" he had called for in his report through "national organizations."

It was, I said, a "dark achievement, but quite an achievement."[14]

It took time for all the pieces to line up. Indeed, there were setbacks after Justice Powell left the Court. Even with uber-conservative Justice Scalia added to the nine, the Supreme Court had a brief reckoning with the realities of money and influence in our political system. In *Austin v. Michigan Chamber of Commerce*, the Court upheld a state law that barred corporations from using general treasury funds to make independent expenditures for or against political candidates— executives spending shareholder money. The state law paralleled a federal statute barring corporations and unions from making independent expenditures in federal elections that dated back to 1947 (a provision the Court would invalidate in *Citizens United*).

The *Austin* Court explained that quid pro quo corruption— crass horse trades like the one Nixon had engaged in with the dairy industry—was a legitimate concern that lawmakers could target with campaign finance laws, but it wasn't the only one. It was also Congress's business to address "the corrosive and distorting effects of immense aggregations of wealth that are accumulated with the help of the corporate form and that have little or no correlation to the public's support for the corporation's political ideas."[15] This was a brief flash of political lucidity. It was also a shot at "immense aggregations of wealth" deployed in politics. It would not last. The Court Republicans would soon power up those corporate "corrosive and distorting effects" in our politics.

Even with *Austin* upholding the ban on corporate independent expenditures, the political system was increasingly awash with corporate money. The Federal Election Commission had decided to allow corporations to give unlimited amounts to political parties, so long as the funds weren't spent directly on a candidate's campaign— so-called soft money. What did these unlimited corporate funds buy? "Issue" ads, those political commercials that only had to avoid the "magic words" that *Buckley* had so helpfully listed for the ad-makers. Corporations were free to funnel money through political parties so long as the political ads avoided the magic words that made an ad "political."

In 2000, nearly half a billion dollars poured into political party soft money funds.[16] It stank so badly that a bipartisan group of lawmakers, led by Senators John McCain and Russ Feingold and Representatives Chris Shays and Marty Meehan, got together and hammered out an update to FECA: the Bipartisan Campaign Reform Act, or BCRA.* Among other things, BCRA replaced the idiotic "magic words" test with a simpler rule: if an ad mentioned a candidate by name or picture and ran in the weeks leading up to an election, the law assumed it was designed to influence the election (as it obviously was) and treated it so for the purposes of limits and disclosure.

What happened next is interesting, in the context of what having "a man on the Court" means. BCRA was immediately challenged in several lawsuits that were consolidated into one: *McConnell v. Federal Election Commission*, named for plaintiff Senator Mitch McConnell. In 2003, Senator McConnell largely lost that round; with a few minor exceptions, the Court upheld the law, including provisions that barred corporate and union executives from using other people's money on independent expenditures. But then in 2005 and

---

* It's worth emphasizing "bipartisan." If you're a lifelong Republican and wonder where your party has gone, remember that as recently as 2002, a Republican-controlled House of Representatives and an evenly split Senate came together to enact significant, meaningful campaign finance reform. And a Republican president, George W. Bush, signed it into law.

2006 came a personnel change at the Supreme Court, with the arrival of Justices Roberts and Alito and the departure of Justices Rehnquist and O'Connor. Justice O'Connor's departure left the Supreme Court for the first time in American history with no member with the practical political experience of having run for office.[17] Roberts's and Alito's arrivals also marked the emerging influence of the Federalist Society over judicial selection.*

Interested amateurism about politics became the order of the day at the Court. The newly constituted Court began dismantling campaign finance restrictions, even if that meant reversing precedent and, often, using cartoonishly inept political theorizing and fact-finding to prop up its outcomes. Rehnquist and O'Connor were both Republican appointees, but they predated the Scheme. The new Federalist Society men on the Court brought a new approach to corporate political spending. Big influencers had loved the "magic words" test that BCRA eliminated. As a first order of business Chief Justice Roberts's Court struck down that BCRA provision and functionally resurrected magic words with an "express advocacy" test.[18] Back came those political "issue" attack ads. It was another obvious flag to the far right (if they needed another one) of how valuable a "man on the Court"—or two—could be.

The fatal blow fell in January 2010, with the Court's appalling decision in *Citizens United v. FEC*. Less than a decade after the *McConnell* Court had reviewed a voluminous record laying out the dangers of corporate corruption and influence, and had upheld BCRA's restrictions on independent political expenditures, the Court reversed itself. Nothing had changed but the membership of the Court.

To make this decision possible, the Republican majority entered

---

*Justices Rehnquist and O'Connor were Republican appointees, but they were not groomed and selected by the Federalist Society and owed nothing to the group or to the dark-money donors who worked through the Federalist Society to propel compliant candidates onto the Court. Justice Alito was nominated only after right-wing donors revolted at President Bush's selection of Harriet Miers, a highly accomplished lawyer but one who operated outside of the Federalist Society's ecosystem. The person who helped the Bush White House pivot from Miers to Alito? The Federalist Society's longtime leader, Leonard Leo.

a fact-free zone—there was zero contemporary evidentiary record, none, in *Citizens United*; indeed, the Chief Justice maneuvered the case through the Court's procedures in a way that fended off any factual record. The Republican majority was free to fantasize about politics, and "find" whatever facts needed to be found to open the floodgates of unlimited "independent" political spending. Justice Kennedy authored the opinion, which journalist Jon Schwarz may have described best:

> Kennedy's ruling contains some of the silliest, wackiest, most preposterous pronouncements in the tens of millions of words extruded by the Supreme Court in its 229-year history:
>
> > [W]e now conclude that independent expenditures, including those made by corporations, do not give rise to corruption or the appearance of corruption. . . .
> > The fact that speakers [i.e., donors] may have influence over or access to elected officials does not mean that these officials are corrupt. . . .
> > The appearance of influence or access, furthermore, will not cause the electorate to lose faith in our democracy.

Kennedy might as well have written, "We now conclude that the sky is green, and everyone in America will agree that that's definitely true."[19]

Insisting that these so-called independent expenditures couldn't corrupt because they are spent "independently" of the candidate was factually wrong. The Supreme Court's conservative justices revealed what former FEC Chairman Trevor Potter (a Republican and, full disclosure, a close friend) called their "profound misunderstanding of how elections . . . operate in practice."[20] When "courts opened our elections to a maelstrom of unlimited spending by 'outside groups,'" Potter explained, they didn't seem to grasp that "an increasing amount of [it] is far from independent by any reasonable assessment." Many groups are dedicated to only one candidate, and emerge and expire for one race, which is hardly a sign of "independence." In fact, as Potter pointed out,

A large and growing number of these groups regularly engage in close relationships with the campaigns they purport to be independent from: super PACs hire close aides and recent employees of the candidate; candidates appear as "special guests" at super PAC fundraisers; super PACs creatively synchronize media strategy with the campaign through vendors, aides, the internet, or other channels; candidates regularly signal to donors which super PAC to direct funds to after they reach the maximum legal limit to the campaign; and much more . . .

Our modern campaign finance system is replete with winks and nods. Indeed, today, it would be highly unusual to see a super PAC aligned with a major candidate's campaign engage in activity that the campaign viewed as "counterproductive." Instead, they usually complement or amplify campaigns' strategies in ways that can be highly valuable—and then major donors who funded those efforts enjoy privileged access to the candidates themselves.[21]

That was not even the majority's worst mistake in *Citizens United*. Its worst mistake was to imagine that this unlimited spending would be "transparent"—and then, when it obviously wasn't, do nothing about its error.* (The majority also foolishly overlooked that even if unlimited political spending actually were "transparent," it still opened the door to very non-transparent threats and promises about when and whether that unlimited spending would be deployed. Give a thug a

---

* In an amicus brief that we filed a few years later in a case called *American Traditional Partnership v. Bullock*, John McCain and I told the Court how easily transparency requirements could be skirted in the wake of *Citizens United*. Our words fell on deaf ears. I could understand why the justices might think they could safely overlook the views of the junior senator from the smallest state, but I thought that it would have some effect when they heard from Senator McCain, a veteran politician and legendary champion of transparency. I revisited the transparency failure again in a brief supporting Congressman Ted Lieu's challenge to super PACs. Again the Court did nothing. At some point, omission becomes commission.

cudgel, and you give him the power not just to swing it, but to threaten to swing it.)

Switching out Rehnquist and O'Connor for Roberts and Alito delivered, big time, for the dark-money forces out to reshape our society. *Citizens United* radically transformed the world of political money just months before the 2010 elections. The right-wing machine saw the decision coming and pounced, with floods of new money not just flipping the House of Representatives, but also pouring into state houses just as they were taking up new redistricting efforts. This powered up a Republican project called REDMAP to gerrymander Congress. The wash of money through state houses produced Republican state legislatures able to gerrymander their states in bulk, throwing the House an additional thirty Republican seats in 2012. In that election, nearly 1.4 million more voters pulled the lever for a Democratic member of the House than for a Republican, but Republican bulk gerrymandering made possible by *Citizens United* dollars produced a counter-majoritarian Republican majority.[22]

None of this seemed to worry the Republican justices on the Court. After *Citizens United* unleashed unlimited political spending, the Court turned a persistent blind eye to the flagrant problem of unlimited dark-money spending.[23] Separately, in *Rucho v. Common Cause*, the Court signaled that it wouldn't be refereeing partisan bulk gerrymandering, either.

At last, all the key pieces were in place to unleash the corporate influence machine that Attorney Powell had recommended. It is an influence machine that dominates much of American politics today, and an influence machine that controls much of what we do in the Senate. Central to much of this remains the Chamber of Commerce, which was Powell's client for the secret report and today is the apex predator of corporate influence in Congress, red in tooth and claw.

A vicious cycle has emerged. Powell encouraged corporations to exert political power and he enabled that corporate political power from the Court. Those Court decisions empowered the political far right; the political far right then used power granted by those decisions to propel more far-right justices onto the Supreme Court. The Court issued rulings that enabled huge, untraceable corporate spending in political races—dark money. This dark money then fueled the right-wing corporate political enterprise, which used its wealth, unhampered by campaign finance rules, to stack more right-wing justices on the Court. Urged on by dark-money front groups, The Court That Dark Money Built would soon carve out new constitutional protections for dark money.

It's a deadly spin cycle for democracy.

PART IV

Co-conspirators

CHAPTER SIX

Mercenaries, Fringe Groups, and Lobbyists

It is difficult to get a man to understand something when his salary depends on his not understanding it.

—UPTON SINCLAIR

IT'S NOT ENOUGH TO HAVE A MOTIVE AND a plan to commit a crime. You also need the instrumentality: the murder weapon. In addition to motives galore, the corporate right wing also had instrumentalities galore.

First, it had a robust mercenary force standing by. To work its will in regulatory agencies, it had lawyers all over Washington. Every major DC corporate law firm competed for corporate clients for their regulatory practice groups, which often melded indistinguishably with the firm's lobbying efforts. They had stables of well-groomed "experts" to provide favorable testimony and comments in regulatory proceedings. Right-wing "think tanks" and sponsored university fellowships provided those stables for corporate "experts" to be trained, groomed, and fed. These mercenaries knew a lot about regulatory capture; that was their world. Repurposing them from regulatory capture to Court capture would be a short step.

The right-wing fringe was also standing by. The nurture and guidance of the Kochs breathed new strength and life—and deregulatory purpose—into the nativist far-right fringe. The existing assortment of oddball groups would not do. The Koch political operation needed a sleeker team to develop and sell an ideology that suited their agenda, while hiding their identity and their true objective. They were almost uniquely well equipped to build a massive secret propaganda machine. If identities needed to be laundered from money they gave, telling lawyers to find or design a way to do things was familiar. If fringe groups needed to coordinate with each other, organizing with others through trade associations and lobbying groups was familiar activity. And if money needed to be spent, so be it; money was no object, the return on investment was tremendous, and getting people to do things for you for money is a familiar practice of the very rich.

Another force stood by: the corporate lobbying effort had exploded after Powell's manifesto. One year after its publication, in 1972, the National Association of Manufacturers moved its headquarters from New York to Washington, DC. The same year, the CEOs of America's biggest companies came together to form the Business Roundtable. Its organizing principle, in the words of co-founder John Harper, was that "business must take an active, aggressive role in developing understanding of and support for the free-market system by reestablishing the public's confidence in business. Without question, we have our work cut out for us."[1] Now where had we heard that before, nearly verbatim?

In 1968, just 100 American companies had public affairs offices in the nation's capital. Within ten years, there were 500. When Powell wrote his secret memo in 1971, just 175 companies even had registered lobbyists. By 1982, 2,500 did. As for corporate PACs, researchers found that "from the late 1970s to the late 1980s, corporate PACs increased their expenditures in congressional races nearly fivefold," twice as fast as labor PAC spending.[2]

Today, of course, these numbers seem quaint.* The Chamber alone outspends by threefold the second-biggest lobbying spender. And the biggest lobbying spenders are all corporate. Unions aren't even close. Journalist and former presidential press secretary Bill Moyers highlighted data showing that "[i]n the early 1970s, business PACs contributed less to congressional races overall than labor PACs did. By the

---

* According to the good government watchdog group OpenSecrets, in 2020, there were about 12,000 registered lobbyists in Washington, DC (and many, many more unregistered lobbyists) and more than $3.5 billion was spent on lobbying.[3]

mid-1970s, the two were at rough parity, and by the end of the decade, business PACs were way ahead. By 1980, unions accounted for less than a quarter of all PAC contributions—down from half six years earlier."⁴ Those numbers, too, seem quaint.* Indeed, the idea of reported contributions seems quaint in our new, grim, dark-money political era.

New groups joined the throng. In 1973, the Heritage Foundation set up shop in Washington, DC. The same year, the "public interest" law firm Pacific Legal Foundation launched in California, with the encouragement of then Governor Ronald Reagan, to file strategic lawsuits and advance the interests of businesses through sympathetic plaintiffs, while obscuring the identities of the real protagonists. In 1974, oil magnate Charles Koch co-founded what was initially called the Charles Koch Foundation but in 1977 changed its name to the Cato Institute and became a prominent libertarian think tank specializing in climate denial.†

Heritage's website brags that nearly two-thirds of the policy recommendations it made to both President Reagan and President Trump were adopted by their respective administrations.⁵ Like Cato, it is aggressively pro-business (in propaganda-speak, pro-"limited government") and anti–majority rule. Heritage and Cato are among literally hundreds of interconnected organizations that would be created over the coming decades by a small assortment of billionaires to convince people that government by the people is the true enemy.

When these groups say "individual liberty," they really mean

---

* In the 2019–20 election cycle, OpenSecrets reports that organized labor made political contributions of less than $250 million. That's a healthy amount, but nowhere close to the nearly $6 billion business interests spent.⁶

† Cato's chief climate denier later made a spectacular "noisy exit" when he realized that climate denial was false and wrote a repudiation of the Cato climate denial operation.⁷ As journalist Marc Gunther reported, it was quite an epiphany:

> Taylor's own conversion began with a cable-TV debate a decade ago with Joe Romm, a fiercely partisan author and climate blogger for the Center for American Progress. In the green room afterward, Romm, who has a PhD in physics, told Taylor that he had misrepresented congressional testimony by noted climate scientist James Hansen. Go look at what Hansen actually said, Romm urged him. "I went back to my office, looked at the information, and it turned out he was right," Taylor recalls. "It was from that point on that I decided I had to do more due diligence."⁸

"corporate deregulation"; when they say "freedom," it's usually "freedom to pollute" or "freedom to discriminate" or "freedom to ignore laws protecting workers" (or, these days, "freedom to expose others to a virus" and "dismantle our health care system"). As for "states' rights"? That's cover for pretty much anything they want the federal government out of (unless, of course, they happen to prefer the federal system—look at the Trump administration's attack on California's emission standards). What they are actually talking about is a world in which those who are rich enough can escape democratic governance.

The regulatory mercenaries, tarted-up fringe groups, and corporate lobbying behemoth provided an immense arsenal of right-wing influence for the Scheme to deploy. But that was not enough for them. They constructed a new archipelago of front groups to work their mischief.

CHAPTER SEVEN

The Front Group Archipelago

Darkness cannot drive out darkness: only light can do that.
—Rev. Martin Luther King Jr.

THE FRONT GROUP ARCHIPELAGO DESIGNED TO CAPTURE THE Court for dark-money donors did not spring into existence out of thin air. It had a history. A bad one. Years ago, the tobacco industry set up front groups and "astroturf" organizations as the health dangers of smoking became more apparent. These groups did a lot of lying. By the 1990s, legal pressure on the tobacco industry culminated in a federal court determination that the tobacco companies "engaged in an overarching scheme to defraud smokers and potential smokers for more than 50 years."[1] This shut down the tobacco fraud operation.*

The timing was ripe: just as the tobacco fraud groups were having

---

* The court's ruling was damning:

> Put more colloquially, and less legalistically, over the course of more than 50 years, Defendants lied, misrepresented, and deceived the American public, including smokers and the young people they avidly sought as "replacement smokers," about the devastating health effects of smoking and environmental tobacco smoke, they suppressed research, they destroyed documents, they manipulated the use of nicotine so as to increase and perpetuate addiction, they distorted the truth about low tar and light cigarettes so as to discourage smokers from quitting, and they abused the legal system in order to achieve their goal—to make money with little, if any, regard for individual illness and suffering, soaring health costs, or the integrity of the legal system.[2]

to shut down, attention was turning to fossil fuel emissions. Tobacco's front groups were quickly repurposed in the service of climate denial. The flotilla of lie-for-hire groups swelled to number in the dozens. Many still exist. Some were let drop after they got too smelly to be useful. In my "Time to Wake Up" climate speeches on the Senate Floor, I referred to this repurposed array of front groups as the "Web of Denial." Think of this front-group array as piano keys, nominally separate but all part of the same keyboard, and able to be played in chords and sequences as their funders direct, whether in tobacco fraud, climate change denial, or Court capture. The method is the same, and so are many of the groups.

Let me offer a few choice examples. In the early 1990s, an organization appeared called The Advancement of Sound Science Coalition, or TASSC. TASSC said that it was an independent grassroots coalition that believed in "sound science in policymaking." TASSC spokespeople hit the airwaves decrying "junk science"—for instance, the EPA's decision to classify secondhand smoke as a known carcinogen. Fox News regularly featured TASSC in a segment attacking *real* science that it called, disturbingly, "Junk Science."

TASSC operated under a veneer of respectability for more than a decade, before it came out that the group was a front organization created by a public relations firm for its client, the tobacco company Philip Morris. TASSC's true objective was not to promote "sound science," but to undermine real science by sowing confusion and distrust, while hiding the true source of the industry propaganda it was pushing. Its founding documents—uncovered years later in the course of the tobacco litigation—clearly stated that its actual purpose was to help Philip Morris promote tobacco use nationally and discourage public trust of actual scientific studies.[3]

Another tobacco front group was called Citizens for a Sound Economy, funded by none other than David Koch. Masked as a grassroots citizens group, CSE pulled in millions from companies like Philip Morris as it railed against the EPA's report on secondhand smoke, FDA efforts to regulate tobacco, workplace smoking rules, tobacco taxes, and lawsuits against the tobacco industry. In 2004, after the gig was up in the tobacco game, CSE morphed into two new Koch dark-money vehicles: Americans for Prosperity and FreedomWorks.*

These groups inherited an initiative that CSE had begun a few years earlier: the U.S. Tea Party project. A few years ago, researchers at the University of California's Center for Tobacco Control Research and Education uncovered a web of connections between tobacco astroturf groups (including TASSC and CSE) and the Tea Party, leading them to conclude that "[r]ather than being a purely grassroots movement that spontaneously developed in 2009, the Tea Party has developed over time, in part through decades of work by the tobacco industry and other corporate interests."[4]

A now-defunct "Annapolis Center for Science-Based Public Policy" took a page from TASSC's book. It was founded by a former vice president of the National Association of Manufacturers—not an environmentally friendly group—to "support and promote responsible energy and environmental health and safety." But—surprise—it too was a disinformation machine, founded to keep from the public the fact that the people telling them global warming was a hoax were in fact a consortium of major polluters.

Brown University professor Dr. Robert Brulle has spent years looking into the disinformation around climate science. He found that the Annapolis Center was a precursor to today's web of climate denial front groups funded by polluters including ExxonMobil, Marathon Petroleum, and the Kochs.[5] Dr. Brulle created a graphic that shows a constellation of organizations devoted to what he calls "institutionalizing delay," and links the groups to fossil fuel billionaires who back them.[6] I used his graphic in my "Web of Denial" speeches on the Senate Floor. It shows how identity-scrubbing organizations like the Kochs' DonorsTrust and Donors Capital fund a whack-a-mole array of disposable groups with misleadingly wholesome names, like the "Heartland Institute" and the "Franklin Center for Government and Public Integrity."

The New York Times profiled a corporate PR firm, FTI Consulting,

---

*This is not the last time Americans for Prosperity will figure in this book, together with its corporate twin, Americans for Prosperity Foundation.

that made a cottage industry of disposable phony front groups with names like "Citizens to Protect PA Jobs," "New Mexicans for Economic Prosperity," "Main Street Investors," and "Texans for Natural Gas" that were all actually industry-funded influence campaigns.[7] Texans for Natural Gas, no one will be surprised to learn, "has downplayed the magnitude of emissions of methane, the prime component of natural gas and a potent greenhouse gas, from oil and gas production."[8] The *Times* reported that, acting in the guise of representatives for Texans for Natural Gas, "FTI employees have launched pro-industry petitions, produced videos and reports on the importance of the Permian Basin oil field, and written opinion pieces for local newspapers supporting fossil fuels."[9] The *Times* also exposed testimonials from three imaginary women on the organization's website, "two of whom are represented with stock photos and one with a photo used without permission from the Flickr page of a photographer in the Philippines."[10]

The fakery went beyond the photos. The *Times* uncovered internal documents that laid out a "strategic communications" tactic of FTI employees assuming false identities to disrupt online discussions. FTI offers its clients a menu of fake personas, including "the Derailleur" (who tries to get the comment thread to focus on a detailed non-issue), the "Drunken Conspiracy Theorist Uncle" (who agrees with a negative viewpoint but then lumps it in with other unrelated and offensive issues), the "Semantic Nitpicker," the "Skeptical Capitalist," the "Patronizing Voice of Reason," the "Confused Time Traveler," the "Concerned Hipster," and—I swear I am not making this up—the "Dog Typing on a Keyboard." For money, FTI "dogs" would disrupt unhelpful Internet debate with a barrage of "very poor grammar, spelling, and punctuation . . . to clutter up the thread and make it very hard to read." Classy stuff, huh?

TASSC, the "Annapolis Center," and FTI are all snapshots from a massive web of front groups and professionals who serve them. It would take too many pages to document them all.

What would justify setting up a disinformation apparatus at this scale? Let's start with $660 billion. That's the amount the International Monetary Fund—a global group of highly trained economists and academics—calculates is the U.S. subsidizes the fossil fuel industry *every year*.[11] How many front groups, how many super PACs, how many lobbying shops, would someone set up to defend an annual subsidy of $660 billion? How many trade associations would they take over? How big a covert operation would it be cost-effective to run?

Make the math easy: someone who spent $6.6 billion every year on this mischief would see a hundredfold annual return on investment. And other industries, with other nefarious purposes, could join in and share the cost. By comparison, in the 2020 election cycle, all the presidential campaigns together spent about $4 billion, congressional campaigns spent $3.8 billion, and parties spent $3 billion.[12] If you want to understand why Republicans in Congress today seem to have no agenda other than to gum up the works, $660 billion—the value their climate inertia provides to fossil fuel oligarchs—is a good place to start. As an example of influencers oppressing the people, it's hard to do better than a covert campaign that manipulates the federal government to pump billions of dollars out of the public's pocket and into a few polluting corporate coffers. The right wing rails against "government handouts" for regular people who are down on their luck; its donors gorge on corporate welfare in the hundreds of billions.

These covert campaigns don't just help fossil fuel groups feed at the public spigot; they do lasting, drive-by damage. The tobacco and climate-denial "think tanks" first questioned the research showing that tobacco causes cancer and that climate change is a real and urgent threat. Then they went after individual scientists who spoke out about these truths, including my friend Michael Mann, whose work produced the "hockey stick" graph that shows the sudden spike in global warming in the twentieth century.* Then they attacked the entire concept of science and expertise itself.

I am writing this in the middle of a pandemic. By mid-2021, more than 99 percent of the Americans dying from COVID-19 were those who decided not to get the vaccine.[13] They don't trust the science. They don't trust the government. What diet of propaganda infected them with these attitudes, after vaccines against polio, smallpox, diphtheria, and other illnesses have saved so many lives? The anti-vaxxers are but

---

* It turned out when they went after Michael that they had grabbed a ferret by the teeth, and they probably now wish they'd left him alone—he is a fierce advocate who recently published *The New Climate War*, his fifth book about climate change and the political forces that oppose doing anything about it.

one deadly legacy of the right-wing dark-money web of science denial and the oligarchs who fund its covert operations.

We can disagree on how to resolve problems, but it's another thing altogether to lie about the science, and it's even worse when the false rhetoric is funded by hidden special interests, so no one knows who's actually responsible for the lying. Unfortunately, there is a lot of money to be made—and so a lot of money being spent—in perpetuating lies. Dark money, thanks to the Supreme Court Republicans, makes that lying possible now at an industrial scale. Front groups are the spreaders.

I've tangled with these front groups. Indeed, I've aggravated the hell out of them. Give the powerful dark-money interests a scare, and I've found their behavior follows a pattern. I've seen this often enough to recognize when the "Scheme machine" has been activated. Let me share two examples.

Years ago, I suggested that climate denial could be actionable fraud under the civil RICO statute. I compared the corporate climate deniers to the tobacco industry defendants whom the DOJ had successful sued in the 1990s for fraud.[14] Hoo-boy, I got a reaction.

Years later, I filed an amicus brief in the first *New York State Rifle & Pistol* case, calling out the Supreme Court's pattern of partisan wins for big donor interests and all the dark money lurking around the Court.[15] Another big reaction. Indeed, the dissent huffed that the Court was being "manipulated in a way that should not be countenanced,"[16] apparently in reference to my brief, and Justice Alito followed up with a speech complaining about "Senators and others with thoughts of bullying the Court."[17]

I touched a nerve both times because denying the reality of climate change and capturing the federal courts are central purposes of the dark-money operation. The reaction both times followed a predictable, orchestrated pattern of what I call "faux outrage."

The first telltale sign of the "faux outrage" operation was that the initial reaction arose entirely out of right-wing media, after little or no splash in the mainstream legitimate press. Perhaps the whole regular media had missed something important that I did, but more likely I had triggered something important to these dark-money interests, who then orchestrated the reaction in right-wing media. The regular media took note only after the noise level from the right-wing mouthpieces itself became newsworthy.

The second telltale was timing. Reaction on the right started up within a few days, persisted at a steady rate for a couple of weeks, and then ended. It came, it stayed, and then it went, like a media campaign. Which makes sense when you look at the network of PR apparatus employed by the dark-money right.

A third telltale is that much of the product was written by the "usual suspects." Some of the authors attacking me deliver right-wing "faux outrage" regularly, over a wide variety of topic areas; others specialize in facilitating the right-wing climate denial or Court-capture enterprises. After a while, the *dramatis personae* of the right-wing outrage machine become recognizable—characters such as Hans von Spakovsky and Diana Furchtgott-Roth, who opine on a marvelous array of topics. In these operations, the same cast member sometimes fired off multiple similar pieces in different outlets—another signal of an artificial effort.

A fourth telltale was strikingly similar analogies, language, and talking points. My personal favorite moment was when the *Wall Street Journal* editorial page had to post an editor's note "apologiz[ing] for the similarity" of its editorial to an earlier article in the *National Review*.[18] (For the record, I accept that the *Wall Street Journal* did not plagiarize the *National Review*; I think the reality was that both pieces copied from the same dark-money talking points.)

The fifth and most telling red flag is that the hook—the locus of the "faux outrage"—wasn't true. People all saying the same true thing doesn't signal much. But when a little bunch of people are all saying the same false thing, that's a signal that something's up, that there is some connection.

When I suggested the tobacco case could serve as precedent for investigating fossil fuel–funded climate denial, the faux-outrage falsehood was that I wanted a criminal investigation, to throw people I disagreed with "in prison." I was Torquemada, the Inquisitor! A very cursory look, either at what I actually said or at the actual record of the tobacco case, would have shown that it was a civil lawsuit. The remedy in that case was an order to the tobacco industry to cease and desist from its fraudulent behavior. No one went to prison. But it's easier to whip up faux outrage over "criminalizing disagreement" than it is over making an industry cease systematic fraud—so that's what they made up.

On my Supreme Court brief, the common fabrication was that we wanted to "pack" the Court with extra justices. This accusation, at a time when right-wing interests are systematically packing the Court with ideologues, is ironic. But more to the point, it's not what we said in the brief. I had publicly supported changes at the Court—a binding code of ethics, better disclosure of gifts and hospitality, less appellate "fact-finding," real disclosure of dark-money funders around the Court, fewer partisan 5–4 decisions—all of which are entirely reasonable. Precisely zero of the "faux outrage" articles addressed any of those proposals. The only proposal they did discuss was a fabricated one.*

Lying to prop up faux outrage against my efforts to enforce the laws and to spotlight dark money in the Supreme Court is symptomatic of a larger plague of lying in the right-wing influence effort. A striking admission of how this big-money fixery depends on lies was written by *Business Insider*'s Josh Barro, a Republican who interned for Grover Norquist at the anti-tax group Americans for Tax Reform and then worked at the conservative Manhattan Institute for Policy Research before leaving the party in disgust over its embrace of Donald Trump. Just before the 2016 election, Barro wrote: "If [conservatives] look honestly enough, they will realize the conservative information sphere has long been full of lies. The reason for this is that lying has

---

*Apparently our brief got under Justice Alito's skin. He was particularly rankled that the Court declined to take up the case (which was the outcome we had urged, for the good reason that the challenged law was no longer on the books). He talked about us at the National Lawyers Convention in 2020. It is, he said, "wrong for anybody . . . to try to influence our decisions by anything other than legal argumentation." Todd Ruger, "Justice Alito Speech Leads to Rare Court-Congress Dialogue," *Roll Call* (Nov. 13, 2020). That's a bit rich from someone whose majority has been created by hundreds of millions of dollars in dark special-interest money, who spends lots of time at swanky conservative conferences and galas.

He was not similarly irked when Laura Ingraham vented that Congress should "circumscribe the jurisdiction of this Court" if it wouldn't overturn *Roe*. Nor when Tucker Carlson called Justice Kavanaugh a "cringing little liberal" on national TV after the justice declined to strike down vaccine mandates for health workers. In court, we would call these excited utterances—admissions made in the heat of the moment. It is evidence that someone sure thinks the Federalist Society justices have been bought and should be delivering. Justice Alito's silence after these right-wing outbursts on national television is pretty telling too.

been the most effective way to promote many of the policies favored by donor-class conservatives, and so they built an apparatus to invent and spread the best lies."[19] They have, he explained, "built a network of think tanks and magazines and pressure groups funded by wealthy donors whose job was to come up with arguments that would sell the donor-class agenda to the masses."[20] This is the opinion of someone who worked at the heart of the right's misinformation web. Insider admissions are telling evidence.* (Just in case the Supreme Court wasn't in on the joke—I never wanted to give up on the prospect of good faith at the Court—I alerted them to this very language in one of my amicus briefs, warning the justices that they are being played.[21] It had no apparent effect.)

With this juggernaut of deceit poised and ready, it's really not out of their way to target lies against one annoying senator. These are the groups that are fronting fact-free appeals to our highest court. The timing of the "faux outrage" surge, its arrival through right-wing media, the matching falsehoods, the near-plagiary arguments, the "usual suspects" authors—all of it suggests organized, orchestrated effort. And that suggests a Scheme.

I guess I should add that there are persistent attempts to mock, undermine, and criticize me in right-wing media, much more than my status as the junior senator from the smallest state would explain. I'm actually a top target. The only reasonable conclusion is that my work on dark money, climate denial, and Court capture is seriously pissing someone off. If there was no there there, I really would not be worth all their trouble. But there is a "there there." Just ask David Brock, another person who worked at the heart of the right wing's web. In yet another insider admission, he called out the right wing's "long game to capture the courts, and the Supreme Court in particular."[22]

---

*These revelations are not one-offs. In November 2021, two longtime conservative pundits, Stephen Hayes and Jonah Goldberg, left Fox News because of its lies about the January 6 insurrection at the U.S. Capitol. A few weeks later, Goldberg was asked by NPR's Steve Inskeep if Fox News personalities had been "lying to [his] family for months." "Yes," Goldberg replied. "The Republican Party and conservative media world is full of people who know the truth and say something else."[23]

CHAPTER EIGHT

Super PACs, 501(c)s, and Corporate Shareholders

Truth never damages a cause that is just.
—Mahatma Gandhi

AS THE SCHEME CLOSED IN ON THE LAST three Court vacancies, it could add to its front-group arsenal a new array of weaponry, thanks to *Citizens United*. According to the 5–4 majority in *Citizens United*, unlimited "independent" expenditures would not corrupt the system—or appear to corrupt it—because there would be transparency. Perhaps the Republican Supreme Court justices actually thought that they would start seeing political ads with taglines like "ExxonMobil approved this message," or "Facebook sponsored this ad." Perhaps. If they believed that, developments quickly proved them wrong as this new weaponry was deployed.

The first development was super PACs. A regular PAC, or political action committee, can contribute only in limited and reported amounts directly to candidates, and the money that comes into a regular PAC is also both limited and reported. A *super* PAC, on the other hand, can accept unlimited amounts of money and spend unlimited money on elections so long as its spending is "independent"—that is, the money doesn't go to a candidate and isn't "coordinated" with their campaign (wink, wink). Since 2010, super PACs have churned through more than $6 billion in donations. More than $1 billion of that came from just eleven donors.[1]

As to "transparency," yes, super PACs come with disclosure requirements. But nothing requires the *real* donor to be disclosed. The real donor can hide behind a front group—after the *Massachusetts Citizens for Life* decision, usually a not-for-profit entity—and only the front group's name is disclosed.

These weaponized political front groups are often referred to by the section of the Internal Revenue Code under which they're organized: 501(c)s. Donations to traditional charities, or 501(c)(3)s, are tax-deductible, and those charities basically cannot spend on elections at all. But those organized under Sections 501(c)(4) ("social welfare" organizations), 501(c)(5) (unions), or 501(c)(6) (business associations, like the Chamber of Commerce) don't face that bar. Instead, although the Internal Revenue Code says these organizations must operate "exclusively" for the public good, IRS regulations interpret that to mean only that they can't have politicking as a "primary" purpose. That in turn came to mean that these nonprofit organizations could spend up to half their funds on elections—a 50 percent rule.

Here's the kicker: they don't have to tell us who's funding them. In fact, under rules issued by the Trump administration, *they don't even have to tell the IRS*—trust, but don't verify.[2] So someone who gives to a 501(c) group that makes independent political expenditures, instead of giving directly to a super PAC, gets complete anonymity.* Of course, the 50 percent rule means they get only half the value of their money in political advertising. But they get secrecy. Basically, they pay a 50 percent secrecy fee for the 50 percent that goes into ads. For donors like the fossil fuel industry, with unlimited funds, that's inconsequential.

And it's often not even a 50 percent fee, because the extra 50 percent spent to maintain anonymity can be routed to another friendly group, which can then spend half of *its* 50 percent on political ads (nothing says so-called independent groups can't coordinate with one another), so now the fee is only 25 percent, and so forth. A crew of

---

*This racket doesn't just keep citizens in the dark about who is telling them what to think about candidates and issues; it creates avenues for foreign influence. A foreign government that wanted to influence our elections could give to a 501(c)(4) organization knowing that their donor identity would never be disclosed even to the IRS. Secrecy is secrecy, protecting anyone, and it's how Russia—or any other country—could influence our elections.

four "social welfare" organizations—perhaps with the same staff and address—could cycle a million-dollar donation through themselves and put nearly 95 percent of the donation into political ads. All of this is further facilitated by the complacent canard that political "issue" ads aren't "political." The whole smelly deal is a racket run to keep citizens in the dark.

When the IRS tried to clean up this mess a few years ago, it ran into its own gale force "faux outrage" storm, also kicked up by the right-wing influence machine. Right-wing news threw a fit. The IRS commissioner was repeatedly threatened by House Republicans with impeachment. A junior IRS official was hauled before Congress and referred for criminal prosecution by the Department of Justice. And the Obama administration rolled over, missing an epic teachable moment. By the time an exhaustive inspector general investigation confirmed that the influence machine's charges were bogus, that the "faux outrage" was in fact very "faux," the damage had been done. Dark money had an avenue into politics no one dared touch.

Organizations with 501(c) designation enjoy the benefit of nonprofit status. But the Court didn't limit its *Citizens United* decision to nonprofits. Now ExxonMobil or Facebook or Merck could use unlimited shareholder money for political purposes, too. These are public companies. Surely they would need to tell their shareholders if that's what they were doing? Nope. In fact, as of 2021, more than half of the Fortune 500 still refuse to disclose donations to 501(c)(4) groups that are laundered into political advertising.[3] It's taken hundreds of shareholder actions to force many companies to make disclosures at all.

The Securities and Exchange Commission could have done something about that. The SEC sets the rules for what information public companies must disclose to investors. After the Supreme Court said that its ruling in *Citizens United* wouldn't lead to corruption because transparency would save us, academics and industry leaders called upon the SEC to make that assurance meaningful with disclosure rules. Public Citizen recently reported that the petition it filed in 2011 calling for disclosure of corporate political spending "has received more than 1.2 million comments—the most in the agency's history—from diverse stakeholders including the late founder of Vanguard, John Bogle, five state treasurers, a bi-partisan group of former SEC chairs and commissioners, Members of Congress, and investment professionals representing $690 billion in assets."[4]

But President Obama's SEC chair, Mary Jo White, decided that she didn't want to get the agency involved in "politics." (I'm guessing she saw the IRS faux firestorm and wanted none of it.) This is another story of where Democrats missed their window to act. Once Republicans took over the Senate and House—just as folks were waking up to the real havoc wreaked by *Citizens United*—they put in the SEC's annual appropriations bill a provision barring the agency from proceeding with a rule requiring political disclosures. That's right: Republicans blocked the SEC, the agency entrusted with safeguarding investors' interests, from requiring companies to tell investors what political viewpoints their money is funding.* They *really* don't want you to know who's behind their gravy train.

In sum, between the mercenary armies targeting regulatory agencies, the coordinated array of Koch-funded right-wingers, the tobacco and climate denial operations, and this new super PAC/dark-money weaponry, did the corporate right have the means to deploy this Court-capture Scheme? Oh, yes, indeed.

---

* Contrast this with unions, which not only have exhaustive reporting requirements, but also have to keep representing employees who refuse to pay them.

PART V

Method

CHAPTER NINE

The Federalist Society Turnstile

[W]e have six Republican appointees on this court after all the
money that has been raised, the Federalist Society and all these
fat cat dinners . . .
                                            —LAURA INGRAHAM, FOX NEWS

AS WE'VE SEEN, THE FAR RIGHT LEARNED THROUGH hard experience
that democracy didn't serve its ends. It's hard to get elected officials to
push an agenda that the American public mostly despises, like eliminating Social Security, Medicare, and the U.S. Post Office—all part
of the 1980 platform that David Koch ran on as the Libertarian Party
vice presidential candidate. So they had a motive. Thanks to the Powell secret report that pointed them at the Court, they had a plan. As
we have shown, they had means galore. And thanks to influence at the
Court and unrelenting pressure on the IRS, FEC, and SEC, they had
the vehicles to funnel huge amounts of secret money into the system.

But a Scheme like this to capture the Supreme Court needs coordination. Here, investigative journalist Jackie Calmes wrote in her book
Dissent, "Republicans had an edge. They had a system to put proven
conservatives on the courts."[1] Remember that because of their lifetime appointments, judges are immune from the wrath of the public.
Stack courts with judges willing to deliver on this mission, and you can
evade democratic accountability. And it's a bargain. Even $580 mil-
lion spent on an elaborate, covert scheme to capture the Court is
more cost-effective than continuously throwing billions into two-year

election cycles, particularly when the people you elect still won't do all the things you want.

Key to that system, and sitting at the center of the Scheme's dark-money web, is the Federalist Society for Law and Public Policy Studies. The organization began as a small group of conservative law students and professors at Yale and the University of Chicago who wanted to provide a counterweight to what they viewed as liberal orthodoxy at law schools (recall Lewis Powell, whose memo called for this kind of initiative).[2] The Federalist Society's first conference, at Yale Law School in 1982, was described as "Woodstock" for the budding conservative legal movement.[3] Speakers included future Supreme Court Justice Antonin Scalia, future SCOTUS nominee Robert Bork, and future Solicitor General Ted Olson, whom history will remember as the man who got the Supreme Court to stop Florida from recounting its ballots and to install George W. Bush as president.

Today, the Federalist Society has chapters at more than two hundred law school campuses, as well as undergraduate, attorney, and academic chapters, and boasts some seventy thousand members.[4] The Federalist Society's Washington, DC, office also serves as a think tank to promote its philosophy of "individual freedom and limited government." (We all know, I hope, what those buzzwords really mean.) In 2018, Politico called it "one of the most influential legal organizations in history."[5] I completely disagree with its extreme anti-government, de-regulatory, pro-corporate, bought-and-paid-for agenda, but this is America. They get to hang out together, and they get to say their piece.

However, that's not the end of the story. As Michael Kruse of Politico observed, "Over the years, the Federalists have honed a disciplined, excessively modest narrative of their origins and purpose—that they are simply a facilitator of the exchange of ideas, a high-minded fulcrum of right-of-center thought, a debating society that doesn't take overtly partisan, political positions. That narrative is not wrong. It's just not the whole truth."[6]

The whole truth is that the Federalist Society wears a third hat: the organization is being used to capture America's judiciary, and it is this role that is dangerous. Today, a shocking six of the nine members of the Supreme Court have all been involved with this dark-money-funded organization—Justices Thomas, Alito, Gorsuch, Kavanaugh, and Barrett, and Chief Justice Roberts.[7]

This is unprecedented. But so was candidate Trump's decision in the wake of Justice Scalia's death to hand over to the Federalist Society and its fixer Leonard Leo the task of identifying candidates for the Supreme Court. Trump made his Supreme Court list public before the election and bragged that all the candidates had been "picked by the Federalist Society," which he called the "gold standard."[8] I suspect that the release of that list (and probably an agreement to populate his environmental agencies with fossil fuel flunkies) explains why the Koch brothers, with their arsenal of hundreds of millions ready to deploy in the 2016 race, quietly dropped their objection to Trump's candidacy.[9] Like medieval baronies, House of Koch made peace with House of Trump. The price was controlling the Court appointments and the climate agenda.

The Federalist Society does not stand alone. It is deeply enmeshed in a right-wing apparatus of funders, think tanks, law firms, marketing firms, academics, pseudo-journalists, shell companies, "astroturf" groups, and "social welfare" organizations. The vast majority of this apparatus is funded anonymously. It is a massive enterprise designed to steer the law steadily in a pro-elite, deregulatory, anti-democracy direction. And it's designed to capture the Court.

In this web, the Federalist Society's role is to groom, vet, select, and then—seemingly by any means necessary—appoint judges willing to impose a specific set of political, legal, and economic theories. (No surprise: these theories coincide almost perfectly with the interests of Federalist Society big-money donors. And when they don't, you can guess which gives way.) The Federalist Society hosts the donor-controlled turnstile through which ambitious Republican judges must pass to get to the Court.

Decades of donor investment in this apparatus paid off under Trump. At least 80 percent of Trump judicial appointees, including all three of his Supreme Court picks, are current or former Federalist Society members, and "FedSoc" donor victories at the Supreme Court are commonplace.[10] The grip of this group is so tight over recent appointees to the Court that Court-watcher Dahlia Lithwick coined the term "Federalist Society sock puppets."[11] If that seems harsh, consider that Ronald Reagan's solicitor general Charles Fried balked at calling the Court's Federalist Society justices "conservative." "They're reactionaries," he said. "That's the only correct term for them."[12]

Let's examine that apparatus. The latest state-of-the-art set-up for dark-money political influence is a twinned 501(c)(3) and 501(c)(4). Two particularly smelly examples of this phenomenon are the Judicial Crisis Network and Americans for Prosperity, both of which play alongside the Federalist Society—in JCN's case, literally alongside—in the Court-capture Scheme.

JCN is organized as a 501(c)(4) organization, which means it considers itself—to quote the Internal Revenue Code—a "civic league or organization not organized for profit but operated exclusively for the promotion of social welfare . . . the net earnings of which are devoted exclusively to charitable, educational, or recreational purposes." JCN has a paired 501(c)(3) organization, the Judicial Education Project, that can accept tax-deductible donations. The two organizations share the same staff and address at a downtown Washington, DC, office building. The overtly political work gets done by the 501(c)(4); the support for that political work—staffing, administration, research, public relations, advocacy, and any other relevant task—can be done by the 501(c)(3), and is tax-deductible (meaning it is subsidized by you, the taxpayer). Sweet deal.

In 2020, Senate Democrats investigated JCN and determined that it had made more than 10,500 ad buys since 2012, mostly on political "issue" ads.[13] We also know through tax filings (filed long after the fact) that in 2016, a single unknown donor gave JCN $17.9 million for an ad campaign to blockade Judge Merrick Garland's nomination from advancing and to land now-Justice Neil Gorsuch in the blockaded seat.[14] All told, JCN received four separate anonymous donations of $15 million or more following Justice Scalia's death, including in 2017 a $17.1 million donation to run a media campaign promoting the troubled nomination of now-Justice Brett Kavanaugh.[15] With all this anonymous money, JCN itself bragged, it was "ready on day one with a $12 million war chest" for the Kavanaugh campaign."[16]

We don't know who wrote those checks, or whether the same

person wrote all those checks. And because of that, we don't know what that person's motive was, nor what particular business they may have had before the Court. Court decisions can sometimes benefit an interest by hundreds of millions, even billions, of dollars. Remember that the Supreme Court Republican justices were willing to engage in procedural overreach of historic proportions to scrap the Obama administration's Clean Power Plan. Analysts predicted the rule would lead to $34 to $54 billion in savings and health benefits for an anticipated direct cost to industry of $8.4 billion.[17] But the fossil fuel industry wasn't interested in the benefits, only the costs. If the fossil fuel industry gave JCN over $60 million to influence the makeup of the Supreme Court, and saved $8.4 billion, it would have been a very rewarding investment.

As for that other 50 percent that IRS rules prohibit "social welfare" organizations from spending for political purposes, here's what JCN does. In 2020, Democratic senators and staff determined that JCN had given more than $38.2 million in "grants"—no surprise, almost half of its total budget—to other advocacy groups since 2011,[18] with the largest contributions going to groups with explicit political aims, such as the Republican Attorneys General Association.* As we noted in our courts report, "[t]hese grants—much like JCN's so-called 'issue ads' targeting 'vulnerable Democrat Senators'—don't count against JCN's political spending limits."[19] Since JCN gets to keep its donors confidential, by the time the money hits the next organization's account, the donor, if reported at all, is listed simply as JCN; the original source remains a mystery. And that organization gets to do the same thing with

---

* The Republican Attorneys General Association, or RAGA, has been captured by the same dark-money groups driving the Scheme. RAGA funded the infamous January 6 rally and used robocalls to bring people to DC that day and march on the Capitol. A *New York Times* investigation found that the group—which for years has carried water for the right-wing interests, launching challenges to the Affordable Care Act, vaccine mandates, environmental regulations, and more—coordinates closely with fossil fuel and other corporate interests, in some cases simply pasting a company's words straight onto their own letterhead. David B. Frohnmayer, a former Republican attorney general of an earlier vintage, explained why it is dangerous to use "a public office, pretty shamelessly, to vouch for a private party with substantial financial interest" without disclosing the connection: "The puppeteer behind the stage is pulling strings, and you can't see."[20] As a former attorney general myself, it is painful to see these states' top lawyers flack for a right-wing agenda and serve corporate interests, not the people's.

50 percent of its capital, and so on down the line, like Russian nesting dolls.

For years, I have been the lead Democrat on the DISCLOSE Act, which would require transparency for any election expenditure over $10,000. (No surprise, Republican senators have blocked it from becoming law.) In our bill, we've gone to great lengths to make sure we'd really be able to follow the money through the multiple screens used to hide the real donors, often behind double and triple layers of concealment.[21] Because that's how the game is played.

Other funds went from JCN directly to right-wing groups like the NRA, which spent $100 million to support Trump and Republican candidates in the 2016 election and poured millions more into the campaigns to confirm Justices Gorsuch and Kavanaugh. Still more flowed to fake grassroots groups like the "Honest Elections Project" and "Concerned Women of America."* These "astroturf" groups are designed to seem like just a bunch of thoughtful, committed ordinary citizens. Not quite.

To understand this fakery better, let's take a look at the "Honest Elections Project." Buckle up. We did a little homework and discovered that a few years ago the Judicial Crisis Network changed its name in Virginia, where it is incorporated, and became the "Concord Fund."[22] Under Virginia corporate law, a company can register a "fictitious name," and operate legally under that fictitious name. Well, the "Concord Fund" registered "Judicial Crisis Network," its old name, as a new fictitious name under which to conduct business. Why the Judicial Crisis Network felt it had to change its name, and then adopt its old name as a new fictitious name, you will have to ask them. But that wasn't all.

The "Concord Fund" also registered another fictitious name to operate under: "Honest Elections Project Action." At the same time, its twinned 501(c)(3), the Judicial Education Project, changed its name to the "85 Group" and also registered *its* old name as its new "fictitious

---

* If you've heard about the "Honest Elections Project," it's because it was in the news in 2020 urging battleground states to purge voter rolls, fighting mail-in voting, and advancing voter suppression measures. After the 2020 election, it challenged the vote count in Pennsylvania, and worked with state legislatures to pass measures to keep more people from the ballot box.

name," and also added a new fictitious name: the "Honest Elections Project." So you have twinned 501(c)s operating out of the same offices with the same staff under multiple "fictitious names." In essence, it's the same operation, trying very hard to convince people otherwise.

The organization that spent tens of millions of dollars ramming through judicial nominations—including nominees far from the mainstream, confirmed by a bare majority of the Senate, representing a minority of the population—is the same entity, now under a "fictitious name," spending millions to suppress the vote. If it is willing to spend so much on such a blatantly anti-democratic project as blocking access to the ballot box, what do we suppose it was buying with its federal court expenditures?

By the way, JCN—sorry, the Concord Fund—and the Judicial Education Project—sorry, 85 Group—also registered the additional fictitious names "Free to Learn" and "Free to Learn Action," so they are prepared to stir up right-wing panic over what they call "critical race theory."[23] As *The Guardian* observed (sometimes the most clear-eyed analyses of what is happening in America comes from outside the country), JCN's "legal maneuver allows it to operate under four different names with little public disclosure that it is the same group."[24] Of course, it's actually eight names if you count the twinned 501(c)(3) groups, and that doesn't count its link with the Federalist Society.

Research done for my Senate Judiciary subcommittee uncovered that, by 2018, outside interest groups linked to the Federalist Society had spent at least $400 million on the campaigns for President Trump's judicial nominees.[25] (This is the number later raised to $580 million by the Center for Media and Democracy.) Some of that money went to shell organizations like JCN. Some of it went to sophisticated right-wing media operators like the innocuously named "Creative Response Concepts Public Relations" firm (now CRC Strategies). CRC was paid millions to provide public relations services to multiple organizations, including JCN, during the judicial confirmation fights. It's CRC we have to thank for Justice Kavanaugh's widely criticized alibi that he had a "doppelganger"—a classmate who looked like him and attacked Dr. Christine Blasey Ford.[26] A few years earlier, CRC had "boasted that online videos, television ads, pundit commentary, opinion essays and other material supporting Gorsuch had been viewed

1.2 billion times."[27] Even once Kavanaugh was on the Court, Jackie Calmes wrote, "CRC flacks sent reporters accounts of his questions from the bench, an article lauding him for having an all-female staff, and a Fox pundit's column favorably predicting that he would support conservatives' priorities."[28]

An extraordinary amount of all this Court-capture activity ties back to the Federalist Society and Leonard Leo, who from his perch as the organization's executive vice president helped execute the Scheme.* Remember, the Federalist Society claims to be just a simple "debating society" that has nothing to do with the judicial confirmation process—and nothing to do with JCN. Yet a *Washington Post* investigation found tax filings that listed JCN's official address as the private home of Ann and Neil Corkery, "close allies of Leo," who have had leadership positions in other organizations Leo has run.[29]

The *Post* reported that while JCN's president officially got no salary from JCN, tax filings reveal he "received more than $1.5 million in fees from the Federalist Society over nine years for media training through a firm based at his home."[30] JCN and the Federalist Society are as close as Frick and Frack.

There's more. When the *Washington Post* outed the dark-money Court-capture operation run through the Federalist Society, the central spider in that web, Leonard Leo, left his office in the Federalist Society and began to help operate the Honest Elections Project. He was replaced by JCN's Carrie Severino, who supplemented her role

---

* We know from new reporting that it was the Federalist Society's Leonard Leo who "laid out the road map for Trump on the federal court system" with the goal of "transforming the foundational understanding of rights in America." Leo came up with the list of "judges that would please the Republican base" from among the "decades of conservative lawyers in the pipeline." He became a "team" with McGahn and McConnell to "keep the judicial nominations effort moving." It was Leo who took to the White House, where he had "extensive access," the revised nominees list that included Kavanaugh and Barrett. The picks were made by advisors, said McConnell, with Trump's role merely "signing off on them," and he "never veered from the lists of candidates suggested by Leo and others."

This was not about calling "balls and strikes." If you want "to have the longest possible impact on the kind of America you want," said McConnell, "you look at the courts." (More accurately, the kind of America the far-right megadonors want, I'd say.) Trump noticed. "Mitch McConnell. Judges. Judges. Judges. The only thing he wants is judges," said Trump.[31]

at JCN with Leo's old role managing the donor turnstile he had run out of the Federalist Society. They may even have bumped into each other in the hallway in this shell-game shuffle. Though JCN's tax filings say it's headquartered at Leo's friends the Corkerys' house, the day-to-day operations of the Federalist Society and the Judicial Crisis Network are run out of offices on the same hallway in the same office building in Washington, DC. In fact, when a *Post* reporter "visited the JCN offices to ask questions, a security guard contacted a longtime employee of the Federalist Society to see whether anyone at JCN was available. A Federalist Society employee then escorted the reporter to JCN's office."[32]

This is sloppy tradecraft from a covert ops point of view. But Democrats are not formidable adversaries, so the Scheme gets away with all of these "fictitious names" run by the same crew with the same donors out of the same hallway in Washington. And this is just one corner of the web of front groups the dark-money donors have spun to capture the Court.

The *Post* investigation gave us a glimpse into the network of organizations connected like Frick and Frack that slosh money around to hide their true donors and dodge tax and disclosure rules. As the 2016 election campaign heated up, Leo became president of three new nonprofits. The groups—"BH Fund," "Freedom and Opportunity Fund," and "America Engaged"—were all formed by a law firm with deep ties to the conservative movement.[33] The nonprofits reported having no employees and no websites. They had virtually no public presence. Leo's role as president of all three groups was not disclosed for nearly three years because of lags in how nonprofit groups report their annual operations to the IRS. All three entities hired CRC for public relations and consulting. (Yes, groups with virtually no public presence somehow needed public relations advice from CRC.) In 2016 and 2017, the three employee-less nonprofits raised about $33 million, with the BH Fund taking in $24,250,000 from a single donor whose identity is still not publicly known. BH Fund then gave a total of almost $3 million to the two other Leo groups, Freedom and Opportunity Fund and America Engaged.

America Engaged then passed along nearly $1 million to the NRA's lobbying arm, which, in a remarkable coincidence, announced a

$1 million campaign to support the nomination of Neil Gorsuch. The other organization, Leo's Freedom and Opportunity Fund, sent $4 million over the next two years to a group called "Independent Women's Voices," which is—no surprise—anything but "independent." Its president and chief executive, Heather Higgins, was a frequent guest on Fox News speaking, supposedly on behalf of "independent women," in support of President Trump and his judicial nominees and sowing doubt about the accuracy of Dr. Ford's testimony about Kavanaugh. A few years earlier, she had explained the advantages of seeming to be "a branded organization . . . that does not carry partisan baggage": "Being branded as neutral but actually having the people who know, know that you're actually conservative puts us in a unique position."[34] Talk about covert ops.

The *Post* scoured IRS filings and reported that "[i]n the two years following its formation, the BH Group received more than $4 million" from JCN and two other groups that were also "connected to Leo through funding, personnel and the same accountant."[35] In all, the *Post* tracked more than $250 million going into the coffers of more than two dozen nonprofits associated with Leo and his allies between 2014 and 2017. Our research later brought that number to $400 million; Center for Media and Democracy's further work raised it to $580 million by the end of 2018.[36]

That's a pretty big slush pile for someone whose day job required him—per the Federalist Society's own website—to "not participate in activism of any kind." And that's a pretty convoluted rigamarole to set up for no purpose.

No surprise that Leo is on record telling a group of conservative activists that "judicial confirmations these days are more like political campaigns."[37] He should know; he's running them—from behind a massive covert operation. And what can we glean about who in the shadows he is running them *for?* Who can write an anonymous check to JCN for $17 million? And three more $15-million-plus donations? And $24,250,000 to the BH Group? Maybe someone spent all this money out of the goodness of their heart. My experience tells me otherwise. My experience tells me there's a Scheme behind those checks.

By the end of 2019, Leo's work stacking the judiciary had paid the big donors extraordinary dividends. It had proved well worth the price for Leo, a deeply conservative Christian Republican, to throw his support behind the candidacy of Trump, a thrice-married former Democrat and vocal supporter of abortion rights. The Scheme had cleaned up on judges. But by 2020, Trump was looking more and more like a loser who would not be making many more judicial appointments.

When Leo left his role as executive VP at the Federalist Society in early 2020 (he remained on its board), he launched a new group called CRC Advisors with—you guessed it—the same guy who runs CRC Strategies.[38] As usual, there was subterfuge involved, linked to all those "fictitious name" groups we discussed earlier. CRC Advisors was involved in the rebranding of the Concord Fund and 85 Fund, through which it planned "to funnel tens of millions of dollars into conservative fights around the country."[39] The "Honest Elections Project" was one of the resulting fictitious names in that rebranding. One investigative website summarized it thus: "Leonard Leo is using CRC Advisors to manage H.E.P. and help ensure strategic coordination across a network of conservative non-profits."[40]

Donors evidently followed, because CRC Advisors committed to spending a "minimum of $10 million for an issue advocacy campaign focusing on judges in the 2020 cycle."[41] And of course, the judicial turnstile moved down the hall, with JCN's Severino now selecting and grooming judicial candidates and, by the end of the year, managing the nomination of Amy Coney Barrett.

The funders lurking behind these front groups weren't just supporting the Scheme with their massive dark-money donations. Big donors at the same time had a free-for-all with political dark money. They hid their hands behind dark-money screens in their political election spending, just as they hid their hands behind dark-money screens in the Court-capture network. Dark-money spigots pour into the Scheme *and* into political races. Because of the ugly effects of Court decisions, wealthy interests are closer than they have been in a century to a quiet capture of our democracy, accomplished through anonymous dark money and through front groups with "fictitious names." The Framers of the Constitution must be rolling in their graves.

Numbers are telling, so let's follow the political dark-money numbers the Dark Money Court set loose.

The election of 2010, just months after *Citizens United* allowed unlimited secret corporate political spending, was an "off-cycle" election—the presidency wasn't at issue. Back in the 1998 election—also off-cycle—outside groups had spent just over $10 million on "independent" expenditures.[42] In 2002, the next off-cycle election, they spent $16 million; in 2006, the following one, $37 million.[43]

Ugly, and growing, but then came the flood.

In 2010, on the heels of *Citizens United*, with less than ten months to gear up from that January decision for the November election, the spending multiplied by a factor of six, from $37 million to $205 million.[44] And it kept going. In last year's 2020 presidential-cycle election, nearly $3 *billion* was spent on federal elections "independent" (supposedly) of political parties or candidates.[45] According to a nonpartisan good-government watchdog, the Center for Responsive Politics, outside groups out-spent *candidates' own campaigns* in thirty-five House and Senate races in 2020.[46] Even before 2020's $3 billion flood, outside spending in the decade following *Citizens United* had clocked in at six times more than it had been in the entirety of the prior two decades.[47]

Citizens United and other Supreme Court decisions empowering all this anonymous influence represent one side of a vicious cycle, the side in which the Court cossets and protects dark money. The other side of the cycle is how dark money has helped the Scheme to stack the Court, just as industry stacks a captured regulatory agency. To perpetrate this is no small deed. It has required an arsenal of tactics, including a doctrine factory where useful legal theories are created, an auditioning process by which judges compete for advancement, a Senate rubber stamp for confirming them, and an armada of amici to signal the donors' wishes to the Court. And the Scheme has it all.

CHAPTER TEN

The Doctrine Factory and Casting Call

Political language . . . is designed to make lies sound truthful and murder respectable, and to give an appearance of solidity to pure wind.

—GEORGE ORWELL

COVER DOCTRINES

The Scheme donors out to capture the Court need legal theories that will deliver the right outcomes for them. It's best for them if these theories can be disguised, so that they can be deployed with some semblance of impartiality by friendly justices. This gives the movement intellectual cover and allows its adherents to shield themselves with "theories" or "doctrines," without confessing the extreme outcomes they seek or the special interests they serve. It's "principle." To do this, the theories need to be fabricated, reverse-engineered from the desired outcomes, then they must be socialized and moved into the mainstream. This requires some kind of machinery. And a doctrine factory exists.

The Scheme's doctrine factory relies, like the Scheme's other elements, on covert work, dark money, and many of the same front groups. The Federalist Society helps cook up and socialize these doctrines, but it's not alone. There's the Koch-funded Cato Institute and the Heritage Foundation, among others. Probably the worst of them all is an ideological hothouse just down the road from Washington, DC, at George Mason University, a public university based in Fairfax, Virginia.

Cooking up cover doctrines has a long history at George Mason. It was where the radical anti-government fringe found a home in the decades after a unanimous Supreme Court ruled in *Brown v. Board of Education* that the Jim Crow "separate but equal" standard violated the Constitution and that public schools would have to be integrated. Objectors didn't argue "keep Black kids out of our white kids' schools"; they argued "states' rights." Giving public vouchers to white students to attend segregated private schools (schools that could avoid *Brown's* desegregation mandate) made it a "school choice" movement, not a "pro-segregation" movement.

As Professor Nancy MacLean recounts in her book *Democracy in Chains*, many of these arguments were originally developed by conservative economists then based at the University of Virginia, who responded to *Brown* by crafting seemingly "neutral" arguments like these to push back against popular and bipartisan civil rights laws.[1] When their activities lost favor at the state's flagship university, the economists found refuge at the fledgling George Mason University.[2] Koch money followed.[3] George Mason became a hothouse funded by anonymous big donors to grow, tend, fertilize, and propagate cover doctrines—doctrines that are doubly outrageous. First, they're faux "doctrines," reverse-engineered to produce a result. Second, they're optional; when they don't produce the right result, they're ignored.

In 2016, George Mason received $10 million from Charles Koch and another $20 million from an anonymous mega-donor, with a few conditions: rename the law school after recently deceased Justice Antonin Scalia, preserve the university's so-called Center for the Study of the Administrative State, and give the anonymous donor veto power over appointment of the school's dean—a flagrant surrender of academic independence.[4] Massive Koch money also backed a nonprofit think tank based at George Mason called the Mercatus Center. The Mercatus Center receives no funding from the university or the state, but its location on the university campus—it calls itself a "university-based research center"—gives its output of donor ideology an academic varnish.

Big right-wing donations to GMU came with other conditions as well. A trove of papers released in 2018 showed how deeply enmeshed donors have been in shaping GMU's "scholarly" output since at least the 1990s.[5] "As George Mason grew from a little-known commuter school to a major public university and a center of libertarian scholarship," the *New York Times* reported, "millions of dollars in donations from conservative-leaning donors like the Charles Koch Foundation had come with strings attached"—like allowing donors to tell the university which professors and administrators to hire.[6]

Who was the legal executor of the 2016 donations? The Federalist Society's own Leonard Leo, the spider at the center of the web secretly controlling judicial appointments.[7] Small world. He got this role as "president of a third-party beneficiary called BH Fund in charge of enforcing the donor agreement with the law school,"[8] operating "as a kind of emissary between the Kochs and the university."[9] The Koch operation could also control the Mercatus Center money pipeline and its hiring. And the Federalist Society was able to move a Scalia Law School professor, Neomi Rao, onto the powerful United States Court of Appeals for the District of Columbia Circuit, with oversight over federal regulatory agencies. Rao, who has suggested that independent agencies are unconstitutional and is no fan of the administrative state, set up the dark-money Center for the Study of the Administrative State and coordinated the anonymous $20 million donor strings that attached to the Center.[10] Had she carried them over to her new court in a backpack, Judge Rao could not more directly insert into American law the hothouse legal theories concocted at the Center for big donors.*

Of all the cover doctrines, the most offensive ones twist the constitutionally enshrined concepts of liberty and freedom to protect power-grabbing, pollution, and cheating. The "freedom" to bust unions is not real freedom, not to union members; it's a power shift between employer and employee. The "freedom" to pollute for free is not freedom

---

* On the bench, Judge Rao has made a name for herself as a fervent auditioner for the Supreme Court, staking out positions that observers have called "dangerous and anti-democratic," "whackadoodle," and the "most shocking judicial opinion I've read since becoming a lawyer."[11] Judge Rao earned the national spotlight when she attempted to block a hearing when President Trump's DOJ tried to drop charges against Michael Flynn years after he had pled guilty to them, a highly unusual situation that she apparently did not want the trial court judge sniffing around—she ordered him to drop all charges without even a hearing, no questions asked. The entire DC Circuit quickly reconvened *en banc* to reverse her.

to those who suffer from the pollution; it's a power shift to polluting interests. The "freedom" for banks or for fraudsters' "boiler rooms" to cheat customers is not freedom; it's a power shift from consumers to the bottom dwellers who commit fraud in the financial services sector. These fake "freedoms" damage the real freedom that comes with being able to live in safety, peace, and prosperity.

When there's hypocrisy in the daylight, look for power in the shadows. There's a lot of hypocrisy around cover doctrines. "States' rights" was an important cover doctrine to protect Jim Crow, but where was it when *Heller* and its progeny overturned local gun safety laws, utilizing an interpretation of the Second Amendment that Chief Justice Warren Burger—a Republican appointee—called "one of the greatest pieces of fraud—I repeat the word, 'fraud'—on the American public"?[12]

The biggest canard of them all is "originalism," the legal theory that launched the Federalist Society and the conservative right-wing legal movement. "Originalism" started as the notion that courts had strayed from the original text and meaning of the Constitution and should return to a mythical "original" interpretation. But *originally*, voting was limited to people who were white, male, and owned property. *Originally*, Black slaves were quantified as "three-fifths" of a person. *Originally*, women had virtually no economic role or property rights. *Originally*, Blacks and whites could not marry, and gays could be prosecuted and imprisoned. And *originally*, an agrarian society needed little consumer protection; without massive industries, it needed no protections from abuse by massive industries. For an arch-conservative, you can see the charm of "originalism." But most normal people don't think that what everyone needs is a bit more 1788 in their lives.

Again, corporations had no role in American politics, *originally*. So where was originalism when the right-wing members of the Court considered in *Citizens United* whether to open American politics to unlimited special-interest political spending? No mention. The Court ignored originalism, and instead concocted fanciful political fairy tales about how "independence" and "transparency" would protect us from corporate-money corruption. The big-donor interests did not object to this departure from "originalist" doctrine. The donors behind the Scheme want victories and are not fussy about philosophy.

AUDITIONS

If all that the right-wing dark-money apparatus was doing was churning out sincere ideas about how to make our system of government
work better, that would hardly be objectionable. No one party or
group has a lock on good ideas. People may forget that the Affordable
Care Act—aka "Obamacare"—was based on a Republican plan implemented successfully in Massachusetts under Republican Governor
(and my Senate colleague) Mitt Romney.

But that is not what is happening. Right-wing oligarchs are using
the Republican Party to degrade government and dismantle its protections. In the words of anti-tax activist Grover Norquist, they want to
shrink government to the size where they "can drag it into the bath-
room and drown it in the bathtub." The more drowned the government, the less it can actually govern; the less it can govern, the better
for the donors. For them, the more gridlock and dysfunction in Washington, the better. It's a win-win: nothing gets done (which means corporations get to continue raking in entrenched subsidies and evading
responsibility) and people lose faith in the government. As people lose
faith in government, it gets easier to strip away government's ability to
protect them, in a darkening spiral.

This is far less about having principled policy disagreements than it
is about raw power. Just look at the official Republican policy platform
in the 2020 election: there was none.

The judiciary is there to defend us and our constitutional system
both from the encroachments of a monied elite and from the tyranny
of a mob majority. Degrading that constitutional protection requires
willing judges. So the monied elite set up the Federalist Society turnstile to ensure that, when a Republican is in the White House, there's
a ready supply of judicial candidates reflecting big-donor interests.

Ambitious judges aren't stupid. They see the turnstile, and they understand what they need to do to get through it. Some years ago, I was
speaking with a circuit court judge (for that matter, a Republican appointee). He was distressed by the conduct of some of his colleagues.
He believed they were going out of their way in legal rulings to opine
on certain issues, perhaps only tangentially related to the actual case
before them, and in doing so sending a signal. A judge takes a pretty

solemn oath to confine his attention to the parties before him, and to resolve their dispute with no one else in mind. But these judges weren't deciding the case just for the litigants, he told me. They were writing to get the attention of the gatekeepers at the Federalist Society turnstile—the big donors who pull the levers of judicial advancement in Washington for the Republican Party. The word the circuit court judge used was "auditioning." That word has stuck with me.

Perhaps the most blatant auditioner of them all was now-Justice Brett Kavanaugh. You might recall Trump's much-ballyhooed list of Supreme Court candidates, all picked by the Federal Society, for Justice Scalia's old seat. Kavanaugh's name wasn't on that initial list. But Kavanaugh had an in. As an associate counsel in the White House during the George W. Bush administration, he had worked on judicial nominations with the Federalist Society's Leonard Leo. He knew the donor influence network. Kavanaugh knew that Leo—his longtime friend at the center of the Scheme—controlled the names that went to Trump.

Kavanaugh got how the Scheme worked. He not only auditioned for Leo; he auditioned at the Federalist Society. Really, no one auditioned harder than Brett Kavanaugh. As a circuit judge, he spoke at fifty-two Federalist Society events, which has to be a record.[13] But simply parroting right-wing doctrine to friendly Federalist Society audiences might not be enough. So he made sure his circuit court opinions signaled his chops.

On abortion, Judge Kavanaugh ruled that it was okay to force an undocumented teenager, who satisfied every federal and state criterion for an abortion, to wait as the first-trimester clock ran out—a decision so beyond the pale that the full DC Circuit reviewed and reversed the ruling just days later.[14] For the social conservatives: check.

On guns, Judge Kavanaugh argued—in a dissent, thank goodness—against DC laws that banned semi-automatic rifles and that required gun owners to register their firearms.[15] The case was a follow-up to *District of Columbia v. Heller*, in which the Supreme Court decided for the first time in our two-hundred-plus-year history that the Constitution secured an individual right to own a gun.[16] Kavanaugh's dissent was even more extreme than Justice Scalia's radical opinion in that case—which is saying something. For the extremist NRA: check.

On the "administrative state," Kavanaugh wrote a dissent arguing that independent agencies like the Consumer Financial Protection Bureau—with leaders that the president can remove only for cause, not political whim—are a "significant threat to individual liberty."[17] For polluters, big banks, and other regulated entities: check.

And most important to this dark-money Scheme was his ruling—a good year before *Citizens United*—that nonprofit front groups "are constitutionally entitled to raise and spend unlimited money in support of candidates for elected office" because it is "implausible that contributions to independent expenditure political committees are corrupting."[18] Yeah, how could that possibly be corrupting? For the big donors: check and mate.

The Trump pledge to choose his justices off the Federalist Society list was a big deal. Kavanaugh was not on the initial list, but thanks to his auditioning, and Leonard Leo's help, Kavanaugh solved it. He got on the next list, locked and loaded for advancement. It has been reported that the price for Trump of Justice Kennedy's retirement was nominating Kennedy's former clerk Kavanaugh, and that this provoked a battle within the White House's Court-packing cabal about whether Kavanaugh was "too much of a 'Bushie' and might not fulfill their hard-line right-wing ambitions."[19] Kavanaugh's auditioning helped dispel that worry.

Kavanaugh wasn't the only one to audition. As a judge, Justice Gorsuch auditioned around a case called *Chevron** that is very important to donors who want to decimate federal agencies.[20] Barrett's dissent as a circuit judge in the Second Amendment case, *Kanter v. Barr*, was described as her "audition tape for the Supreme Court.[21] Gorsuch spoke at numerous Federalist Society events, as did Justice Barrett, and Justices Gorsuch and Kavanaugh took victory laps at "FedSoc" gatherings after

---

* *Chevron* is precedent that constrains federal courts from substituting their own judgment for expert agency action authorized by Congress. If you haven't heard of it, that is the advantage of capturing the Court—other than a few high-profile cases each term, judges can use theory and jargon to hide the true impact of their rulings from much of the public. If you care about the environment, a case talking about something called "*Chevron* deference" is unlikely to alarm you, especially if the decision drops around the same time as a hot-button social issue—say, abortion or birth control or LGBTQ+ rights. You'll likely be reading about that headline-making case, not about *Chevron*. When the Court applies that decision a few years later to gut an environmental regulation, it will be too late.

their confirmations. Less than a year after her confirmation, Justice Barrett was the featured speaker at a thirtieth-anniversary celebration for the McConnell Center at the University of Louisville—as in Mitch McConnell, the senator who rammed her confirmation through the Senate. She either has a great sense of irony or none at all, because the argument she chose to make at the event, as Senator McConnell looked on smiling, was that despite all evidence to the contrary, the Supreme Court justices aren't "partisan hacks." [22]

In nature, when we see behavior, we can draw conclusions. When we see, for instance, a vulture wheeling, we can expect something dead below. It is not always true; the vulture may just be wheeling in an updraft. When we get a number of vultures wheeling, it's pretty reliable evidence that there's something dead below. And when so many judges start auditioning for advancement that their behavior acquires a name from other judges, you can be pretty sure there is an audience for their auditioning—a casting agency, so to speak.

It's important to understand how brazen and beyond the bounds of constitutional norms all of this was. It is not unusual for a president to consult with outside organizations and solicit recommendations for potential judicial candidates. It is entirely another thing to outsource a core executive duty to a private organization unaccountable to the people or the government. That's what happened. When former Senate Judiciary Chairman Orrin Hatch was asked whether judicial picks were "outsourced" to the Federalist Society, he said, "Damn right." [23] Or perhaps I should say "insourced," which is what former Trump White House Counsel Don McGahn—yes, also a Federalist Society member—called it at a Federalist Society gathering in 2017. [24]

Worse yet, the private organization accepted massive anonymous donations while performing as the "insourced" turnstile. Because Federalist Society contributions can be undisclosed, or come through shell companies, we may never know what role donors like the Chamber of Commerce or the Koch operation got to play in selecting the justices who will be hearing their cases for the next several decades. But we do know that as the Scheme ramped up, the Federalist Society started receiving a lot of money from dark sources. In 2002, before it got so deeply involved in federal judicial appointments, the Society received just $5,000 from DonorsTrust, the 501(c) organization that

serves as the Kochs' "dark-money ATM."[25] DonorsTrust has no business and makes no product. Its sole function is to launder the identities from big right-wing political donations. In the most recent year
on record, 2019, the Federalist Society received $7 million via Donors-
Trust, up 140,000 percent.[26] If there's an innocent explanation, I'm all
ears.

The credibility of the judiciary derives from judges' political independence and judicial temperament. Ordinarily, judges have not
been ideologues whose identity and professional success are bound
to a single group. This spirit of judicial independence is a good thing.
We want jurists with a host of diverse personal and professional backgrounds that enrich their lived experience of the law. It's one of the
ways we ensure the system is working for everyone.* But for those who
seek to capture the Court, none of that is desirable.

A particular sore point for conservatives was Justice John Paul Stevens, a Nixon appointee who came to vote regularly with the Court's
liberal wing. The Scheme needs to eliminate the risk of such independent thought as much as possible. Ardent auditioning by a candidate
can reassure the donors watching at the turnstile, "No Stevens here.
You can count on me!"

Even people close to the president can flunk this turnstile test. A
New Yorker profile on the Federalist Society credited the group with
scuttling George W. Bush's first White House counsel, Alberto Gonzales, as a possible nominee to the Supreme Court, and then scuttling the actual nomination of his next White House counsel, Harriet
Miers.[28] According to Amanda Hollis-Brusky, a professor who studies

---

* For example, when conservative Chief Justice William Rehnquist surprised Court-
watchers in a case called *Nevada Department of Human Resources v. Hibbs*, Justice
Ruth Bader Ginsburg suggested that the Chief Justice's life experience may have
played a role in a decision many called feminist. At the time, his daughter was recently
divorced with a challenging job and occasional child care problems; sometimes the
Chief Justice left work early to pick up his grandchildren after school. This prompted
scholarly research finding that judges who had at least one daughter were about 7 percent more likely to vote "in a feminist direction" on civil rights cases with a gender
component, even if their voting record on civil rights cases overall was not particularly
liberal. The existence of daughters appeared to have no impact on a judge's civil rights
rulings where gender wasn't on the table.[27]

   To be clear, this research doesn't show bias either way. It simply demonstrates that
judges are human in their understanding of how the law affects others.

the Federalist Society, "By the time of the Miers nomination, the Federalist Society had created a signaling mechanism within the conservative movement. . . . The message Leonard [Leo] and others had sent was: If you want to rise through the ranks, we need to know you. And that's what they were all saying about Miers—'We don't know her. She is not one of us.'"[29] "One of us," of course, means someone who takes their cues from the Federalist Society and its donors—someone who is not, as Justice Stevens turned out to be, an independent thinker. Auditioning is how judicial candidates show they're "one of us."

In a 2020 *New York Times* article about how the Federalist Society big donors are reshaping the federal courts, law professor Stephen Burbank explained, "The problem as I see it is not that judges differ ideologically—of course they do—nor is it that a Republican president would look for someone with congenial ideological preferences. . . . It's that in recent decades the search has been for hard-wired ideologues because they're reliable policy agents."[30]

The Federalist Society Court-packing effort that selected these eagerly auditioning "policy agents" now enjoys a two-thirds majority on the Supreme Court.

CHAPTER ELEVEN

The Senate Conveyor Belt

A senator of the United States is an ambulant converging point
for pressures and counter-pressures of high, medium and low
purposes.

—WILLIAM S. WHITE

IF THE FIRST STEP IN THE SCHEME TO capture the courts is indoctrina-
tion and grooming, and the second is vetting and selecting—or, from
the judge's perspective, auditioning—the third step is appointing and
confirming. This means cultivating politicians willing to do whatever
it takes to jam through candidates who may be not only out of the
mainstream, but also rated downright "unqualified" by the nonpartisan American Bar Association, which has reviewed judicial candidates
from both parties since the 1950s. The Trump presidency set a record
for such "unqualified" nominees. The Federalist Society turnstile operators were looking for something different than "qualified."

After the Federalist Society justices were through the turnstile, the
donors needed a Senate conveyor belt to rapidly and reliably deliver
the justices to the Court, no matter the reservations or concerns. This
wasn't "no more Stevenses" time; this was "no more Borks."

Was there any sign of suspicious activity in the Senate, where
justices must be confirmed? You bet there was. Even before the
2010 *Citizens United* decision, Republican senators had been bend-
ing decades-old norms to stall and block President Obama's judicial
nominees. Once the Court unleashed that "tsunami of slime" and

dark money tightened its loathsome grip on Republican politics, the Republicans started violating those norms altogether. When Justice Scalia died suddenly in February 2016, Senate Republicans went into norm-breaking overdrive. They notoriously abandoned their constitutional duty to advise and consent, refusing to give President Obama's nominee Judge Merrick Garland even the courtesy of a hearing.

I was in Munich when the news about Scalia's death broke, getting coffee in the American break room at the Munich Security Conference, where John McCain and I were leading the American delegation. I remember immediately starting to think of "stealth" Republican candidates, whom it would be hard for Senate Republicans to oppose, but who would fight back against the dark-money direction the Court had taken. Who might Obama nominate, who John could lead support for in a Republican Senate? But almost instantly the message came from Mitch: no one. No Obama nominee would be considered.

How did this happen? One theory is that Mitch McConnell is an evil genius, able to see around corners. A more likely theory is that big donors—the ones who had set up and rebranded the Judicial Crisis Network to address the "Judicial Crisis" of an Obama presidency— were ready with a plan for Mitch to execute and told him what to do. We know that Scheme operative Leonard Leo contacted McConnell's judicial team in that early interval. The notion that this was a plan backed by big donors, and not McConnell freelancing, is buttressed by the way Republican senators lined up, even if awkward reversals were required—hypocritical 180s in the daylight, betraying power in the shadows. The speed with which Republican senators all scampered into line certainly makes one wonder if the big donors behind the JCN operation were also behind the Mitch McConnell dark-money political operation that goes to bat for Senate Republicans.

It's one thing for dark money to pick Supreme Court nominees. It's another thing to get U.S. senators to line up like ducklings. Why might this have happened? Let's turn our gaze to the political side.

I remember being told, in Democratic Senate lunches nearly a year earlier, the happy news that former Democratic Senator Evan Bayh (with over $9 million in leftover political funds) would run for his old seat in Indiana, that former Democratic Senator Russ Feingold would run for his old seat in Wisconsin, and that former Democratic

Governor Ted Strickland would run for the Senate seat up that cycle in Ohio. Each announcement was greeted with cheers. The 2016 Senate cycle looked good. All three, we were told, had significant polling leads. Their appearance in these races was a harbinger of Democratic victories in all three states, victories that would give Democrats control of the Senate.

But something intervened. Things went bad. Things went so bad that by the end of our 2016 August recess, with the last frantic months still ahead before the November election, Wisconsin had moved to a dead heat, we'd lost a double-digit lead in Indiana and were trailing by five points, and the Democratic Senate Campaign Committee had abandoned our "winning" Ohio candidate to focus on defending other races. We went from expecting victory to losing all three.

What had intervened? A flood of dark-money spending that would ultimately amount to $70 million had bombarded these three candidates.[1] The attack ads had started way early, in April 2015. Campaigns are rarely up on the air that far before an election. With our candidates still setting up their campaigns, the dark-money attacks went unanswered. It was like strafing aircraft still on the runway—a strafing with ultimately tens of millions of dollars of attack ads by dark-money front groups, the new political weaponry launched by *Citizens United*. As I poured my coffee in that Munich control room, the barrage was at its peak. Its success kept Mitch McConnell in as majority leader, able to control the Senate—and control the confirmation of judges.

If, at that moment, Mitch was counting on these bombardments by dark-money funders to stay in power, and if Republican senators knew that these donors were pummeling into oblivion Democrats' chances to retake the Senate, adherence to the Scheme makes political sense: you help us win; we follow your plan.

This was new political warfare, by the way. Customarily, candidates announce early in the year before the election, after the clamor from the previous election subsides. A fundraising battle then follows, a sort of proxy contest with each side trying to raise the most money, to show the strength of the campaign and bank cash for the air wars to follow. An unknown candidate may run an intro ad to push up name recognition, but otherwise the media blitz comes at the end of the campaign, when voters are paying the most attention. Unlimited money, dark money, anonymous front groups, early attack ads, and spending in the tens of millions—all of this disrupted the traditional cadence of campaigning, just as the blitzkrieg disrupted the ordinary cadence of warfare.

The shift was possible only in a world of determined big-money donors, because regular campaign contributors aren't usually engaged enough to be donating that kind of money so early. Without big-money willingness to spend early and keep the money coming, most candidates wouldn't want to spend too soon and risk not having enough cash for the final push. With unlimited money, attackers can spend whatever, whenever, and destroy opponents before they're off the ground. Instead of the usual campaign rhythm, there's "total war."

One of the problems with all this dark money being dark is that it's hard to connect the dots between the millions pouring into the Court-capture operation and the millions pouring into campaign coffers, party committees, and so-called independent attack ads. But behaviors are a tell. And the Senate's behavior was telling.

Confirming judges and justices nominated by the president is one of the most solemn and important duties the Constitution gives the Senate. One of the long-standing Senate traditions around judicial nominations is something called the "blue slip." For nearly a century, the chair of the Senate Judiciary Committee, whether Republican or Democrat, has agreed to hold a hearing on a nominee only after that nominee's two home state senators each return a "blue slip" indicating that they don't object to the candidate. Exceptions to the blue slip rule have been rare. Before 2017, there was no record of any judicial nominee confirmed without any blue slip and over the previous sixty years, just three were confirmed with only one blue slip.[2] This tradition held through the presidencies of Bill Clinton, George W. Bush, and Barack Obama; not a single judicial nominee was confirmed without two blue slips while they were in office.

The last two years of the George W. Bush administration were my first two years in the Senate. From my vantage as a junior senator on the Judiciary Committee, the judicial confirmation process seemed to work smoothly and with mutual respect. Senate Democrats controlled the Senate, and the Judiciary Committee honored the blue slip process and worked with the Bush White House to ensure that the Senate performed its "advise and consent" duties efficiently. In those last two years of President Bush's second term, we confirmed sixty-eight judicial nominees. Most of President Bush's nominees waited less than twenty days between clearing the Judiciary Committee and receiving a confirmation vote by the whole Senate.[3]

It wasn't long into President Obama's first term, however, that it became clear that something was up. Democrats controlled the House and Senate, but Senate rules still allowed Republicans to filibuster nominees, and Republican senators could stop a home-state nominee by simply not returning their blue slips. Republicans took advantage of both of these procedural tactics against President Obama's nominees. A report by Senate Democrats found: "During President Obama's first term, the average circuit court nominee waited more than seven times as long for a vote as the average Bush nominee during his two terms. According to the Congressional Research Service, 60 percent of President Bush's first-term circuit court nominees were confirmed within 30 days on the Senate Floor. In contrast, 80 percent of President Obama's first-term circuit court nominees waited more than 90 days."[4] Delaying a colleague's chosen nominee is not a small thing, and the absence of that Senate courtesy is a telltale sign of outside pressure.

During the first five years of the Obama administration, Senate Republicans filibustered thirty-six of the president's judicial nominees.[5] To put that in perspective, that was the same number filibustered in the previous *forty-two years* before his presidency.[6] Many of those filibustered nominees were eventually confirmed with strong bipartisan support. In some cases, more than ninety senators voted for the judge who'd been filibustered—clear evidence that the purpose of the filibuster was to slow the confirmation process.

Those were the nominees who got to the Judiciary Committee. Dozens of seats were left open—some for years—because Republicans refused to support *any* nominee to that seat. In eighteen cases, the president went ahead and nominated anyway, but the nominee did not advance because one or both home-state senators failed to return a blue slip.[7] No blue slip; no hearing. In some cases, Republican senators refused to return blue slips on nominees *they had recommended* to the White House.[8]

In January 2015, control of the Senate shifted to the Republicans. Mitch McConnell became majority leader, and Chuck Grassley became the chairman of the Judiciary Committee. Republicans no longer needed to filibuster; they could outright block. In contrast to the sixty-eight nominees Senate Democrats confirmed in the last two years of the Bush administration, in the last two years of the Obama administration Mitch McConnell let just five circuit court nominees get a hearing before the Judiciary Committee, and only twenty-two judicial nominees were confirmed to any court.[9] This was the lowest number of judges confirmed in a Congress since the Truman administration.[10]

Bad turned to worse in the Senate when Donald Trump won the presidential election in 2016. President Trump entered office with 112 backed-up judicial vacancies to fill; including the Supreme Court seat that Mitch McConnell held open for nearly a year, and seventeen circuit court seats.[11] Republicans quickly moved Gorsuch into the "Garland seat." But those seventeen vacancies on the courts of appeal were also a big prize. Unlike the Supreme Court seat, these were protected by the blue slip . . . until Senator Grassley killed the blue slip tradition at Mitch McConnell's behest. Grassley had embraced the process when he became chair of the Judiciary Committee in 2015, writing in his hometown paper:

> For nearly a century, the chairman of the Senate Judiciary Committee has brought nominees up for committee consideration only after both home-state senators have signed and returned what's known as a "blue slip." This tradition is designed to encourage outstanding nominees and consensus between the White House and home-state senators.
>
> Over the years, Judiciary Committee chairs of both parties have upheld a blue-slip process, including Sen. Patrick Leahy of Vermont, my immediate predecessor in chairing the committee, who steadfastly honored the tradition even as some in his own party called for its demise. I appreciate the value of the blue-slip process and also intend to honor it.[12]

Now that a Republican president was nominating judges, grabbing those appellate seats was too vital, and that intention went out the window. The conveyor belt had to be rapid and reliable.

We senators are ordinarily jealous guardians of Senate prerogatives. A senator's claim to home-state circuit court seats is a valuable prerogative. Rhode Island has claim to one seat on the First Circuit Court of Appeals, and Senator Jack Reed and I take our responsibility to recommend a nominee very seriously. But Republicans willingly gave up their own claims, in order to take away Democrat senators' claims and open circuit court seats for Federalist Society nominees. That is a sign of the power behind the Scheme. I warned Republicans at the time about what this meant, but against the Scheme's pressure for judges, this old Senate prerogative stood no chance.

The Senate conveyor belt was dialed up to high speed. Republicans accelerated the vetting process by stacking multiple circuit court candidates in a single hearing, which also meant our five minutes of questions was spread across a broader panel. To keep up speed, Republicans voted candidates out of committee even when the nominees hadn't yet provided all the information requested by the committee. On the Senate Floor, Majority Leader McConnell used the "nuclear option" to slash debate time on nominees from thirty hours to just two.

The Trump administration also eliminated the American Bar Association's long-standing role evaluating judicial candidates before their nominations are announced, something it had done from 1953 until the presidency of George W. Bush and resumed during the Obama administration. The nonpartisan ABA is one of the nation's oldest legal organizations. Its mission is not to advance any particular reading of the law but simply "to serve equally our members, our profession and the public by defending liberty and delivering justice as the national representative of the legal profession."[13] Since the Eisenhower administration, a standing committee of the ABA has reviewed the backgrounds of thousands of federal judicial candidates and offered its independent analysis of whether they demonstrated the integrity, professional competence, and judicial temperament the role demands, rating them "well qualified," "qualified," and "not qualified."

Killing the ABA preclearance process saved time, and the Trump White House, urged on by the Federalist Society big donors, was in a hurry to get judges confirmed. But that wasn't how they framed their decision. Instead, President Trump and his cronies trotted out the notion that the ABA was "biased" against conservatives. In fact, prior to the Trump administration, a majority of the ABA reviewers had given potential jurists "not qualified" ratings just thirty-six times—nineteen times to a Democratic nominee, and seventeen times to a Republican nominee.[14] Four presidents had no judicial nominee rated "not qualified" by the ABA: Nixon, Reagan, George H.W. Bush, and Obama. In my experience, if there was a bias at the ABA, it was for corporate big-firm lawyers over plaintiff's lawyers, and prosecutors over public defenders—a mildly conservative bias.

Instead of pre-nomination review by the nonpartisan, experienced ABA—and instead of a process that looked at only ability, integrity, and temperament, not judicial philosophy—Trump handed his judicial nominations over to the right-wing ideologues of the Federalist Society. Here's Steven Calabresi, a co-founder of the group and member of its board of directors, speaking to *The Hill* in 2017: "I would say I think the Federalist Society has come to play over the last 30 years for Republican presidents something of the role the American Bar Association has traditionally played for Democratic presidents. The last two Republican presidents have disregarded ABA ratings, and I think they are relying on the Federalist Society to come up with qualified nominees."[15] This is a stunning insider admission of a role we have not seen before: "to come up with" the nominees.

In his letter to the ABA announcing that the Trump administration was eliminating its preclearance role, White House Counsel (and Federalist Society member) Don McGahn wrote, "we do not intend to give any professional organizations special access to our nominees."[16] This sounds reasonable—until you remember that their own highly partisan professional organization, fueled by millions of corporate and right-wing dollars, was actually *coming up with* their nominees. For the right-wing dark-money groups looking to capture the courts, the ABA's problem was not that it's partisan, but that it's not. The *Economist* magazine, with the benefit of an outsider's perspective, may have said it best: "The federal courts look stronger for including a range of legal philosophies. . . . The problem is that conservatives are not striving for balance, but conquest."[17]

In all, the ABA rated ten of Donald Trump's nominees "not qualified" versus Obama's record of zero.[18] Eight of those ten were confirmed to lifetime appointments on the federal bench over the objection of every Democratic senator. For the first time, the Senate voted to place a candidate on the federal bench who had been rated "not qualified" based on concerns of bias.[19] For the first time, the Senate voted to confirm a candidate whom the ABA committee *unanimously* rated "not qualified."[20] And for the first time since at least the Ford administration, the Senate placed a candidate rated "not qualified" onto a federal court of appeals. Indeed, Senate Republicans placed three judges with a "not qualified" rating onto our nation's second-highest courts—one of them the nominee the ABA unanimously agreed was not fit to be a judge.[21] Again, this Senate behavior was a measure of the pressure the Scheme could produce.

Over the Trump years, Senate Republicans moved at a pace never before seen to install judicial nominees, many of whom stood out for their lack of courtroom experience, their youth, and their naked partisan extremism. When youth, inexperience, and partisanship are assets, it's not a sign that equal justice is the goal. In his first year in office, President Trump and the Senate Republicans—putting aside almost all other work to focus on judicial confirmations—confirmed twelve circuit court judges, the fastest pace of any president since the Judiciary Act of 1891 created the circuit courts.[22] A pace like that is not normal, and signals outside pressure as surely as a bent-over palm tree signifies a gale.

Roughly two-thirds of Trump's nominees were white men (compared to 31 percent of the U.S. population).[23] Twenty-four percent were women (compared to 51 percent of the U.S. population). Less than 4 percent were Black (compared to 13.4 percent in the general population) or Hispanic (17 percent). Not a single appellate court appointee was Black. These judges are likely to be around for a very long time. Nearly half of Trump's appellate judges were under forty-five when appointed, compared to 5 percent under President Obama and 19 percent under President G.W. Bush.[24] Many had carved out extreme right-wing positions even if they had spent little time in the courtroom.

For example, Sarah Pitlyk is a former Kavanaugh clerk who served as special counsel to the Thomas More Society, a conservative anti-choice organization. The briefs she wrote for them didn't just oppose abortion and contraception, but also opposed reproductive health advances that have helped many families become parents, including surrogacy and fertility treatments. She had barely any litigation experience—she had never taken a deposition, never picked a jury, never argued a motion, never been involved in any criminal case whatsoever. The ABA unanimously rated her unqualified based on her lack of courtroom experience.[25] She now has a lifetime appointment to the federal district court in Missouri.

Several nominees had criticized the Affordable Care Act and were involved in lawsuits to strike it down, but none so egregiously as Chad Readler. Readler served as an acting assistant attorney general in Trump's politicized Department of Justice. DOJ attorneys are meant to be the government's lawyers, not the president's. Their job, except in rare circumstances, is to defend federal laws regardless of their own political inclinations. Attorney General Merrick Garland has defended several controversial positions taken during the Trump administration. He explained that this is the essence of the rule of law, even as he acknowledged, "It is not always easy to apply that rule. Sometimes it means that we have to make a decision about the law that we would never have made and that we strongly disagree with as a matter of policy."[26]

Readler, by contrast, used his DOJ position to ram through a brief in *Texas v. United States* arguing that the Affordable Care Act was unconstitutional—the very law that DOJ had spent years defending, and that the Supreme Court had already upheld twice. The filing was so nakedly partisan and inappropriate that several career lawyers at DOJ refused to put their names on the brief, and at least one senior official resigned over it. Even politicians thought it was a bridge too far: Republican chair of the Senate HELP Committee Lamar Alexander called the arguments Readler was pushing "as far-fetched as any I've ever heard."[27] The Supreme Court apparently agreed with Senator Alexander. It rejected Readler's arguments, upholding the ACA for the third time.[28] But things worked out okay for Readler: he is now a federal appellate judge on the Sixth Circuit.

I could go on. A *New York Times* investigation found that Trump's appellate judges "were more openly engaged in causes important to Republicans, such as opposition to gay marriage and to government funding for abortion" than prior administrations' nominees and "notably more likely than their peers on the bench to agree with Republican appointees and to disagree with Democratic appointees—suggesting they are more consistently conservative."[29] Based on the "no more Stevenses" concern, partisan posturing actually became a positive criterion for the Senate conveyor belt. The impression that courts pick sides is ultimately fatal to courts in a free society. But the folks behind the Scheme didn't care. Results, not reputation, was the donors' goal. They sought "conquest."

In the last two years of the Trump administration, with Democrats back in control of the House, the Senate was sent hundreds of bills that did important things like lowering health care costs, reducing corruption in politics, and combating climate change.[30] Nearly 90 percent had bipartisan support. Virtually all died in Mitch McConnell's legislative graveyard. His singular focus was packing the courts. My Democratic colleagues and I called this out as a scorched-earth judicial power grab, one undertaken at significant cost to the prerogatives of the Senate, but our protests were no match for the dark money fueling the Scheme.[31]

One last Senate prerogative was sacrificed on the dark-money altar: we surrendered our powers of congressional oversight by yielding to wanton claims of executive privilege. Since Nixon famously asserted executive privilege to conceal documents from Congress, there has been tension between the branches of government over these assertions: the executive branch generally wants a broad privilege, and the ability to delay compliance; Congress generally wants quick compliance, with narrow exceptions. Congress ordinarily jealously protects its oversight prerogative. Executive privilege confounds that prerogative.

But when it came to clearing, for instance, the troubled Kavanaugh confirmation, Republicans meekly accepted flagrantly improper assertions of executive privilege. The White House turned over to us thousands of blank pages stamped "Constitutional Privilege," a made-up term that reflected how improbable an assertion of executive privilege would be. As for process, the Trump White House ignored procedures to resolve conflicts about executive privilege that were established by the Reagan White House and followed by every White House since. It withheld over 100,000 pages of records from its initial submission to the Senate, only to release 42,000 pages just hours before

Kavanaugh's hearing was about to begin, scuttling any chance of true due diligence—the very purpose of the Senate's "advise and consent" function.

Ordinarily, senators would have been furious about this gross incursion into Senate prerogatives, but this was Kavanaugh, the Great Auditioner; he had cleared the Federalist Society's turnstile and was on Mitch McConnell's conveyor belt, and the donors, I'd hazard, were insistent—"donors who might be enraged if Kavanaugh goes down in flames," as *Politico* reported.[32] As Democrats fumed in the minority, Republicans let these preposterous assertions of "Constitutional Privilege" go. It takes political force of considerable magnitude to get a body like the Senate to meekly surrender its institutional prerogatives. The Republican executive privilege rollover is a measure of the power of that force—another palm tree bent over in the gale.

The Judiciary Committee air was thick with tension the morning of Dr. Christine Blasey Ford's testimony. We knew that the right-wing trolls had been working her over savagely (another clue of the pressure brought to bear), to the point where she'd had to stop teaching, move from her home, and hire a personal security detail. We knew she'd had no experience under that kind of pressure, let alone the exposure of the hearing. We knew that our Republican colleagues had given up their cherished right to ask questions (another signal), so that a professional prosecutor could try to discredit her testimony. She looked awfully alone sitting at that big witness table.

As it turned out, she was a charming and disarming witness, poised and candid and calm, and the professional prosecutor never landed a punch. Dr. Ford came across as a very nice person who'd had a horrible experience and was still honestly grappling with it. She was believable. I believed her. When the hearing broke up for lunch, I let my colleagues at our caucus gathering know that, as a former prosecutor, I felt she had come across as a very credible witness, that it had been a horrible morning for Kavanaugh, and that the Republicans had to be thinking about withdrawing his nomination.

Boy, was I wrong. Over lunch, the Republican game plan changed. We heard no more from the ineffectual prosecutor. There was no effort to grapple with Dr. Ford's testimony. The new play was to go full-bore on offense: ignore Ford, run the tribal flag up the flagpole, and go to the Republican "go-to" stance of anger, grievance, and resentment.

Lindsey Graham was the pivot. (He is also my friend.) Lindsey came out snarling with anger. An opening question, "Are you a gang rapist?" was definitely a first for a Supreme Court nomination hearing.[33] The new strategy was to paint Kavanaugh as the victim of Democratic evil. "What you want to do is destroy this guy's life, hold this seat open, and hope you win in 2020," Lindsey raged. "This is the most unethical thing I have seen in my time in politics."

"Boy, you all want power," he railed at us. "God, I hope you never get it. I hope the American people can see through this sham." He called the hearing bringing Dr. Ford before the committee "the most despicable thing I have seen in my time in politics." His last question to Kavanaugh was, "Would you say you've been through hell?" Kavanaugh answered, "I've been through hell and then some." After all that Dr. Christine Blasey Ford had been through, now Kavanaugh was the victim. Mission accomplished.

As we left the hearing later, Lindsey and I crossed in the anteroom. "Lindsey, you were a total asshole out there," I told him. He looked surprised that I'd said that. "And," I said, "you just put on the most consequential five-minute performance I've ever seen in the Senate. Kavanaugh was dead meat. You revived him." He had. His snarling performance didn't just set the tone of defiance, it also set the bar so as to take the sting out of Kavanaugh's own snarling tirade to the committee.

The Kavanaugh hearing was a telltale in many ways. One telling clue was the behavior of the FBI. Before joining Congress, I'd worked with the FBI for years. Just three attorneys general in the country have full criminal jurisdiction, meaning they prosecute all crimes in their state. As Rhode Island AG, I was one of them. I'd also been the U.S. attorney for Rhode Island, appointed by President Clinton. In those jobs, I'd learned a few things about the FBI.

First, I learned that the FBI was proud to the point of prickly. They don't like being told what to do. Part of that pride is a sense that they are custodians of a legacy. They take the reputation of the FBI very seriously.

Second, I learned that they have procedures for nearly everything, and they take following procedure very seriously. They have lots of offices and lots of agents, and making sure everything gets done right take lots of procedure.

Third, though I didn't even think about it since it seems so obvious, the FBI is all about gathering information. It's the Federal Bureau of Investigation, and investigation is the purposeful collection and sorting of information.

So the FBI's behavior in the Kavanaugh investigation stood out like a sore thumb. The first sign that something was weird was when the FBI became impervious to information. People who knew Kavanaugh and had something to report about his behavior found the drawbridges drawn up and the shutters slammed shut at the FBI. There was no way in for their information. Some of those people came to senators on the Judiciary Committee to ask what to do, so we saw this firsthand. An FBI that repels information? Very strange.

When we made inquiries seeking the entry point for information about Kavanaugh, there was a weird stall. Ultimately, the FBI said it was setting up a tip line to collect information. In the end, the FBI also did a few terse interviews (restricted by the White House), but without follow-up, and with many witnesses left out. As one key witness said, "I never imagined they would never contact the people that support my story."[34] To anyone who'd been around FBI investigations, which tend to be very thorough, this was weird. In this "supplemental background investigation" that followed Dr. Ford's allegations, the FBI never interviewed either the alleged victim or the perpetrator.[35]

When we asked about this strange investigation, FBI Director Christopher Wray said that the Bureau was following its standard procedures. That wasn't true. What he meant by that, we later came to find out, was that in background investigations ("BIs," as they're called)—as opposed to regular criminal investigations—the FBI viewed itself as the agent of the White House, and it followed White House direction rather than its ordinary procedures. So the "standard procedure" Wray said it was following was to *not* follow its standard procedures. How about that.

But even *that* explanation seemed weird, because the FBI has standard procedures for everything, and the idea that it didn't have standard procedures for background investigations didn't ring true. Sure enough, setting aside the whole "standard procedure of not following standard procedure" malarkey, there actually *are* standard FBI procedures for background investigations. There are also standard FBI procedures for a tip line. Neither set of procedures was followed.

As we dug further, we then heard from the FBI that the FBI procedures for background investigations didn't apply to Kavanaugh, because this was a "supplemental BI." Our briefer told us that in a supplemental BI, as opposed to a "full and logical BI" (that's what they call it), there were no procedures and it was up to the White House to direct not only who would be questioned, but what questions they could be asked. The FBI could point us to no document that gives the White House that kind of operational control of supplemental BIs. And it makes no sense—a supplemental BI is necessary only when an issue arises, so proper investigative procedure is even more important. Sure enough, when we asked White House counsel whether they had operational control over FBI supplemental background investigations, they said no, they did not.

If such a "no-procedure procedure" existed, you'd think the Senate, the ultimate consumer of FBI background investigations, would know about that. Direct political control by the White House of background investigations (supplemental or otherwise) would degrade our trust in the background investigation process, through which hundreds of executive appointees must pass on their way to Senate confirmation. No one had ever heard that before. It appears to have been invented for this case. As someone who's worked with the FBI for years, I know that takes some pressure.

The mystery no-procedure procedure for supplemental BIs is a fig leaf for the fact that the White House's direction of the Kavanaugh investigation violated the FBI's protocols for background investigations. In essence, these protocols say that the FBI must keep investigating and reporting to the "client" (the White House or appointing agency) whatever derogatory information it finds on the supplemental allegation or issue, until the investigation is complete (until, in the FBI's words, "all aspects of the allegation or issue are thoroughly explored") or until the "client" stops the investigation by withdrawing the nominee.[36] There is no "procedure" where the FBI hands over investigative control of a background investigation to the White House, or leaves aspects of an allegation or issue unexplored. Yet they did.

Worse, the FBI "tip line" was a fake. The tips didn't go through the regular FBI tip line analysis. If tips were relevant to Kavanaugh, they were just sorted from general FBI tip line traffic and then handed over to White House counsel, uninvestigated. [37] It was more a "tip dump" than a tip line. We don't know what happened at the Trump White House, but it looks like the tips were buried by White House political operatives. Worst case, they were used by the White House to steer the FBI away from witnesses with damning or corroborating testimony.

Believe it or not, as I write this we still don't have an answer from the FBI on its tip line protocol. We did find a YouTube video in which the FBI discusses its tip line. Here's how the FBI agent ends the presentation: "I think one of the most important things to know about the FBI's tip line . . . is every single piece of information that's submitted by an individual is reviewed by FBI personnel and FBI headquarters. So there is nothing that goes unaddressed. We basically listen to everything that people want to submit, and we give it its due diligence." [38] That wasn't true for Brett Kavanaugh.

The result in the Kavanaugh "supplemental background investigation" was something that looked like an investigation but wasn't one—an unprecedented simulacrum of a background investigation designed to bury, not discover, information. This is not what the FBI is known for.

This all took time and trouble to find out, because for years the FBI stonewalled, then slow-walked, my colleagues' and my efforts to get information, refusing to answer even basic questions like "Do you have standard tip line procedures?" and "Do you have standard background investigation procedures?" and "Please show them to us." The FBI was being far, far too secretive. Something was up.

The information blockade was particularly frustrating because at the time Republican senators on the Judiciary Committee were instantly getting everything they wanted from the FBI for their investigation into the Trump/Russia investigation, "Crossfire Hurricane." We watched all that FBI investigative information fly past us to Republicans, while we couldn't even get a simple policy document. The

FBI information logjam was selective—another sign that something was up.

There's a whole separate book to be written about how the FBI tanked the Kavanaugh investigation and who was behind it. It's enough here to say how unique and unprecedented this was: how weird it was that relevant information was repelled, how unusual that the FBI would be pressured to violate its tip line and background investigation procedures; indeed, how unusual that the FBI would yield to that pressure. Nothing like this had ever happened before in any background investigation that I'm aware of. The FBI's mission, after all, is to "Protect the American People," and its priority is to "combat public corruption on all levels." These machinations and prevarications put at risk the Bureau's reputation and credibility, not to mention the Senate's ability to trust FBI background investigations in the future.

It was not just a disgrace; it was a signal. It was a signal of the power of the drive to jam Kavanaugh onto the Court. It's a signal when the White House puts that kind of political pressure on the FBI, and it's a signal when the FBI rolls over for that political pressure. The FBI doesn't easily roll over, and doesn't normally violate procedure, and doesn't ordinarily have its director claim to be following "procedure" without letting us know that the procedure was "there's no procedure."

Like I said, that's gale force stuff.

The Grand Old Party outsourced the selection of judicial candidates, allowed private special-interest money to infect the nominations process, ran roughshod over long-standing norms of judicial nomination and confirmation, tanked an FBI investigation, and fought to conceal the Scheme's donors from the public. The decision to abandon the Senate's advise-and-consent role and instead hold the Court seat open through the 2016 elections left the Supreme Court without its full roster of justices for nearly a year, and it tarnished, perhaps irretrievably, the reputation of our highest court as a place where justice, not politics, presides. This was particularly plain when the imaginary "principle" that had supposedly barred Merrick Garland from receiving a hearing evaporated upon the death of Justice Ginsburg.

In the words of Senator Graham before the Ginsburg vacancy, the Garland blockade was about principle: "if an opening comes in the last year of President Trump's term, and the primary process has started, we'll wait for the next election."[39]

"Hold the tape," he said.[40]

Justice Ginsburg died not months but weeks before the 2020 election. We all know what happened next. Republicans reversed their own recent "Garland principle," holding the Barrett confirmation hearings while early voting in the presidential election was actually under way. Think how embarrassing it must have been for Republicans first to have to take an imaginary stand on a nonexistent principle, and then to have to pull an immediate 180 and violate that supposed "principle." But the forces behind this didn't care. This was raw power at work.

CHAPTER TWELVE

Plaintiffs of Convenience
and Friends of the Court

Procedure is the bone structure of a democratic society.
—ABE FORTAS

THE NEXT STEP IN THE JUDICIAL TAKEOVER SCHEME, once a judge has been groomed, selected, and confirmed, is to put him or her to use. That requires a whole apparatus to get the right cases before the Court, to get them there fast, and to let the justices know what the dark-money donors want. Here's how that works.

PLAINTIFFS OF CONVENIENCE

Despite the fail-safes built into our system, right-wing forces readily get their pet issues before the Supreme Court. In theory, judges are supposed to rule on real-world disputes, not hypothetical challenges. Evidence is to be introduced and tested in the trial courts; appellate courts shouldn't go off fact-finding on their own. Supreme Court justices ordinarily allow an issue to "percolate" for a few years to let the parties develop all the relevant facts and lawyers test out all the best arguments. Often the Court waits for a conflict to develop between different circuit courts before it intervenes. All of that has taken a beating of late.

The Scheme uses an armada of outside groups, most funded by a few billionaire trusts and families, to design "test lawsuits" that challenge legal principles they seek to overturn. They design the best strategy to get a favorable, tasty case teed up. Then they go shopping for a plaintiff.

I've been a lawyer a long time. In the real world, a client comes into your office, and you start to build a case. When you start with the case and then go looking for the client, that's abnormal—and a sign of ulterior purpose. Lawyers for the conservative movement make no bones about the fact that they're challenging a law or policy that they just don't like. This is hard to jibe with the Constitution's "case or controversy" requirement, which implies a real case with a real plaintiff with a real grievance who went and chose a real lawyer.

When the group behind the case is funded anonymously, the real party in interest remains hidden. That, too, is not normal. The goal of these front groups is to remake policy for the hidden donors behind the case, not to advocate for a real client. A great many front groups are out there, prowling around looking for opportunities to overturn laws and decisions they (or, more accurately, their donors) don't like. They hide who's paying for their operation and bring plaintiffs of convenience into court as if this were normal. It's not.

Right-wing operatives recruit plaintiffs to stick at the front of a pre-packaged lawsuit. The recruits are not always people. Edward Blum is a failed candidate for Congress from Texas who has spent the bulk of his career battling civil rights protections. Blum isn't a lawyer, but he reportedly recruited Shelby County, Alabama, to challenge the "preclearance" requirements of the Voting Rights Act.[1] These preclearance provisions required jurisdictions with histories of persistent voter suppression to get federal approval before changing local election rules or procedures. Dark-money front groups brought and supported the litigation. The resulting decision, *Shelby County v. Holder*, was a big success for the Scheme: a partisan majority of the Supreme Court decided 5–4 to abolish the key "preclearance" provision of the Voting Rights Act, whose reauthorization had passed the Senate 98–0 as recently as 2006. Justice Ginsburg's famous dissent observed that the majority's decision to throw out preclearance "when it has worked and is continuing to work to stop discriminatory changes is like throwing away your umbrella in a rainstorm because you are not getting wet."[2] State legislatures in the preclearance states immediately passed laws benefiting Republicans by disenfranchising minority voters, in some cases "with almost surgical precision."[3] Dark money had teed up the right case, and dark-money donors savored a big victory.*

Another example went beyond just client-shopping. Justice Alito took the opportunity, in a 2012 case called *Knox*, to signal that he was open to overturning a landmark precedent allowing public sector unions to collect a "fair share" fee from non-members for whom the unions advocated. Before Justices Roberts and Alito arrived, the Court had set a reasonable balance: if a majority of employees voted to unionize, the union was obligated to represent all employees in negotiations or in workplace grievances. Employees who benefited from these union services but were not union members were charged a "fair share fee" for this representation. This avoided the "free rider" problem of employees enjoying the benefits of union membership without sharing the costs.† Even Justice Scalia had accepted the balance.

Then, in *Knox*, a fairly unremarkable case about the propriety of a midyear dues assessment, Justice Alito went out of his way to volunteer several paragraphs critiquing *Abood v. Detroit Board of Education*, the 1977 "fair share fee" case. This wasn't the only time the Republican justices have sent such signals. Ruth Marcus, the editor who covers the Court for the *Washington Post*, has described their signaling to the front groups as a "bring-it-on invitation for future mischief-making."[4]

With that invitation, conservative special-interest groups fell over themselves to race up to the Court to seize this proffered prize

---

* This was not Blum's only effort to get the Court to take up pet conservative causes that had been rejected in democratically elected legislatures and prior Supreme Courts. He founded "Students for Fair Admissions," an astroturf group suing Harvard University over its admissions policies. Blum claims that the group has more than twenty thousand members, but no member—or even member list—has ever been seen. It's unclear who's paying his bills. Harvard won that lawsuit, incidentally, and the appeal as well. As this book was going to press, the Court announced it would review the Harvard decision along with one challenging the admissions policies of the University of North Carolina.
† The benefits of riding along can be considerable. In 2021, the Bureau of Labor Statistics reported that union members had median weekly earnings of $1,169 compared to $975 for non-union workers—meaning that the average non-union worker earns 83 cents for every dollar earned by the average worker covered by a union. According to BLS, union members are also more likely to have access to health care benefits, retirement benefits, life insurance benefits, and paid leave benefits.

from their 5–4 conservative majority. At the time, two justices were in their eighties, Barack Obama was president, and no one foresaw Mitch McConnell's refusal to allow the president to fill a Supreme Court vacancy; so the rush was on. The groups rushed to overturn the "fair share" case, not because it didn't work, or because any facts had changed, but because they didn't like it. Or more exactly, a big donor, the Bradley Foundation, didn't like it and had been grousing about it for years. This was their chance.

Leading the charge was a "public interest" firm called the Center for Individual Rights, an organization backed by Bradley and Koch money. The Center heard Alito's signal, built its case, found a plaintiff (a California teacher named Rebecca Friedrichs), and brought its lawsuit.

Just as a client usually comes to a lawyer, not vice versa, usually that client wants to win, not lose. Not here. The front group asked the lower courts to rule *against* their plaintiff, and as quickly as possible, please. Like I said, I've been a practicing lawyer a long time. I can't recall seeing a case where the plaintiff wanted to lose. This is not normal. But here the plaintiff was decorative; the decisions were being made by donors behind the law group, and what they wanted was not a trial victory, and certainly not a well-developed trial record on the question of union "fair share" dues, but a fast lane to the Supreme Court whose majority had signaled that they were eager to throw out the law.

As it turned out, even with all the rush, they were too late. Justice Scalia died before the case was decided, depriving the union-busting Center of its anticipated Supreme Court majority. Once Justice Gorsuch was appointed in 2017, however, the 5–4 door reopened and the special interests rushed right back in. The party in that second case, Mark Janus, a home health aide, was actually thrown into the lawsuit *after* the case was filed. Mr. Janus was substituted as a plaintiff when the first nominal plaintiff, a Republican governor, couldn't show he'd been harmed by the law in question. So the litigating front group swapped in Mr. Janus.

The front groups also did some swapping among themselves. The group that had brought the case in *Friedrichs* became an amicus supporting the plaintiff in *Janus*. The group that brought the case in *Janus* had been an amicus supporting the plaintiff in *Friedrichs*. And the groups that brought the two cases and groups that chimed in as amici were funded by the same organizations.[5] Lots of piano keys; same piano players.

Just as in *Friedrichs*, the attorneys representing Mr. Janus asked to lose as quickly as possible, to rush back to the friendly Supreme Court—with no record, no witnesses, no experts, no evidence of the likely consequences of the ruling. So up the case went through the right-wing fast lane, Gorsuch voted as predicted, and out went a precedent that unions, cities, and states had relied on for forty years.

Usually in situations like this, the Supreme Court will correct whatever legal error they found, and "remand" the case back to the lower court for a trial judge to develop the relevant facts and apply the corrected framework. Not here. The majority was on a mission. As for the plaintiff, Mark Janus, he's no longer a home health aide for the state of Illinois. He became a "Senior Fellow" at the Liberty Justice Center, the Koch-backed group that brought "his" case before the Supreme Court.

Usually, clients choose lawyers, lawyers try to win, and clients pay the lawyers rather than go on the lawyers' payroll; here all this was stood on its head. The Supreme Court has turned a conspicuously blind eye to these cases that reek of political stratagem and procedural abnormality. A captured Court wouldn't be too fussy about "standing" or "case or controversy" concerns or respect the value of a case winding its way to the Court through regular litigation with a solid record of evidence. A captured Court would *want* to take up the cases rushed to them outside ordinary procedure by groups funded by right-wing interests that helped get them on the Court in the first place.

As a lawyer myself, I've often thought of the grim feeling those union lawyers in the *Janus* case must have had on argument day as they walked into the Supreme Court. The original invitation from Justice Alito, the "fast lane" travel of the case, the overhang of *Friedrichs*, the political litigant group with its hidden anonymous funders, the plaintiff of convenience, and the predictable vote of Gorsuch: everything signaled that the fix was in and the argument day a charade. It's a horrible feeling for a lawyer.

Another way to create a "case or controversy" requires a bit of local legislative effort. Say there's a law or decision you hate, like *Roe v.*

Wade. And say you've built a Court majority ready to put a few dings in that law. Well, a web of right-wing groups awaits, ready to draft bills and slip them to friendly state legislators. It only takes one state: the friendly local legislators introduce the outside group's bill, often verbatim, and a Republican-controlled legislature rushes it to passage. It might even be that the Republican legislators and the right-wing groups get funding from the same donors, and that the whole exercise is coordinated in advance.

The most prominent of these groups is the American Legislative Exchange Council, or ALEC. In 2012, Bloomberg reported that approximately one thousand model bills drafted by ALEC were being introduced by sympathetic legislators every year, with about two hundred becoming law annually.[6] ALEC and its sidekick array of "State Policy Council" groups are heavily funded by the Koch political operation (though ALEC's climate denial work made it too toxic even for ExxonMobil to support).[7]

So you have the law you hate, a Court you think wants to change the law, a group that has access to state legislatures, and legislators who will pass a bill for the group. The rest is easy. You get the group to get the legislature to pass the bill that violates the law that you don't like. Then you sit back and wait for someone to challenge your new law. The litigation comes to you.

Think that's a stretch? In Texas, a Republican-controlled legislature pushed through a blatantly unconstitutional new state law to give the Supreme Court a chance to ding *Roe v. Wade,* barring abortions before many women even know they are pregnant. The Center for Reproductive Rights sued to challenge the new law. The case went up to the Supreme Court for what should have been an easy stay of the law while the case worked its way through the lower courts, something the Court has done many times before when a law is a patent violation of existing precedent.

But that's not what happened. In September 2021, the 6–3 reactionary majority controlling the Court let the law go into effect. As I write this, the 10 percent of American women who live in Texas have effectively lost their constitutional right to get an abortion. The whole setup may have been scripted charade, but the consequences in those women's lives were very real.

AN ARMADA OF AMICI

Now your case is at the Court, "fast-laned" or otherwise. You need to tell your friendly justices what you want them to do. For that, dark-money donors maintain an armada of "public interest" law groups, which they send into the Court in orchestrated flotillas. In the Amy Coney Barrett hearings, I called out a leaked memo from a Bradley Foundation grant officer explaining that "it is often very important to orchestrate high-caliber amicus efforts" in the Supreme Court.[8] The memo followed an email from the Bradley Foundation to Leonard Leo asking him to recommend "a 501(c)(3) nonprofit to which Bradley could direct any support of the two Supreme Court amicus projects."[9]

The Center for Individual Rights and the Liberty Justice Center appeared in the *Knox/Friedrichs/Janus* saga. Other right-wing "public interest law groups" are handy by the dozen, with names that sound like they came straight out of a propaganda handbook: the Alliance Defending Freedom, the American Center for Law and Justice, the Becket Fund for Religious Liberty, the Center for Law and Religious Freedom, the Christian Legal Society, the Eagle Forum Education & Legal Defense Fund, the Honest Elections Project (Leonard Leo's "fictitious name" group), and the Institute for Justice. Heritage and Cato are also frequent fliers in the courts. As my staff and I have documented, connections among these groups abound.

None holds a candle to our old friend the U.S. Chamber of Commerce, where the Court-capture idea first surfaced. The Chamber's largest division, launched in 1998, is its "Institute for Legal Reform." Since 2010, the "Institute" alone has spent more than $250 million—a quarter of a billion dollars—lobbying lawmakers to make it harder for consumers and workers to sue big corporations.[10] (The Chamber itself has spent more than $1 billion on lobbying during that time.[11]) It hasn't been shy in the courts, either. My colleagues and I reported that "from 2006 to 2016, the Chamber was involved in 1,100 lawsuits, either as a plaintiff or *amicus curiae*."[12] (This is particularly ironic given that the Chamber and the Institute love to complain that there's too much litigation in the country.)

The Chamber has been particularly active in the Supreme Court, where it has filed briefs in hundreds of cases—far more than any other organization—to let the justices know how to resolve a case. Most of its filings are amicus, or "friend of the court," briefs. Historically, amicus briefs have allowed parties or interest groups to offer the Court additional information, expertise, insight, or advocacy. Sometimes amicus briefs offer a truly fresh perspective or unique analysis; other times they do little more than offer an end-run for parties to circumvent the page limits the Court sets on their filings. Amicus briefs have become one of the primary vehicles for the Chamber of Commerce and others in the dark-money web as they lobby to push judicial doctrine rightward. Consistent with the Powell memo, the Chamber can act as the intermediary organization, protecting a corporation from having to "get too far out in front and to make itself a target." The Chamber refuses to answer questions about its funding and discloses nothing to the Supreme Court about who is behind its amicus briefs.

In the last few decades, amicus filings in Supreme Court cases have ballooned to dwarf the actual litigants' own submissions. In the Supreme Court's 2014 term, amici submitted nearly twice as many briefs as they had in 1995 and *eight times* the number submitted in the 1950s, before the right-wing Court-capture Scheme began to take shape.[13] The Court increasingly relies on these briefs. One study found that from 2008 to 2013, the Supreme Court cited amicus filings 606 times across 417 opinions.[14] I have submitted many amicus briefs myself, especially in recent years, so I certainly do not question their value. But when I write one, I put my name on it. I don't operate through front groups. I own what I say, and anyone and everyone can assess my motives.

For the Court-capture crew, these briefs serve several ends. They are tools for judicial lobbying, telling the justices how certain organizations want the case to come out. They lend anonymity. They also signal to the conservative justices what's a priority for their benefactors. When the case *really* matters to the big donors, the front groups appear in armadas of as many as fifty, to make sure the justices know how important it is.

Too often, these briefs are written by organizations that have helped justices get on the bench—groups that have feted these justices with awards, invited them to give keynote addresses to adoring crowds, and welcomed them to swank conferences. In the Senate, we call this lobbying. Senate and House rules—and federal law—require lobbyists to file regular public disclosures identifying themselves and the sources of their funding.[15] This helps the public understand who is advocating for or against a piece of legislation and better recognize when supposedly public-minded statements are simply dressed-up self-interest.

Not on the Court. The rules that apply to amicus briefs make it painfully easy to hide behind a feel-good name that means nothing to the public—but one that the Dark Money Justices likely recognize. Without transparency, there is no meaningful way for the parties and the public to know who is behind amicus briefs. In the vicious cycle between Court and Scheme, the Court indulges this secrecy for the big donors.

The big-money right has mastered the art of submitting multiple amicus briefs in a single lawsuit. Each may argue a slightly different aspect of the same case, but all drive toward the same conclusion. It's a practiced ruse: allowing the parties to evade the Court's efforts to limit page counts, creating a drumbeat of self-reinforcing viewpoints, introducing fringe theories using repetition to add the gloss of acceptability, and steering the justices to doctrinal springboards that set up friendly decisions in later cases.

Sometimes the groups bumble and confess to a "project" of the Court: in the first *New York State Rifle & Pistol Association* case, the NRA let slip its awareness of what it called the Court's "project" to expand gun rights.[16] That was quite a slip. Justices aren't supposed to be deliberately steering the law in a pre-planned direction over a series of cases; they're supposed to decide each case on its merits. They're not supposed to have "projects." *

An example of a right-wing amicus flotilla came in a case about the Consumer Financial Protection Bureau, the federal agency established in the wake of the Great Recession to protect American consumers

---

* The term *project*, like a verbal Forrest Gump, keeps turning up. The Bradley Foundation had its "Supreme Court amicus projects." Mitch McConnell called his packing of the Court his "court project." Senator Mike Lee, in a speech to the 2018 Federalist Society gala, crowed, "Thanks to President Trump and the Senate Republican majority, we have a Supreme Court that should be ready to do its part on this project."[17]

from predatory or manipulative financial products. Incidentally, this was one of Brett Kavanaugh's audition cases at the circuit court level, a sign of its importance to the right. The corporate right hates the CFPB. In 2020, my Democratic colleagues and I reported that "since 2014, 16 right-wing foundations [have] donated a total of nearly $69 million to 11 groups that filed amicus briefs in favor of scrapping the CFPB. Over the same period, the same 16 foundations donated over $33 million to the Federalist Society."[18] They *really* don't like the CFPB.

The Federalist Society made the CFPB case a rallying point for something called "unitary executive theory"—a cover doctrine grown, fertilized, and propagated in dark-money-funded hothouses. For decades, Congress has kept expert administrative agencies outside the direct political control of the president. Presidents can drive policies, appoint people to lead the agencies, and argue for rules they want, but presidents do not get to direct outcomes at an independent agency or replace its leader without cause. Congress chose indirect executive control, not direct political control, because agency expertise often serves the public better than a president's politics.

Though not under direct executive control, the agencies aren't rogues. Congress can change the laws they enforce, cut their budgets, or kill them off completely if they try to go rogue. We want regulatory agencies doing their job protecting the public, not playing politics, and we don't want politics subverting expert analysis, so we make the agencies quasi-independent.

For decades, this premise was uncontroversial. Eighty years ago, the Supreme Court unanimously supported this form of supervision and oversight, and it did so again with only one objection (from Justice Scalia) thirty years ago.[19] But it nagged at billionaire owners of big regulated entities. So they propagated the "unitary executive" theory. As none other than President Nixon's former chief of staff, John Dean, explained, "In its most extreme form, unitary executive theory can mean that neither Congress nor the federal courts can tell the President what to do or how to do it."[20] Pretty sweet for a special interest, when the president owes you big.

Big-money donors don't much like honest, transparent, and fact-based agency decision-making. It would be so much easier to buy political influence with the White House and end-run the experts. So when they had a 5–4 Court and a chance to blow up the CFPB *and* push "unitary executive theory," it was irresistible. They deployed their amicus flotilla in a case called *Seila Law v. CFPB*, which the Supreme Court decided 5–4 in 2020. Unfortunately for them, the agency still stands, though it lost some independence. But the hothouse "unitary executive" theory got a warm reception from the Federalist Society justices, and it's now ready as a springboard for favorable decisions in future cases.

Seila Law was awash in industry-funded amicus briefs. At least thirteen amici who share common funding (but didn't report it) wrote separate briefs to the Court.* I wrote a brief with several colleagues that included an unusual appendix for the Court, in which I cross-referenced those amici and their common donors. We warned the Court what was up: "These amicus briefs may appear to be a broad outpouring of support for a legal position, but publicly available information gleaned elsewhere suggests them to be an echo chamber funded by a small and powerful cabal of self-interested entities. We are all thus deprived of knowing how real or artificial this florescence of briefing is."[21] The Dark Money Court took no interest in that concern.

Who is standing behind this echo chamber of amici, playing the keys? We don't know anywhere near enough about that, but we can start with a name that is familiar, the family that bankrolls major dark-money groups like Americans for Prosperity and DonorsTrust (yes, the "dark-money ATM of the conservative movement"): the Kochs. David Koch died in 2018, leaving his brother Charles to continue their crusade to push anti-government ideology using billions from the family's fossil fuel empire. They go big, publicly pledging, for example, to spend $889 million to support Republican candidates in just one election cycle.[22] Most of that spending ended up channeled through a web of dark-money groups. It's a savvy tactic: they made a public splash about the money they would deploy against anyone who crossed them,

---

* The Supreme Court asks amici to disclose if a party's counsel authored the brief or if someone made a contribution "intended to fund the preparation or submission" of the brief. In 2018 a group took to GoFundMe to raise money to support an amicus brief. Even though most donors only gave tens or hundreds of dollars, the Supreme Court rejected the filing because they could not attach a name to every single dollar behind it. Yet the Court allowed these groups to sidestep its rules to funnel undisclosed millions into amicus efforts.

so the threat got out there; but in making good on the threat, they went dark, so the American public couldn't know which messages broadcast at them through front groups were really from a couple of creepy anti-government billionaires with a fossil fuel empire.

The Kochs went similarly big on the effort to capture the courts. Koch network money underwrote *all* of the eleven right-wing briefers in *Seila Law*.²³ In the *Janus* union-busting case, thirteen separate amicus briefers were funded by the Koch-linked DonorsTrust and Donors Capital.²⁴ None of the briefers disclosed these connections to the Court.

Notwithstanding the use of legal smokescreens, shell companies, and other identity-laundering entities, and despite delays in reporting and straight-up failures to report, researchers have managed to glean enough information about right-wing dark-money funding sources in recent years that a picture emerges. Behind all the organizations pushing the anti-government agenda—and there are literally hundreds—lurk just a handful of individuals, trusts, and families.²⁵ They would probably fit on a bus. (They'd be a bit disoriented, though; it's not really a public transportation crowd.) This all masquerades as a people-driven movement, but it's funded by a handful of billionaires who resent majority rule, taxes, and what they pejoratively call the "administrative state."

Books such as Jane Mayer's *Dark Money*, Nancy MacLean's *Democracy in Chains*, and Naomi Oreskes's *Doubt Is Their Product* have done an excellent job at tracing the network of right-wing funders. The specific parts of the dark-money apparatus that produce climate denial have also been well traced in scientific studies by Michael Mann, Robert Brulle, Justin Farrell, Riley Dunlap, and others. Their work reveals a massive disinformation campaign, managed like a covert intelligence operation, run through many dozens of front groups, funded with billions of dollars of dark money, and out to manipulate our government. Up against it, Democrats have made virtually no systematic effort to expose or spotlight the mischief. It is one of our failings.*

A few of the funders they identify deserve special mention for

---

*While the focus of this book is the Republican-backed dark-money Scheme that has captured the Court, a moment of reflection—and confession—on our side is in order. On a great many occasions, Democrats at many levels failed to fight back or give public warning as the Scheme progressed. It was worse than appeasement; it was acceptance.

their work to capture the Court. One big donor is the Scaife Family Foundation, which traces its funds to the family's banking and fossil fuel fortune. The Scaife family has given millions to "public interest" law firms that fight environmental regulations, as well as to groups including the American Civil Rights Institute (a brainchild of Edward Blum of the *Shelby County* lawsuit, which is, no surprise, anti–civil rights), the Federalist Society, the American Legislative Exchange Council, the Cato Institute, Heritage Foundation, and the Center for Immigration Studies (which is, no surprise, anti-immigrant).

But the Scaifes are pikers compared to the Lynde and Harry Bradley Foundation, which since 2000 has funneled more than a half a billion dollars into dark-money projects including voter suppression, initiatives to privatize public schools, and attacks on labor rights and renewable energy. Millions have gone to organizations such as the Federalist Society and the Becket Fund for Religious Liberty. In *Seila*

Walking away from the climate fight in the Obama years set the tone, as so many of the dark-money players were the same in climate denial and the Scheme. Those players learned a lesson about the size of "the fight in the dog" on our side. A few years later, walking away from the IRS 501(c) fight squandered a teachable moment, opened a dark-money sluicegate, and again set a tone of weakness. We didn't even respond when Republicans began to run attack ads accusing Democrats of being the dark-money party—a cynical but clever gambit out of the covert ops playbook: accuse your adversary of your own misbehavior.

For years, Democrats failed to direct attention to the increasingly obvious marks of the Scheme; indeed, we too often didn't even pay attention. For years, we didn't force a vote on DISCLOSE. For years, we let donor-friendly 5–4 partisan Supreme Court decisions pile up; they'd grown to seventy-three by the time anyone blew the whistle. Individual bad decisions that we should have decried often went totally unremarked. In confirmation hearings, we concerned ourselves more with nominees' stances on "the issues" than on the machinery that put them there. We were sleeping sentries.

When warnings did come, they were too often ignored. It's said that French pilots actually saw the German armor divisions massed along roads outside the Ardennes Forest, readying for the blitzkrieg, and French high command simply refused to believe the pilots' eyewitness reports. The analogy seems apt.

During Trump's debauched presidency, he was a dazzling distraction from these creeping encroachments. As a party, we fixated on the shiny object and did little to expose the Scheme. In the first year of the Biden administration, the White House's official website reveals, the president and vice president each publicly used the term "dark money" exactly once. Worse, the President's Commission on the Supreme Court papered over this entire problem without a mention.

Our sins were of omission not commission, for sure; we were the sleepy guard, not the crafty burglar. Nevertheless, they must be faced, and I acknowledge them here. *J'avoue.*

Law v. CFPB, the Bradley Foundation funded groups behind eight of the eleven coordinated amicus briefs, to the tune of $5.6 million.[26] In *Friedrichs*, the first case that took aim at public sector unions, the Bradley Foundation gave money to the law group that crafted the lawsuit and to eleven of the amici.[27] In *Janus*, the sequel to *Friedrichs* after Justice Gorsuch joined the Court, the Bradley Foundation bankrolled both *Janus* plaintiffs and twelve of the amici.[28]

On the very day the Supreme Court agreed to hear *Janus*, who should show up as the keynote speaker at an event organized by the Bradley-backed "Fund for American Studies" but the newly confirmed Justice Gorsuch himself.[29] (And yes, he went on to vote for the Bradley-endorsed view, overturning a forty-year precedent and forcing unions to work for free for covered employees who gained the "freedom" to freeload.)

Funny story: in the Amy Coney Barrett hearings, I made a presentation that used the Bradley Foundation's secret funding of multiple briefs to explain this Court-capture problem. The *Wall Street Journal* editorial page, which shills for the fossil fuel industry (it derided climate change as a "hoax" as late as 1999), constantly attacks me when I point out that dark money has captured the Court (I'm up to more than two dozen hostile editorials from them, which may be a record of some kind).[30] The paper reacted with particular rancor to my Barrett presentation after the presentation went viral. Something had them hot under the collar. Turns out, the Bradley Foundation has cooked up something called the "Bradley Prize." Right-wing groups love to ape legitimate groups, so I guess this is the right wing's alt-reality version of the Pulitzer Prize.* But they don't kid around with their money. It's a $250,000 cash grant. And guess what? Four—yes, four—of these $250,000 "Bradley Prize" cash grants had gone to people associated with the WSJ editorial page—a cool million bucks cash, thank you very much.[31] Somehow the WSJ ed page failed to disclose that little fact when it lambasted me for my factual Bradley presentation.

---

* Talk about alt-reality: Joseph Pulitzer said, "There is not a crime, there is not a dodge, there is not a trick, there is not a swindle, there is not a vice which does not live by secrecy." The Bradley Foundation lives by secrecy.

PART VI

A Susceptible Victim:
The Compromised Court

CHAPTER THIRTEEN

Ripe for Capture

We are apt to shut our eyes against a painful truth, and listen to
the song of that siren until she turns us into beasts.
—Patrick Henry

IN FRAUD CASES, SOMETIMES THE VICTIM IS A dupe, and sometimes
the victim is in on the fraud. It's worth a look at what kind of victim
the Court has been in the Scheme to capture it. The fact that the
Court has indulged many of the methods of its own capture begs the
question of how vulnerable—or even willing—a victim the Court has
been.

Unfortunately, many of the safeguards to limit capture in agencies and influence in Congress don't exist for the Supreme Court. For
much of our history, this wasn't a major concern. Appointments to the
Court weren't controlled by dark money, and the prevalence of jury
trials and the independence of judges and the rules about "cases or
controversies" all helped safeguard our legal system.

But with jury trials eliminated in 98 percent of lawsuits—which
is the current state of our federal courts—and with dark money persis-
tently stocking the pond via a captured federal judicial conveyor belt,
the odds of finding a friendly judge go up significantly. Let's say you're
bold enough to steal a Supreme Court seat in plain view, manufacture
a "principle" to explain your theft, and then immediately reverse that
"principle" to grab a second seat. You'd probably be bold enough to
look for ways in which the Court is vulnerable. And there are plenty.

Justices make their own calls on a wide range of sticky ethics situations—including whether to recuse themselves from a case—without a binding code of ethics. The Court's recusal policies are a problem. Consider how the Court addressed the saga of coal executive Don Blankenship in 2009. Back in 1998, a rival company run by a man named Hugh Caperton sued Blankenship's company, A.T. Massey Coal, for fraud and contract interference, and in 2002 a West Virginia jury returned a $50 million verdict for Caperton. In West Virginia, state judges are elected. As the 2004 elections approached and his $50 million defeat worked its way through the appeals process, Blankenship took an intense interest in the state supreme court candidacy of Charleston lawyer Brent Benjamin.

Blankenship wasn't shy about his support. He dumped $2.5 million—more than two-thirds of the group's total haul—into a pro-Benjamin group called "And for the Sake of the Kids." Then he spent over half a million dollars more on so-called independent expenditures in support of Benjamin. "To provide some perspective," Justice Kennedy would write, "Blankenship's $3 million in contributions were more than the total amount spent by all other Benjamin supporters and three times the amount spent by Benjamin's own committee."[1]

Three million is a lot to spend—unless it's actually saving you $50 million. Then you're net $47 million to the good. It's not hard to guess what happened next. Benjamin won the election, refused to recuse himself, heard the appeal, and cast the deciding vote for Blankenship's coal company, reversing the jury verdict by a 3–2 vote. Caperton took his case to the U.S. Supreme Court, arguing that the Constitution's Due Process Clause requires a judge to recuse himself or herself when he or she has "a direct, personal, substantial, pecuniary interest" in a case, and that Blankenship's political spending created just such an interest. The Supreme Court agreed. That's the good news.

The bad news is that the *Caperton* case was a squeaker of a 5–4 decision. Believe it or not, four justices were okay with a judge deciding a case for the dominant funder in the political campaign that put him on the Court while the case was pending. The bad news is that the new composition of the Court probably makes *Caperton* a dead letter. And the bad news is that, after Americans for Prosperity spent millions to help Amy Coney Barrett get on the Court—a situation that mirrored the Blankenship saga—Justice Barrett failed to recuse herself from a case involving its twin, Americans for Prosperity Foundation. Ditto Gorsuch and Kavanaugh, who had been favored with similar AFP spending.

To make matters worse, the principal dissent in *Caperton*, written by Chief Justice Roberts, stood on a familiar false premise. The Chief Justice argued that there was no evidence of undue influence because Blankenship had spent his $3 million "independently" of the justice's campaign. As experts know, and as we have seen in practice, "independence" is illusory, a judicial fiction used in *Citizens United* to open the door to unlimited spending. A Court with no political experience can indulge in these motivated fantasies, but anyone with experience in politics knows it's a joke.

If a litigant spending $3 million to support the candidacy of a judge about to hear his case isn't corrupting in the Chief Justice's view, what is? The answer, apparently, is a judicial candidate soliciting $25. Just a few years after the *Caperton* case, the Supreme Court upheld a Florida state law that barred judicial candidates from directly soliciting campaign funds.[2] Chief Justice Roberts wrote the majority opinion. I don't disagree with the Chief Justice that "[t]he judiciary's authority . . . depends in large measure on the public's willingness to respect and follow its decisions."[3] I'm just a bit surprised that he didn't see that problem in the context of big "independent" spending. Here's what he said in the Florida case:

> Even if judges were able to refrain from favoring donors, the mere possibility that judges' decisions may be motivated by the desire to repay campaign contributions is likely to undermine the public's confidence in the judiciary. In the eyes of the public, a judge's personal solicitation could result (even unknowingly) in a possible temptation. . . . That risk is especially pronounced because most donors are lawyers and litigants who may appear before the judge they are supporting.[4]

I have no argument with any of this. I just don't believe that the only donations that can corrupt are personally solicited campaign contributions. And I definitely don't believe that the only judges whose decisions might be "motivated by the desire to repay" are those who are elected rather than appointed.

Unfortunately, Supreme Court justices operate free of most ethics rules that govern other federal officials, including other federal judges.[5] They are explicitly *not* bound by the Code of Conduct for United States Judges that sets the standards for federal judicial behavior.[6] Each justice decides for himself or herself where the line is, and they do not weigh in on each other's decisions. Each is judge in his or her own cause.*

In 2011, Chief Justice Roberts defended the Court's freewheeling approach. He argued that the Court had "no reason to adopt the Code of Conduct as its definitive source of ethical guidance" because it was just one of many sources that the justices could "consult" in making their own ethical decisions.[7] He noted that, unlike lower court judges, if a Supreme Court justice recuses himself or herself, the case will be heard by fewer than the full Court.[8] Also, the Chief Justice pointed out, the Court does not operate completely free of ethical obligations: a federal statute requires all federal judges to recuse themselves if they have a financial interest or close relative in a case, for example. Another law includes the justices among federal officials who are subject to federal disclosure of gifts and outside income, and the Court has voluntarily agreed to follow Judicial Conference guidance when it comes to gifts.

None of these rules has teeth, however, and many are easily avoided. James Bryce, in *The American Commonwealth*, wrote that many misdeeds "shun the light; to expose them is to defeat them." Shining a light on some Supreme Court practices reveals the monumental failure of allowing the justices to self-regulate.

AMICI

The previous chapter described how amicus briefs have become a vehicle for big influencers to lobby courts. It is not unusual to see the Court

---

*The principle that one should not be a judge in his or her own cause is a principle of such antiquity that it originated—and is still sometimes quoted—in Latin: *nemo judex in causa sua*.

flooded with dozens of briefs backed with money from shadowy sources. That's because the Supreme Court's procedural rules let donors bankrolling these judicial lobbying efforts hide behind front groups. A donor can write a $10 million check to a group and hand it over with a wink saying, "I think you know how to use this," or "I'd like to support your work," or even, "Please tell me you'll use this to take down the CFBP." So long as they don't publicly say, "I know you're writing an amicus brief in *Seila Law* and I want my money to support its preparation or submission," disclosure can be evaded. This is because of the way the Court has chosen to enforce its own amicus disclosure rules.

I found this so troubling that I wrote a letter to the Supreme Court suggesting that it update its disclosure rules to reflect the modern-day realities of dark money and judicial lobbying.[9] The Clerk of the Court responded in a letter that told me, politely, to buzz off. I tried again with nominee Amy Coney Barrett during her confirmation hearings.[10] Watchdog groups had discovered that in the case *Oracle v. Google*, Oracle had given hundreds of thousands of dollars to organizations that filed amicus briefs on Oracle's behalf without disclosing the connection. Some excellent investigative reporting documented Google doing the same thing.[11]

"Isn't that the kind of stuff that parties ought to know, that the public ought to know, and that the court ought to know?" I asked Judge Barrett.[12]

"I didn't know that until you just shared that information with me," she replied.

"Please think about these things," I urged her. "There is something that is not right about the way this is happening, and I urge you, and I urge anybody from the Court who is listening, to try to—sincerely try to—clean this mess up because it is not good for the Court."

Judge Barrett had been trained well for her hearing. "Thank you, Senator Whitehouse," is all she said. Now that she is Justice Barrett, I'm not holding my breath. The Court seems content with nondisclosure by big dark-money amici. Not so the Judicial Conference, the federal court system's administrative policy-making group. It takes the issue seriously enough to have set up a special committee to consider improved amicus disclosure. As DC Circuit Court of Appeals Judge

Patricia Millet has said, it's important to see the "power behind the throne" when front-group amici show up.* Perhaps that concern will filter up to the Supreme Court.

GIFTS

The Court claims to comply voluntarily with the gift provisions of the Ethics in Government Act, and Justice Roberts says this claim should assuage any concerns about the absence of ethics rules. Yes, the rules do require the justices to disclose gifts, and they prohibit justices from accepting gifts from litigants or honoraria for outside speeches. But they allow justices to accept travel and lodging in connection with those speeches. And they allow a good deal more.

There is a particularly egregious loophole in the disclosure rules for "hospitality extended for a nonbusiness purpose by an individual," which is called the "personal hospitality" exemption. It gives justices a huge out in their gifts reporting. The Court has made profligate use of this loophole, starting with not requiring that there actually be a personal relationship with the donor providing the "personal hospitality."

This so-called personal hospitality exclusion doesn't just cover stays "at the personal residence of that individual or his family," but also "on property or facilities owned by that individual or his family."[13] That means it's not limited to someone's home. It could include their hotel, their golf course, or even their Florida resort at Mar-a-Lago. Because the exemption spares justices from even reporting these gifts, we have no idea how often they have taken advantage of this loophole. We don't know whose "personal hospitality" they have accepted, who they spent their time with, for how long, or how much their visits might have cost. But we do know about one justice, thanks to the diligence of two lawyers.

When he died, Justice Antonin Scalia was in Texas at the Cibolo

---

* The Judicial Conference created a subcommittee to consider the issue, which in October 2021 released a preliminary report agreeing that control and funding of amicus briefs "are important and complex issues that deserve further investigation and consideration." The subcommittee also recognized that "parties may enjoy more influence over amicus briefs than the current disclosure regime reveals," and that the existing disclosure provisions "may need to be revised." I hope the full committee will give the subcommittee's report the attention it deserves.[14]

Creek Ranch, a five-star resort that he and a guest had flown into on a private charter plane for a gathering of the International Order of St. Hubertus, a secretive all-male hunting society. Justice Scalia was staying for free as a guest of the ranch's owner, Texas millionaire John Poindexter. That one weekend, which some have valued at $10,000 for the Justice and his guest, might deserve a raised eyebrow, particularly since Poindexter's business just had a case before the Court. But it wasn't just one weekend. (And it was more than that other, notorious weekend Justice Scalia spent hunting with Vice President Cheney— and traveling there and back with him on Air Force Two—even as the Bush administration had important cases before the Court, including one in which Cheney was a named party.)

Every once in a while, a regular lawyer does something very impressive. A famous example was Boston lawyer Joseph Welch challenging Senator Joe McCarthy in a Senate hearing after McCarthy's attack on a young staffer. "Let us not assassinate this lad further, Senator. You've done enough," he said. "Have you no sense of decency, sir? At long last, have you left no sense of decency?" It was a tipping point that went the 1954 equivalent of viral, and it can be seen today in the documentary *Point of Order*. I require all my Senate interns to watch it. Another was a local real estate lawyer, Watson Bryant, standing up against the FBI and the full weight of federal law enforcement in the early days of the effort to pin the Atlanta Olympic bombing on his innocent client, Richard Jewell. His efforts were featured in the movie *Richard Jewell*.

I would add the unheralded duo of Stephen Bruce, a Washington, DC, pension lawyer, and his associate Allison Pienta, who noticed something odd when Justice Scalia died on that all-expenses-paid Texas hunting vacation. As people reminisced about the Justice, more and more stories emerged on the internet and in the press about Scalia's many hunting vacations, stories that piqued these lawyers' curiosity. The two began to dig, scouring public records for mentions of Scalia's hunting trips. Ultimately, they posted a comprehensive report.[15] Here's what their determined digging unearthed.

First, there were many trips—indeed, many dozens. This was not an occasional thing. The report chronicles more than eighty hunting vacations taken by Justice Scalia in the two decades before his death, and there may well have been many more. Eighty is a lot.

Second, these were expensive trips. Some venues hold themselves out as commercial operations, so you can look up the rates they charge—sometimes a thousand dollars a day or more.[16] A complete accounting would likely put the value of these trips well into the hundreds of thousands of dollars, especially if the "personal hospitality" was also extended to family or friends of Scalia.

Third, the Justice often was accompanied on these trips by Republican political figures and, in some cases, individuals with interests before the Court: Republican elected officials, Republican Party officials and donors, representatives of pro-gun advocacy organizations, fossil fuel industry folks, and so forth.[17] These were not "personal" affairs in the ordinary sense.

Fourth, the hunting vacations appear to have been "comped" to the Justice. He seems to have seldom paid for them. If the venues comping the Justice were reimbursed by a third party, that makes it all even messier, but we don't know.

Fifth, the reason we don't know is because none of these trips was reported under Supreme Court disclosure rules. When Senator Graham and I made a bipartisan inquiry about the justices' receipt of gifts, travel, or hospitality, the Court assured us that the justices "take care to ensure that any items received are in full compliance with" judicial branch rules.[18] Maybe "items" was a trick answer. But these dozens of expensive comped vacations were never disclosed.

Last, a specific system was used to evade disclosure. Here's how it worked. The Supreme Court's "personal hospitality" exemption obviously implies a personal relationship, but it doesn't *explicitly* say so. So Justice Scalia or his intermediaries would arrange a hunting trip at a suitable venue and get the owner of the venue to invite the Justice. The owner of the venue often had no personal relationship with the Justice, yet the invitation from the owner made it "personal hospitality."

One Georgia lawyer described how the conversation would go. When asked if he would give a speech to the Georgia bar, the lawyer recalled, Justice Scalia "smiled and said, 'I've always enjoyed hunting quail in Georgia.'"[19] A team of lawyers immediately got to work planning a symposium—and a quail hunting trip on a south Georgia plantation. As Justice Scalia's colleague Justice Sandra Day O'Connor advised a Texas lawyer trying to get Scalia to come address his alma mater, "He'll do anything if you take him hunting."[20]

Under this practice, any justice could solicit any trip, from any resort owner, and get a free holiday without ever reporting it, so long as they or their intermediary arranged for the resort owner—whom they don't even have to know—to "invite" them. Indeed, big donors could go to the owners of the fanciest resorts in the world—private islands in the Caribbean, charter yachts in the Med, ski chalets in the Rockies— and ask the owner to invite a friendly justice and give him a wonderful free undisclosed vacation. They could arrange for political interests to come along and get the ear of the justice in a congenial and very private situation. They could even arrange a nearby speech to cover the justice's airfare.

This secrecy kept the public from knowing that for well over a decade before he rewrote the Second Amendment in a case called *District of Columbia v. Heller*, Justice Scalia had been entertained at some of the most luxurious hunting resorts in the country in the company of senior NRA leaders and other wealthy conservative donors, including some who filed or funded briefs in the *Heller* case.

One Scalia trip took him to Nuremberg, Germany, in March 2007, for the "World Forum for the Future of Sports Shooting Activities." At the time, *Heller* was headed for the Court's docket. Justice Scalia's opinion in this case would radically redefine and expand the scope of the Second Amendment right to bear arms, delivering a landmark win for the NRA and the firearms industry. Groups funding the Nuremberg conference, including the NRA, were amici curiae in the case. At the conference, Scalia talked with gun-rights activists Alan Gottlieb of the Second Amendment Foundation and Stephen Halbrook of the NRA. After Justice Scalia's death, Gottlieb described the conversation in a right-wing talk radio interview as follows:

> So we didn't talk directly about the case itself because it would have been like sort of a conflict, but he did say . . . "You know, Alan, it takes four votes on the Supreme Court to hear a case, and it takes five to win it. If I don't think we have the five to win it, there won't be four to hear it." And that just made me feel like

I knew at that point in time that if the Supreme Court took the *Heller* case, that we were going to win it.[21]

This revelation, in a case that the Court hadn't decided yet, to a known advocate filing briefs in support of that outcome, presaged the result. It was not proper.

To put Court capture in context, let's put these undisclosed gifts to a U.S. Supreme Court justice side by side with gifts to government employees in instances of regulatory capture—say, the Minerals Management Service's relationship with oil and gas interests exposed after the 2010 Deepwater Horizon explosion in the gulf. My Senate colleague Bill Nelson called this a "cozy, incestuous relationship."[22]

The Interior Department inspector general revealed that MMS inspectors who oversaw oil drilling in the Gulf of Mexico accepted freebies from companies they monitored.[23] Gifts chronicled in the inspector general's report included a trip to the 2005 Peach Bowl on a private airplane, skeet shooting contests, hunting and fishing trips, and golf tournaments. What resulted? Interior Secretary Ken Salazar reported that MMS employees who had accepted gifts were fired and referred for prosecution. When gifts like that cause scandal in the regulatory world, and result in employee firings and referrals to DOJ, it is hard to see how this pattern of dozens of undisclosed, comped luxury hunting trips to a Supreme Court justice is not a problem. In theory, justices are held to the highest standard. Yet Scalia's trips went on for years.

The Supreme Court needs to clean this up, with a proper ethics code and real disclosure requirements.* The fact that this "personal hospitality" system was allowed to run up a pattern of more than eighty

---

*When Lindsey Graham and I wrote to the Court about its gifts disclosures, we received a bland, clerical answer from a Court functionary. The Court asserted to us that "Justices follow the same financial disclosure rules that are applicable to other federal judges," and "the same restrictions on gifts and outside activities that are applicable to the rest of the federal judiciary" and that "the Justices have complied with them." Indeed, the letter assures us, "Justices and their chambers staff take care to ensure that any items received are in full compliance with those rules." On this set of facts regarding gifts of "personal hospitality," it is hard to see how those assertions are true. If they are true, it suggests a crying need for better rules.[24]

free, undisclosed vacations for just one justice signals plainly the need for improvement.

In 2011, the *New York Times* uncovered other ways justices could sidestep the gift rule: justices can enjoy generous "gifts" of friendship in the form of donations made on their behalf. So long as they don't touch the money (they just direct it), they can decline to disclose it.[25] The article described the relationship between multimillionaire donor Harlan Crow and Justice Clarence Thomas:

> Mr. Crow has done many favors for the justice and his wife, Virginia, helping finance a Savannah library project dedicated to Justice Thomas, presenting him with a Bible that belonged to Frederick Douglass and reportedly providing $500,000 for Ms. Thomas to start a Tea Party-related group. They have also spent time together at gatherings of prominent Republicans and businesspeople at Mr. Crow's Adirondacks estate and his camp in East Texas.[26]

What drew attention in 2011 was a much bigger, multimillion-dollar donation that Mr. Crow made to finance a historic restoration project and launch a nonprofit of personal significance to Justice Thomas. In fact, the Justice appeared to have solicited the donation himself. The solicited gift wasn't in Justice Thomas's disclosures—after all, the millions weren't given to him directly.

Mr. Crow, like Justice Thomas, is conservative. He had given a hundred thousand dollars to the "Swift Boat Veterans for Truth" group that attacked presidential candidate John Kerry, and five times more to organizations that ran ads on behalf of President G.W. Bush's Supreme Court nominees. Mr. Crow served on the boards of two conservative organizations involved in a total of eleven cases before the Supreme Court. Justice Thomas voted with the Crow-affiliated groups every time.

Of course, we have no way of knowing how or whether Justice Scalia's long history of free trips with the NRA and other gun and hunting groups affected his vote in *Heller*. Nor do we know how or whether the millions Justice Thomas received for his pet projects affected Thomas's thinking.* But at the very least, other interests appearing before the justices—interests thinking they were facing impartial jurists who would apply the law, honor precedent, and approach their case with an open mind—deserved to know that the justices they were appearing before had friends on the other side, friends who had done them considerable favors. Whether or not the justices should have given serious thought to stepping aside and not hearing those particular matters, this stuff should have been disclosed.

SCHMOOZING

The German novelist Goethe wrote, "Tell me with whom you associate, and I will tell you who you are." After the financial crash of 2008, commentators wondered how in the world federal regulators could have missed all the warning signs that banks were over-leveraged and poised to bring our entire financial system down with them. The answer researchers came up with is that the SEC had been "culturally" captured—they had come to see themselves as part of the industry they were supposed to regulate, bound together by (as law professor Jonas Anderson explained), "identity, status, and relationships."[27]

The Federalist Society has excelled at wrapping the Republican justices they put on the Court into the Society's "identity, status, and relationships." Court culture allows conservative judges to maintain such close ties to the Federalist Society that it's hard to tell where their true loyalties lie. The Federalist Society's black-tie galas, for example, are fertile ground for high-end partisan Washington, DC, schmoozing. Held in the fall, these glitzy affairs sport "all the trappings of a classic Washington fundraiser"—including big-name corporate sponsors prominently featured in the program brochure at donor levels of "platinum," "gold," "silver," and "bronze."

In 2012, Justice Alito was the featured speaker at the FedSoc gala. Many saw it as returning a favor for this group that had been instrumental in his own ascension to the highest court. The following year, Justice Alito attended the gala again, as a guest—this time, Justice Thomas had the headlining honors. Justice Alito's consolation prize?

---

* Also curious: in the fifteen-plus years since Justice Thomas attracted media attention as the Court's leading gift-getter, he has not reported receiving a single gift.

A seat at the table with the head of the Scaife Foundation, one of the dark-money organizations bankrolling the flotillas of amici appearing before the Court. The next year, Justice Alito again headlined the big fundraising gala. Then, in 2017, it was the newest member of the Court, Justice Gorsuch. In 2019, it was Justice Kavanaugh's turn for top billing.

These tribal gatherings of the big donors, the right-wing litigating groups, the dark-money amici, and the Dark Money Justices should make us queasy. If I were a litigant with a case before the Supreme Court, and I saw sitting Supreme Court justices hobnobbing with wealthy donors who were funding briefs against me, I would question their partiality. I would especially question it if I knew that the groups had helped orchestrate those justices' selection and ascension onto the Court. I would wonder about justices so eager for attention and praise from so flagrantly partisan a group. Justices who headline conservative legal group fundraisers do not send a very reassuring message about the Court's impartiality.

Put yourself in a justice's shoes attending one of these partisan pep rallies. You are treated like a rock star at Federalist Society events. You walk through a conference hosted by a group that has shaped your judicial philosophy, groomed you and auditioned you for the bench, put your name on a candidate list for the White House, and coordinated millions of dollars to ensure your confirmation. You are on the Supreme Court thanks to their effort. These are your people. You are their product, and you are their prize. How likely are you to turn your back on your tribe?

The Court missed a big chance to clean up its act in 2020. The U.S. Judicial Conference proposed an advisory opinion to address the "grave concern raised by perceived judicial endorsement of liberal or conservative causes."[28] It's not just a question of general endorsement; specific doctrines and policies pressed by the Federalist Society can be applied in real cases to affect outcomes between parties. Indeed, it's the intention of the big FedSoc donors that doctrines and policies pursued by the Federalist Society will affect outcomes in their cases—and in their favor. That's the point.

The proposed advisory would have banned active membership in the Federalist Society (and the American Constitution Society, a mild progressive answer to the Federalist Society without nearly its influence) as "inconsistent with obligations imposed" by the Code of Conduct for United States Judges—namely, the obligation to avoid involvement with any groups that might "cast doubt on the judge's impartiality."[29] Though membership in these organizations would be prohibited, speaking at events and participating in panel discussions at either advocacy organization would still be fine. This should have been easy.

The draft advisory opinion was released in January 2020, and the Judicial Conference was immediately hit with a barrage of responses from conservative judges—including many Trump appointees—offended at the very notion that someone would try to insert any daylight between them and their precious Federalist Society. Mitch McConnell rounded up dozens of Republican senators to sign a letter of umbrage. (I helped Democratic members of Congress write in response that this was a good idea, even if it meant ACS losing any members who were on the bench.) By July, however, under withering barrage from the Federalist Society right, the proposed rule was withdrawn.

ACCOUNTABILITY

Hidden amici, unreported free travel, huge donations for pet projects, and gobs of partisan schmoozing—all of that sure smacks of access and influence. But even on the rare occasions when we're able to connect the dots—and to do it before a case is actually argued before the Supreme Court—there's not much we can do about it.

Yes, the Court's rules—and, for that matter, federal law—require a judge to disqualify himself or herself "in any proceeding in which his [or her] impartiality might reasonably be questioned."[30] And in some cases, they do. For example, shortly after Justice Elena Kagan joined the Court, the justices heard an affirmative action case that she had weighed in on when she was still solicitor general. Even though her vote was likely to be decisive, she took herself off the panel considering the matter. Justice Thomas recused himself in a case involving Virginia Military Institute's policy of not admitting women because his son was then enrolled there. Interestingly, Justice Rehnquist recused himself from cases argued by an attorney who had testified against his confirmation; he never explained his reasoning (they don't have to), but I suspect it was an honorable decision.

In his 2011 report discussing judicial ethics, Chief Justice Roberts explained that Supreme Court justices "may consider recusal in response to a request from a party in a pending case, or on their own initiative."[31] They may "examine precedent and scholarly publications, seek advice from the Court's Legal Office, consult colleagues, and even seek counsel from the Committee on Codes of Conduct."[32] But it's up to each of them, and their decision is unreviewable. As the Chief Justice wrote, "[t]here is no higher court to review a Justice's decision not to recuse in a particular case," and "the Supreme Court does not sit in judgment over one of its own Member's decision whether to recuse in the course of deciding a case."[33] So no one is overseen, and no justice has to answer for his or her decision.

Where better rules might better protect the Court as an institution, the Court accepts the status quo. A culture of coziness with corporate right-wing activist groups, who are seeking to drive an agenda through the courts, prevails. Justices are human, and as open to peer pressure, group signaling, and tribal applause as the rest of us.

For big donors looking for a vulnerable target, this is all good news indeed. And if any justices have serious qualms about what is happening at the Court, there is little public sign of it. The Court's institutional *omerta* inhibits the justices' acknowledgment that it has a problem, which inhibits the Court from fixing the problem—another bonus for the captors.

My book *Captured* documented the history of regulatory capture and chronicled its grim effects: "When a regulatory agency is captured, it becomes the industry's tool, overlooking errors and misdeeds, setting rules that favor the industry, and keeping out competition that might challenge the big incumbents. That's when regulatory agencies stop working for us and become pawns of the industry they were supposed to regulate."[34]

Sound familiar?

PART VII

Payday: The Captured Court

CHAPTER FOURTEEN

The 80 (aka The Prize)

Where enough money calls the tune, the general public will not
be heard.

—Justice Stephen Breyer, *McCutcheon v. FEC*

I LOVE THE LAW. I ACTUALLY REVERE THE law. As a boy, I wanted to
be Atticus Finch. I loved Thomas More in A *Man for All Seasons*
schooling his acolyte: "And when the last law was down, and the Devil
turned 'round on you, where would you hide . . . the laws all being
flat? This country is planted thick with laws, from coast to coast, Man's
laws, not God's! And if you cut them down . . . do you really think you
could stand upright in the winds that would blow then?"[1] So it's not
an easy thing for me to call out our U.S. Supreme Court, which many
have viewed as standing apart from politics. But to me, the evidence is
compelling, and I fear that until someone points out that the emperor
has no clothes, the emperor's naked parade is likely to go on.

Sadly, one of the consequences of this era of extreme partisan politics is that many people will not heed my warning about what is happening in our courts, especially in the Supreme Court, simply because
of who I am: a sitting U.S. senator and a Democrat. I get it. But if you
were to walk away from this book thinking I've simply set out my list of
political grievances with recent Court rulings, I have not done my job.

I am not alone in my concerns. Court watchers from the right
and left report that the Supreme Court today is polarized "in a fash-
ion we have never seen."[2] Veteran *New York Times* reporter Linda

Greenhouse, who for years had rejected efforts to attach political labels to Supreme Court justices, finally admitted that it is "impossible to avoid the conclusion that the Republican-appointed majority is committed to harnessing the Supreme Court to an ideological agenda."[3] Norm Ornstein, of the right-leaning American Enterprise Institute, has called out the "tribal" politicized Court to the point of calling for term limits for the justices.[4]

After Justice Alito's draft abortion ruling overturning *Roe* was leaked in May 2022, the condemnation language grew even hotter. "The conservative majority's radicalism will deepen the crisis of American democracy," said E.J. Dionne. Jennifer Rubin said a "partisan, radical majority" had "burst through the bounds of judicial restraint" in a "play for theocratic supremacy." Under the headline "The Supreme Court's Legitimacy Is Already Lost," Dahlia Lithwick called it "one of the most brazenly political acts to ever come out of the court," showing "staggering lack of regard for its own legitimacy"; that "there are simply no rules left at an institution that is supposed to be the one making the rules." Charles Blow warned: "The robes can go rogue. This is the power Republicans want—the power to overrule the will of the majority." The *Star-Ledger* described the Court as "irretrievably broken," thanks to "political capture . . . driven by the dark-monied interests of the Judicial Crisis Network."[5]

Recently, two members of President Biden's Supreme Court Commission, retired federal judge Nancy Gertner and Harvard Law professor Laurence Tribe, published a disquieting op-ed headlined "The Supreme Court Isn't Well."[6] This title mirrored the sentence in my amicus brief that provoked Justice Alito's ire and the right's "faux outrage." The "anti-democratic, anti-egalitarian direction of this court's decisions," they wrote, move our democracy "toward a system in which the few corruptly govern the many, something between autocracy and oligarchy." They called out in particular "the dubious legitimacy of the way some justices were appointed."

Now we come to the last category of evidence: the payoff. We've seen the motive behind the Scheme, even the plan; we've seen the means the right-wing elite had to work with; and we've seen the front-group method by which the Scheme was accomplished. We've seen the gale-force political pressure in the Senate, and how vulnerable a victim the Court was. We've even seen actual "admissions against interest" by the Trump White House (that the Federalist Society was "insourced") and by the Federalist Society (that it "came up with" the nominees). We've seen how Trump outsourced judicial selection to that private operation while it was anonymously funded by unelected, unaccountable big donors.

We've also seen how corporate, libertarian, and socially conservative forces merged in the 1970s and '80s to create the right-wing anti-government movement that slowly infiltrated and took over the Republican Party. And how money in politics—especially the tsunami of unlimited dark money unleashed by *Citizens United*—accelerated the takeover. We've seen the Federalist Society use its 501(c)(3) arm to indoctrinate, groom, and audition candidates, and its associated web of shadowy 501(c)(4) affiliates raise and spend hundreds of millions of dollars. We've seen how similar Court capture was to the "regulatory capture" researchers have been documenting for years in administrative agencies, and how inadequate the Court's own rules are at guarding against outside influence. And we've seen the judicial confirmation process in the Senate go from meaningful review to partisan rubber stamp, leaving a wreckage of norms, rules, prerogatives, and FBI integrity in its wake.

Now let's look at the loot, the booty, the proceeds of the Scheme. In assessing guilt, the principle of looking at who benefits has ancient roots. Cicero, talking about the murderous conspirator Clodius, said, "for such an audacious, nefarious monster it is enough to show that he had a great reason," and cited the proverb of Cassius "who profits?"—a phrase still alive today in Latin, "cui bono." So who benefited from the Scheme?

By the time Justice Barrett joined the Court on the eve of the 2020 election, the partisan parade of civil cases under Chief Justice Roberts that gave big wins to big-donor interests had grown to number more than eighty cases—more than the Supreme Court's typical total annual output. For the big-money donors, it's been a feast.

In 2020 and 2021, I worked with my fellow Democrats in the Senate to produce a series of "Captured Courts" reports showing what was at stake: women's right to choose and to access contraception; communities' ability to fight dirty fossil fuel companies making their children sick; workers' rights to come together to negotiate for better pay and working conditions; consumers' ability to hold companies that defraud them accountable in a fair trial; parents' ability to keep their children safe from guns; and all of our rights to enjoy the free and democratic society that our Founders created and left for future generations to perfect. These "Captured Courts" reports can be found online. They are scrupulously researched, and they make for sobering reading.

Those reports had their roots in an article I wrote in 2019 about what was then a seventy-three-case run of partisan 5–4 decisions for the big donors from the Roberts Court.[7] It had seemed to me that something was terribly wrong at the Court as these decisions piled up, but it wasn't enough to intuit that. I needed to confirm this intuition.

First, I needed to make the case to my Senate Democratic caucus. My initial suggestions to the caucus that something was seriously wrong at the Court had not gone well. My colleagues were still heavily invested in the instinctive tradition of protecting the Court's reputation. I owe Senator Patrick Leahy my gratitude for being the first to stand up to support me. As the dean of our caucus, our Senate president pro tempore, a chairman of Judiciary, and the senior Democrat on Appropriations, he's seen a few things. So when Patrick spoke, people listened. And when he said, "Sheldon's right. We need to listen to him," it had a big effect. Thank you, Patrick. Still, for both our sakes, I needed to check and double-check and test with rigorous analysis what my eyes and ears and lawyer's sense were all telling me. Today, I don't know of a single senator in the Democratic caucus who doubts that there is a serious problem at the Court; the evidence drove that conclusion.

To assemble that evidence, my staff and I began digging into the record. We initially looked at Supreme Court decisions from the beginning of its 2005–2006 term, when Chief Justice Roberts joined the Court, through the 2017–18 term. During those years, four justices were associated with the Court's "liberal" wing (including, for a time, Justice John Paul Stevens, a Nixon appointee). The five newer Republican justices made up its conservative, Federalist Society wing.

We looked at the Court's civil cases, where most battles over corporate and political issues play out. We looked first at the Court's 5–4 decisions, 212 cases that came down to a single vote. The number of decisions decided by this slim margin has been historically high in the Roberts Court.[8] In seventy-eight of those single-vote decisions, the Court split along ideological lines, with the majority consisting entirely of the Court's bloc of five "conservative" justices. We homed in on those.

In those seventy-eight 5–4 cases where the Court's five conservative members had banded together, we found that seventy-three cases— almost all of them—implicated issues of obvious concern to the Republican Party and its dark-money special-interest donors. And we found a staggering pattern: in every one of those seventy-three cases, 73–0, the conservative big-money interests won. Every. Single. Time.

As I noted recently in the *Harvard Journal on Legislation*, "Some of these victories go beyond donor interests just pocketing a win in a particular case; the most dangerous victories actually tilt the political or legal or regulatory playing fields in favor of the donor interests in ways that will enable streams of future victories."[9] Indisputably, the big, dark-money special interests have gotten what they paid for: in an ostensibly neutral and nonpartisan Court that's supposed to be deciding issues on the basis of law, evidence, and quality of argument, the dark-money donors have achieved a highly suspect unbroken pattern of victories in four categories where victories matter most to them:

(1) controlling the political process to benefit Republicans;
(2) protecting corporations from accountability (like letting polluters pollute);
(3) restricting civil rights and condoning discrimination; and
(4) advancing a far-right social agenda.

Let's look.

CHAPTER FIFTEEN

Cases Controlling the Political Process

Knowledge will forever govern ignorance. And a people who mean to be their own governors must arm themselves with the power which knowledge gives.

—JAMES MADISON

CAMPAIGN FINANCE CASES

Just a few years before Chief Justice Roberts joined the Supreme Court, two Republican-appointed justices joined its decision in *McConnell v. FEC*, which largely upheld Congress's strengthened campaign finance law. One was Justice Sandra Day O'Connor, the last justice with any experience of running for office, thus the last justice with any firsthand sense of the role money plays in electoral politics.

The lawmakers drafting that campaign finance law had understood how big money—or even the threat of big money—could manipulate political outcomes, facilitate corruption, and drown out citizen voices. They saw outside front groups push wildly misleading if not downright false attack ads. They came together to stop the pollution of our political environment, and they did it with pragmatic, balanced, bipartisan legislation informed by their own experiences. The bill wasn't just bipartisan; it was signed into law by a Republican president, George W. Bush.

The dark-money donors hated it. The ability to hide unlimited political spending is a powerful weapon for the big donors, with real political effects, and they desperately want no one to be able to "follow the money." The captured Court has obliged. Instead of justices with actual elections experience, the Court was filled with justices whose experience was as partisan warriors in political litigation.*

There's a challenge to regulating campaign finance and dark money: money is always trying to find a way in—and trying to find a way to avoid disclosure. So some defensive thinking is required. It wasn't hard to anticipate that dark-money forces would establish new nonprofits to hide donors and slosh money among like-minded organizations. Or that they would co-opt trade associations like the U.S. Chamber of Commerce (as Lewis Powell told them to do).† Or that once they were given an inch they would seize a mile, forming super PACs to spend unrestricted amounts of money in elections and hide their donors.

The Court should stand as a vigilant watchdog of our constitutional order. The entire purpose of the Constitution is to establish a government that is both legitimate in the eyes of the people and able to operate free of undue influence. The Court should encourage Congress to guard those barricades. Instead, the Roberts Court has acted more like a sleeper agent, quietly unlocking doors and disarming long-standing anti-corruption systems. In decision after decision it allowed uncapped, untraceable, and barely regulated funds to flow into our political process—and into our TVs, radios, and mailboxes—ushering in the era of dark outside groups manipulating our elections.¹ It tossed

---

* A full third of the Supreme Court—the Chief Justice, Justice Kavanaugh, and Justice Barrett—participated in the lawsuits that led to one of the most nakedly anti-democratic and partisan moments in the Supreme Court's nearly 240-year history, the decision to stop Florida's recount and hand the election to George W. Bush. The 5–4 ruling by the Court's conservative members (who set aside their customary concerns for states' rights) lent "credence to the most cynical appraisal of the work of judges throughout the land," as Justice Stevens wrote in his dissent, and handed the presidency to a man who lost the popular vote by half a million votes.

† The Chamber of Commerce has ranged from affirming to doubting to denying climate change. Today the Chamber (along with the National Association of Manufacturers) is one of the worst climate obstructors in the country. But back in the 1980s the Chamber prepared an entire briefing for Congress on the coming climate change and possible policy responses. Today, some of its most prominent members claim to want to do something about climate change, and some companies left the Chamber because of its lobbying against policies to address climate change. But the Chamber continues its anti-environmental lobbying. I can only imagine how much money the fossil fuel oligarchs have spent to capture the Chamber.

restrictions on political advertisements. It lifted long-standing caps on aggregate campaign contributions, in a case called *McCutcheon v. FEC*. Before that decision, a big donor couldn't contribute more than $123,200 directly to candidates and parties over a two-year election cycle—a healthy amount by most Americans' reckoning. The day after the decision, they could give more than $3.6 million—and that's before their super PAC and 501(c)(4) money for "independent" expenditures.

Ignoring states' sovereignty to set their own rules within their borders, the Roberts Court handed down decisions that dismantled long-standing, commonsense state campaign finance laws in Arizona and Montana. Montana's ban on corporate money in state races had stood for a century. The state law at issue in Montana governed only state elections, based on that state's particular experience with election interference, and had recently been upheld by the state's own supreme court. But the Dark Money Justices threw it out.

The Montana case was personally significant for me. It was the first Supreme Court case where I decided to write a brief as an amicus—a "friend of the court." I believed I had a special responsibility, as an elected official, to alert the Court to the fact that two of the key assumptions in its recent *Citizens United* decision were demonstrably false: first, "independent" political expenditures were not actually independent; and second, "disclosed" political funders were not actually disclosed. Instead, there was secrecy. I told the Court that "existing campaign finance rules purporting to provide for 'independence' and 'disclosure' in fact provided neither."[2] (Back then, I still thought this might have been innocent error.)

I didn't file my brief alone. Senator John McCain stood alongside me. He caught hell from Leader McConnell for doing so. At the next vote after we'd filed the brief, John approached me on the Senate Floor. "Goddammit, Sheldon, that brief of yours has McConnell hopping mad. I've never seen him so mad," he said. "You mean that brief of *ours*?" I responded. He smiled, shook his head, rolled his eyes, and walked away. How I miss him. We were close—I was the only senator among the pallbearers at John's funeral—and I respected him greatly and miss him deeply.

Regrettably, the Court ignored us both.

I tried again in the *Lieu* case. The Court had allowed super PACs to *spend* unlimited money in politics, but it hadn't said they could *raise* unlimited money. Perhaps the inflow could be limited, even if the outflow couldn't; and perhaps the inflow could be made transparent, as they had said in *Citizens United*. I made the point plainly: unlimited and non-transparent money was flowing into politics through super PACs and corrupting the political system. They refused to take up the case.

The result of this dark-money deluge wasn't just more money—literally billions more dollars—swamping our elections, but more power for party leaders, and a deluge of slime. Mitch McConnell has a leadership PAC that gives him millions of dollars to help keep party members in line. Two of his aides set up major super PACs that are supposedly "independent" but work hand-in-glove with the leadership PAC. It's negative stuff. In the 2020 election cycle, the "independent" Senate Leadership Fund spent $278 million attacking Democrats and just $8 million supporting Republicans.[3] Another dark-money outfit, American Crossroads, spent $76 million attacking Democrats and just $3 million supporting Republicans.[4] A collateral consequence of the Court's campaign finance decisions is the dark and slimy tenor of political campaigns.

Democrats were almost embarrassingly slow to get into the dark-money game. We seem constantly a generation behind in the political arms race, giving Republicans several cycles of unanswered dominance before we awaken. A few years ago, I spoke with a Republican colleague in the Senate about the scourge of dark money driving polarization, negativity, and lies. He agreed that the stuff was disgusting. Then he told me that if we wanted to do anything about it, "Democrats had better start raising a lot more dark money." Why, he asked in his practical way, would Republicans want to fix a system where they had about a ten-to-one advantage? Fair point. Now Democrats are in the dark-money game too, and it's even worse for the public. In fact, some say we raised even more dark money than the Republicans in 2020. I am afraid my colleague's hope for some kind of détente was ill-founded; my DISCLOSE Act, which would clean this mess up and require real transparency for political contributions over $10,000, still can't get a single Republican co-sponsor. The word is out among Senate Republicans that for Mitch McConnell, this is a party "red line" not to be crossed.

That's the key and defining difference between Democrats and Republicans on the topic of dark money: every Senate Democrat is fighting and voting to *get rid of* dark money, whereas every Republican is following Mitch McConnell and voting to *defend* it.* I was the floor manager for the DISCLOSE Act when it last got a roll-call vote on the Senate Floor. We got every Democratic vote and no Republican votes, and the measure died by Republican filibuster. More recently, every Senate Democrat declared support for our democracy and voting reform bill, which includes an updated DISCLOSE Act. No Republican has. (To her credit, Republican Senator Lisa Murkowski voted to allow us at least to bring the bill to the floor for debate and start the process, but one Republican vote was not enough. The measure died by Republican filibuster.)

The conservative dark-money donors, who fund the "independent" political entities that Mitch counts on to barrage Democratic Senate candidates, must be quite insistent, because Republicans dare not cross them. And their takeover of the Republican Party is complete; it's probably accurate to say that the Republican Party is now the political wing of the dark-money apparatus.

GERRYMANDERING CASES

Even as Democrats catch up in the dark-money race, other political process decisions by the Roberts Five help Republicans to rig the system. Take gerrymandering. For centuries, lawmakers from both parties have twiddled with district boundaries to help their political friends and punish their political enemies. But today's "bulk gerrymandering" aims at a state's entire congressional delegation. John McCain and I again joined forces to brief the Court on this issue—even after John had attracted McConnell's ire at our first amicus filing together. We explained to the Court that partisan gerrymandering is

---

*Check the record: in 2012, every Democratic member of the Senate present voted to get rid of dark money. Every Republican present voted to keep it flowing, using the filibuster to block us. All fifty Democrats now in the Senate are on record supporting the Freedom to Vote Act, which includes the DISCLOSE Act.

now accomplished using sophisticated technology—including mapping software, census data, and voting algorithms—to redraw a state's district lines to maximize partisan advantage across an entire state by packing the other party's voters as densely as possible into as few districts as possible.[5]

This came to pass after *Citizens United* unleashed a flood of right-wing special-interest money well timed to win Republican state legislatures in 2010. Those state legislatures could then redraw congressional legislative districts for 2012. In those first months after *Citizens United*, the Republican gerrymandering "Project REDMAP" raised more than $30 million—much of it dark money—and the investment paid off. In 2010 Republicans won state legislative majorities in battleground states that included Ohio, Michigan, North Carolina, Pennsylvania, and Wisconsin. Congressional districts in those states were then gerrymandered to create more Republican districts and fewer, super-saturated Democratic districts. In the 2012 House elections, Democrats got more votes, but Republicans got more seats—and "majority" control. In North Carolina and Pennsylvania, the actual vote split almost evenly between the parties, but "bulk gerrymandering" won Republicans a 10–3 delegation in North Carolina and a 13–5 delegation in Pennsylvania.[6]

When federal courts called this out for what it was—an unconstitutional partisan gerrymander—and struck down the gerrymandered state maps, the Roberts Five stepped in to announce that partisan gerrymanders were "nonjusticiable," or beyond the purview of any U.S. court.[7] (Never mind all the lower and appellate courts that had successfully "justiciated" partisan bulk gerrymandering cases.) Translation: Republicans, we won't stop you; do your gerrymandering worst. And they did.

VOTING RIGHTS CASES

Then there's voting itself. In *Shelby County*, a 5–4 Supreme Court gutted a key section of the Voting Rights Act. When the law was first enacted in 1965, just 6.7 percent of the Black population of Mississippi was registered to vote. Two years later, 59.8 percent of the Black population was registered.[8] Under this law, those states with histories of discrimination were required to get federal sign-off on changes to their voting rules or processes. The Department of Justice got to "preclear" local practices to make sure they would not suppress the minority vote. In *Shelby County*, the Court dismantled this protection.

The Chief Justice wrote the majority opinion with reasoning that defied logic: the law was no longer needed because, with it in place, there were fewer instances of discrimination. After *Shelby County* nuked preclearance, Republican-controlled state legislatures immediately enacted a slew of laws to limit minority access to the ballot box, in some cases targeting minority voters "with almost surgical precision."[9] Here is how Attorney General Merrick Garland assessed the effect the Court's decision to those of us on the Judiciary Committee in September 2021: "The Supreme Court's decision in *Shelby County* . . . effectively eliminated the preclearance protections of the Voting Rights Act, which had been the Department's most effective tool to protect voting rights over the past half-century. Since that decision, there has been a dramatic rise in legislative efforts that will make it harder for millions of citizens to cast a vote that counts. So far this year, states have enacted more than two dozen new laws that make it harder for eligible voters across the country to vote."[10] NPR's longtime Supreme Court reporter Nina Totenberg said that *Shelby County* made "close to a dead letter the law once hailed as the most effective civil rights legislation in the nation's history."[11]

Congress had refused to dismantle the Voting Rights Act—indeed, Congress had recently reauthorized it with a huge bipartisan vote—so the far right went to the Court to get what it wanted.

The right-wing scheme to capture our courts and the Republican voter suppression effort are connected—witness the "Judicial Crisis Network" link to the "Honest Elections Project." These efforts converged again in the early months of the Biden administration. With Trump out of the White House, and the Federalist Society and its handmaiden Judicial Crisis Network out of the judge-picking business, where did they redirect their efforts? To running ads against President Biden's pick to lead DOJ's Civil Rights Division and the associate attorney general who will supervise the position. These are odd targets, trust me—the third-ranking person in the department and a DOJ division head are usually not targets of political smear ads. But these two women would be in charge of investigating and prosecuting voter suppression.

Other dark-money groups got behind voter suppression. An operative from the Heritage Action, a sister organization of the Heritage Foundation, was secretly recorded in 2021 telling dark-money donors that their group was behind the surge of voter suppression state laws being passed across the country. In order to "create the echo chamber"—her words—in the state, the group worked through "activists and sentinels." "In some cases, we actually draft [the voter suppression law] for them," she said, "or we have a sentinel on our behalf give them the model legislation so it has that grassroots, from-the-bottom-up type of vibe."[12] The video is a creepy thing to watch—a behind-the-scenes peek into one corner of the dark-money apparatus at work.

The attack ads against Kristen Clarke and Vanita Gupta at DOJ were so blatant, and so false, that the full *Washington Post* editorial board came together to condemn the ads as a "categorically dishonest video hit job by a far-right outfit,"[13] and I defended the two in speeches on the Senate Floor. The hit on these two women looked much like radical right-wing hit jobs I had experienced—the same venom, the same falsity, the same dark money—more evidence of the connections among the voter suppression movement, dark money, and the campaign to capture the Court.

Writing in dissent in *Rucho*, the gerrymandering case, Justice Kagan argued that one of the Supreme Court's roles in our system of government is to "defend its foundations."[14] "None is more important," she wrote, "than free and fair elections." Sadly, it appears that a partisan majority of the Supreme Court no longer agrees.

DARK MONEY CASES

It's one thing to have a Court that *allows* dark money to flow, as this Court did after *Citizens United*; it's another to have a Court that provides *a constitutional right* to dark money. A case that would let the Court Republicans provide that right sat quietly, session after session, on the Court's docket, waiting in the wings. The case is called *Americans for Prosperity Foundation v. Bonta*, and it was formally taken up on January 8, 2021, while the nation's attention was fixed on the January 6 attack by Trump rioters on our Capitol. That date also fell shortly after Justice Barrett was confirmed, giving the dark-money operation a 6–3 Court majority. With no more worries about a possibly wobbly Roberts vote, the Dark Money Justices took the case.

Here the dark-money amicus armada made its most impressive showing yet. At the "cert stage," the early stage when the question is only whether the Court should take up the case, over fifty dark-money-funded right-wing amici showed up to urge the Court to "grant certiorari" and take the case. It didn't hurt that the plaintiff was the Koch political operation's Americans for Prosperity Foundation.

The puppet masters could have picked an unassuming little charity as the plaintiff of convenience. Instead, they went with a battleship. Americans for Prosperity Foundation is the 501(c)(3) sibling organization of the 501(c)(4) group Americans for Prosperity, the Koch brothers' primary political advocacy group. When I say "sibling," I mean that there is substantial overlap between the two entities. And when I say "substantial," I mean they are effectively identical. If you compare AFPF's 2019 tax filings with AFP's current website, you discover that the organizations share the same address. They also have the same CEO, the same senior VP of policy, the same board chairman, and the same president. Want a difference? The person who is senior VP of state operations at AFPF is the senior VP of grassroots at AFP.

Both groups get millions from the Koch family via the Charles G. Koch Foundation and the David Koch Family Foundation, as well as several other Koch vehicles, including Freedom Partners (now called "Stand Together"), DonorsTrust, and Donors Capital Fund. The Foundation also gets money from several "usual suspects," including the DeVos family, the Bradley Foundation, and the very non-independent "Independent Women's Forum."

Americans for Prosperity helped launch the Tea Party, opposed the Affordable Care Act, and fights to protect massive polluting subsidies for fossil fuel. Since its founding in 2004, AFP has spent hundreds of millions of dollars on "independent" political ads, and it has distributed millions more in untracked donations across a vast web of right-wing influence organizations, including the fifty-plus front groups that came together to defend nonprofits' right to hide their big donors.

This case was about a California tax provision similar to the federal one that governs charities organized under 501(c)(3).* Like federal law, the state law required charitable nonprofits organized in the state to give the state taxing agency a list of their big donors and, like the federal law, it also barred the agency from making that list public.

Scroll back to the 1950s—the beginning of the civil rights era. In the deep South, civil rights leaders were gunned down, racial lynchings terrorized communities, churches were fire-bombed, and activists were targeted by racist mobs that often had the support—sometimes the open support—of the local government. So back then, when the state of Alabama demanded the NAACP's membership list, the NAACP fought back, arguing that releasing its member list to the state authorities would expose its members to the threat of violence. The Supreme Court agreed, unanimously, as it should have.[15]

Now scroll up to the current dark-money era. The dark-money faux "social welfare" groups saw this 1950s Alabama case and thought, "Hmmm, that could be handy." The goal of hiding their big donors could not have been more different from the NAACP's goal to protect ordinary members from Jim Crow violence. But the dark money crew decided they would try to use this case to push secrecy for 501(c)(3) donors—even from authorities needing the information to prevent people from committing tax fraud. From that tiny fulcrum of a required state tax disclosure, the perpetrators of the Scheme would lever a constitutional right to donor anonymity out of the Dark Money Court. They got it. In a decision that equated being a conservative mega-donor today with being an NAACP member in Jim Crow Alabama, the Court created a new right to donor confidentiality, perverting the reasoning that protected the NAACP.[†]

---

* On the federal level, 501(c)(3) groups (charities that can accept tax-deductible donations and are barred by law from any political activity) have to report their major donors to the IRS to help the agency prevent tax fraud and donor self-dealing. The IRS has always kept nonprofits' donor lists private (they are reported separately from the 990s that eventually become public). One of the many gifts the Trump administration gave big donors in the dark-money web was a change to IRS reporting requirements for many nonprofits, so 501(c)(4) and (c)(6) organizations—like JCN and the Chamber of Commerce—no longer need to report the names of their donors even to the IRS. The rule change just makes it harder for the IRS to be on the lookout for tax code violators, and harder for all of us to spot foreign influence in our elections.

† In 2021, Judge Bruce Selya, a Republican appointee to the First Circuit Court of Appeals, shot down a challenge to a Rhode Island campaign finance disclosure law,

It is difficult to reconcile the dark-money majority's decision in *Americans for Prosperity Foundation v. Bonta* with its reliance on "transparency" in *Citizens United* to prevent corruption in a system awash in money—and the Court didn't even try. All six Republican members—the justices that the dark-money-funded Federalist Society had picked for the Court, the justices whom the dark-money-funded Americans for Prosperity had spent millions to put on the Court—joined together to advance the cause of dark money for the dark-money-funded Americans for Prosperity Foundation. The message to the dark-money donors who put them on the Court was loud and clear: don't worry, fellas, we have your back. Dark money is here to stay.

For more than a decade, I have been tracking the profusion of right-wing amici who share the same funders, the same directors, and even in some cases the same address. This case marked an unprecedented showing from the conservative dark-money armada; no other case came close. It wasn't hard to understand the reason. The first organizing principle of the dark-money apparatus is self-preservation, and disclosure threatened to do what sunlight always does to darkness.

Americans for Prosperity is no stranger to the Court-capture scheme—and makes no secret of its role. When Brett Kavanaugh was nominated, the organization announced a seven-figure "grassroots" campaign to shore up his nomination, bragging that "AFP activists across the country have contacted more than 1 million Americans with door knocks, phone calls or mail, resulting in more than 100,000 calls or letters directly into Senate offices."[16] In 2017, one of its press releases celebrated the fact that "AFP invested heavily in grassroots efforts to pressure the Senate to confirm him to the bench."[17] AFP was part of the Koch network that made the $889 million political spending threat. When Amy Coney Barrett was nominated in the twilight days of the Trump administration, AFP did it all again, spending millions to advance her confirmation under the very circumstances that

---

specifically rejecting any analogy to NAACP. "Equating the production order invalidated in NAACP with the disclosure requirements of the Act is like equating aardvarks with alligators," he wrote, refusing to sign off on "appellants' attempt to place this case under the carapace of NAACP."[18]

Republican senators in 2016 had insisted required them to wait until after the presidential election.

I urged Judge Barrett at her confirmation hearing to recuse herself from the pending AFPF case when she took the bench, to no avail. Just a few months later, all three new justices helped onto the Court by AFP's millions gave their dark-money benefactor a major win for dark money. Not a single one recused. Instead they created a brand-new constitutional right to dark money.

Watch for this evil weed to grow.

CHAPTER SIXTEEN

Cases Protecting Corporate Interests

If any of the great corporations of the country were to hire adventurers . . . to procure the passage of a general law with a view to the promotion of their private interests, the moral sense of every right-minded man would instinctively denounce the employer and employed as steeped in corruption, and the employment as infamous.

—Justice Noah Swayne, *Trist v. Child*

THE RECORD IS HARD TO DISPUTE: WHEN A case presents issues core to our democracy's health, the Roberts Five go AWOL or worse; when the issues align with big-money corporate special interests, the Roberts Five stand at the ready. Former White House Counsel McGahn could not have been more up-front about packing the Court to deliver for corporate interests opposed to regulation: "There is a coherent plan here where actually the judicial selection and the deregulatory effort are really the flip side of the same coin."[1] It's a stunningly blunt confession: the justices are chosen to deregulate for the corporations.

The Court's corporate decisions have been a one-two punch: they've limited the ability of government agencies to regulate corporate acts, and they've made it harder for individuals harmed by corporate acts to have their rights vindicated in court. It's not hard to understand why. Powerful corporate special interests are accustomed to disproportionate sway in Congress, where they enjoy outsized influence through political spending and lobbying. When they can get a president elected, or make a deal with him, they can get what they want from the Oval Office. Money talks. Size matters.

In court, things are different. In court, corporations may find themselves having to turn over documents that reveal corporate malfeasance. They may find themselves having to tell the truth, under penalty of perjury. And they lose their influence advantage; they may find themselves being treated equally with regular people—and their actions judged by regular people too. In response to this corporate frustration, the Roberts Five have made it increasingly hard to hold corporations accountable.

Look at the environmental arena. The Roberts Court handed 5–4 victories to a fossil fuel industry determined to preserve its "freedom" to pollute,[2] rejected claims brought under the Endangered Species Act and the National Environmental Policy Act,[3] made Clean Air Act analysis more sympathetic to polluters' interests,[4] limited environmental group suits under federal environmental laws,[5] tipped the law against state and local governments in favor of developers,[6] and blocked the Obama administration's Clean Power Plan before it even took effect, a procedural first for the Court.[7]

In the fall of 2021, as I was working on this book, the Dark Money Justices performed an even brasher procedural gambit. Here's what happened. In 1970, Congress gave the EPA the authority to regulate any air pollutant that can "reasonably be anticipated to endanger public health or welfare."[8] In 2007, the Supreme Court agreed that this mandate includes greenhouse gases.[9] In 2015, the Obama EPA promulgated a new Clean Power Plan that would require utilities to start moving away from dangerous greenhouse emissions and toward safe renewable energy. That's the plan the Court blocked in 2016, shortly before Justice Scalia's death; it never went into effect. The Trump administration came in and withdrew the Clean Power Plan and replaced it with an "Affordable Clean Energy" rule (which by EPA's own estimates would have lowered power plant emissions by a whopping 1 percent by 2035—another Trump sell-out to fossil fuel). That too went to court.

When the legal dust settled in the lower courts—coincidentally, the last day of Donald Trump's presidency—the bogus Trump plan was rejected, and the blocked Clean Power Plan was upheld. But the

Biden administration had already announced that it was withdrawing the Obama-era plan and starting fresh. So there was no rule left in play. It's hard to see how, with no rule left standing, there could be any "case or controversy" for the justices to adjudicate.

But count on Federalist Society justices to be "policy agents" first and foremost where fossil fuel interests are concerned. In October 2021, they announced that they would hear a challenge to the defunct Clean Power Plan anyway, apparently "just in case." [10] Professor Richard Lazarus of Harvard Law School recognized that the "policy agents" on the Court could deliver some major goods again for the fossil fuel industry in the case, *West Virginia v. EPA*, and called the Court's decision to take it "the equivalent of an earthquake around the country for those who care deeply about the climate issue." [11]

The right-wing justices have hinted at reviving a long-dead conservative pet theory called the "non-delegation doctrine." Doing so could cripple Congress's ability to delegate authority to independent agencies like the EPA.* As Ian Millhiser explained in *Vox*, *West Virginia v. EPA* could "fundamentally alter the structure of the US government, stripping away the government's power on issues as diverse as workplace safety, environmental protection, access to birth control, overtime pay, and vaccination." [12] It could prove to be among the "most consequential court decisions in recent US history." [13] And it's pending as I write, brought by polluters, with no actual rule at stake.†

---

*This is a topic worthy of an entirely new book, but let me just say this here: since its earliest days, Congress has delegated significant power to executive officials and agencies in order to ensure the smooth, apolitical, and expert functioning of government. We don't want representatives and senators debating the proper parts-per-million of a particular chemical in the water. We want a body not prone to gridlock, one that is staffed with people who are experts on that particular question. Dismantling our system of administrative government is one of the key prizes of the radical right. For an authoritative exposition of how this doctrine violates long-standing principles of American governance, see Julian Davis Mortenson and Nicholas Bagley's article "Delegation at the Founding." 121 *Colum. L. Rev.* 277 (2021). They demolish any notion that non-delegation has a credible foundation in law or history. Professor Mortenson filed an amicus brief in *West Virginia v. EPA* to bring this important scholarship to the Court's attention.

† In early 2022, the Supreme Court doubled down on *West Virginia v. EPA*, agreeing to take a case, *Sackett v. EPA*, that could severely limit the scope of the Clean Water Act. As in *West Virginia*, the agency rule at issue in *Sackett* hasn't been finalized. There was no significant circuit split on the question at issue. And the EPA had told the couple at

Beyond protecting polluters, the Roberts Five have weakened anti-trust protections,[14] shielded corporate executives from shareholder suits,[15] protected drug manufacturers from state tort laws,[16] taken away fair pay protections from entire categories of workers,[17] restricted class actions that redress low-dollar mass frauds (like adding a small wrong-ful charge to a million customers' bills),[18] and made it more difficult for individuals to sue companies that harmed them.[19] It's almost as if the Republican majority didn't want corporations to have to face the people they've harmed in front of juries.

Which brings us to mandatory arbitration. Companies like to say that arbitration is just like court—except it's generally conducted in secret with little regard for precedent and few procedural safeguards. Plus, arbitrators' decisions can't be appealed. Oh, and the arbitrator is selected—and paid for—by the company that is on the other side of the table. But other than all *that*, arbitration is just like court!

Arbitration is sold as a great convenience, and it can be, for disputes between big corporations. But when it's big corporation against little individual, the system is rigged. One arbitration group was so rigged that attorneys general from several states got a court order putting it out of business.

Mandatory arbitration is a corporate stratagem to steer people away from public courtrooms into private, corporate-funded "dispute resolution"—on the corporations' terms, with arbitrators chosen by them. It is now nearly standard in employment and consumer con-tracts with big corporations. Thank the Roberts Five for that.

Remember when Wells Fargo surreptitiously opened 3.5 million bogus bank and credit card accounts in the names of real custom-ers? A jury trial would have shone a public spotlight on the bank's chicanery, but instead the fraud went on for years because whenever the bank's customers complained, they were shunted into mandatory confidential arbitration. As long as the process was secret, Wells Fargo had every cynical incentive to continue its bad behavior. Protected in

---

the center of the case that it would not prosecute past violations. So there was no rule, no split, and no harm needing redress. Every principle of judicial restraint counsels against taking a case like this. But the Federalist Society big donors put justices on the Court to deliver policy wins, and they now have the numbers to do just that.

arbitration, it didn't have to worry about public shame or (as eventually happened) catching the eye of federal regulators. All it had to do was calculate the price of occasionally having to pay out to the odd "client" versus the value of the fraud overall.

Arbitration tilts the scales against workers as well as customers. The National Employment Law Project estimates that in 2019 alone, mandatory arbitration helped employers who committed wage theft keep $9.2 billion from employees earning less than $13 an hour.[20] Cornell University professors found: "Employees are much less likely to win their claim under arbitration (21.4 percent) than they are in federal (36.4 percent) or state (51 percent) courts. And even when they do win, they tend to recover much less money than they would in court: a median of $36,500 in damages under arbitration, compared to $176,000 in federal courts and $86,000 in state courts."[21] Sweet deal for the corporations.

My Senate colleagues and I found that arbitration allows thousands of cases to be "snuffed out each year without anyone noticing." For example, we reported, according to an American Association for Justice study of arbitration cases from 2014 to 2018:

- Only 1,909 consumers won a monetary award over the five-year period. That works out to just 6.3 percent of cases arbitrated over the five years resulting in consumers winning a monetary award.
- Of the 60 million employees subject to forced arbitration, only 11,114—0.02 percent—tried to pursue a dispute in forced arbitration. Just 282 of these employees were awarded monetary damages over the five-year period.
- Forced arbitration clauses allow nursing homes to avoid accountability for everything from negligent care to sexual assault. Over five years, consumers pursuing nursing home claims won a monetary award in only four cases.
- Consumers pursued 6,012 forced arbitrations involving financial claims, claiming at least $3.7 billion in damages. They won monetary awards in just 131 cases (2.2 percent), totaling $7.4 million—0.2 percent of the claimed damages.[22]

The Roberts Five have taken the hundred-year-old Federal Arbitration Act and warped it far beyond its original purpose, making the Arbitration Act a weapon for powerful and wealthy interests systematically to deny ordinary individuals, like employees and customers, access to a jury of their peers. It's been a veritable torrent of partisan 5–4 arbitration decisions. In 14 *Penn Plaza v. Pyett*, the Roberts Five said unionized employees could be forced to have their age discrimination claims heard in arbitration. In *Rent-A-Center v. Jackson*, they said that the very arbitrator whose legitimacy is challenged can decide if an arbitration agreement is "unconscionable" (adopting, as Justice Stevens noted in his dissent, a rule that neither party asked for but the Roberts Five just made up).²³ In *Lamps Plus, Inc. v. Varela*, they prohibited an employee from bringing class-action arbitration unless the company explicitly agreed to it (how often do you think a company does that?). In *AT&T Mobility LLC v. Concepcion*, they overturned a state consumer protection law and allowed companies to block consumers from bringing class-action arbitrations to remedy low-value/high-volume frauds. In *American Express Co. v. Italian Colors Restaurant*, they reversed long-standing Supreme Court precedent that contractual arbitration clauses are enforceable only so long as they actually give individuals the opportunity to vindicate their rights. And in *Epic Systems Corp. v. Lewis*, they said that employers could force employees to arbitrate away labor rights granted by law. That's six cases, each decided 5–4, each with only Federalist Society justices in the majority, each making it harder for workers and consumers to have their day in court.

The Roberts Court rulings recall the long-reviled *Lochner* case, the 1905 decision that held that employers' "freedom to contract" trumped laws to protect worker health and safety.* "If these untoward conse-

---

*If you're not a lawyer, you may not be familiar with *Lochner v. New York*, but its history is instructive. At the beginning of the last century, business elites promoted a "laissez-faire" economic philosophy that argued that nothing—not unequal bargaining power, not public health, not children's rights, not the risk of a catastrophic financial meltdown—should get in the way of "freedom of contract." Not at all coincidentally, this came as the robber-barons of the Industrial Revolution were cramming more and more people into factories with unsafe and unsanitary working conditions. Against this backdrop, New York passed a law that limited bakery workers' hours to no more than ten a day or sixty a week. In a 5–4 decision in what became one of the

quences stemmed from legislative choices, I would be obliged to accede to them," wrote Justice Ginsburg in her dissent in one of these arbitration cases. "But the edict that employees with wage and hours claims may seek relief only one-by-one does not come from Congress. It is the result of take-it-or-leave-it labor contracts harking back to the type called 'yellow dog,' and of the readiness of this Court to enforce those unbargained-for agreements."[24]

It is easy to see why big-money special interests would want to move as many cases out of court as possible. The jury is intended to dethrone the powerful and wealthy, to make them come down and stand (annoyingly to them) equal before the law. Juries remain the one corner of our constitutional system that rich special interests haven't figured out how to capture. As former Chief Justice Rehnquist explained, "the founders of our Nation considered the right of trial by jury in civil cases an important bulwark against tyranny and corruption, a safeguard too precious to be left to the whim of the sovereign, or, it might be added, to that of the judiciary."[25] Juries weed through facts, evaluate witnesses, and determine fault in matters as simple as a car crash and as complex as an industry-wide class action. Even when cases settle before going to trial, the risk to companies that their conduct will be

---

most reviled rulings in the Court's history, a majority of the justices said that this law, enacted to protect worker health and safety, was barred by the Constitution. The great Justice Oliver Wendell Holmes dissented. In language that would echo through the decades, he wrote:

This case is decided upon an economic theory which a large part of the country does not entertain. If it were a question whether I agreed with that theory, I should desire to study it further and long before making up my mind. But I do not conceive that to be my duty, because I strongly believe that my agreement or disagreement has nothing to do with the right of a majority to embody their opinions in law. It is settled by various decisions of this court that state constitutions and state laws may regulate life in many ways which we as legislators might think as injudicious, or if you like as tyrannical, as this, and which, equally with this, interfere with the liberty to contract. Sunday laws and usury laws are ancient examples. . . . But a Constitution is not intended to embody a particular economic theory, whether of paternalism and the organic relation of the citizen to the state or of laissez faire. It is made for people of fundamentally differing views, and the accident of our finding certain opinions natural and familiar, or novel, and even shocking, ought not to conclude our judgment upon the question whether statutes embodying them conflict with the Constitution of the United States.[26]

reviewed by twelve ordinary citizens helps ensure they negotiate in good faith.

As attorney general, I came to appreciate the function juries serve in our constitutional system. Juries shore up our democracy by getting citizens involved. They are a direct popular exercise of constitutional power, and a reminder that with power comes responsibility. There is a reason that the play *Twelve Angry Jurors* continues to be performed nearly seventy years after it was first released as (in a sign of the times) *Twelve Angry Men*. Watching Americans from different walks of life come together to deliberate and find a way to resolve the question before them is . . . well, it's what America is supposed to be about. Yet the number of federal jury trials has plummeted in recent decades.

Corporate special interests squawk about juries as if they were a bug in the system. They systematically attack and smear the trial bar—the lawyers who bring cases against them. In fact, their complaints demonstrate that the system is working as our Founders intended. I said as much in an amicus brief to the Supreme Court in one of its more recent cases that ended up extending corporate arbitration "rights":

> The very annoyance of the "more powerful and wealthy" that they should be subjected to equality in the courtroom; the very intensity of their desire to divert conflicts away from juries to forums where their power and wealth gives them more advantage—these are predictable and positive attributes of the civil jury's role as the element of government designed to resist "the encroachments of the more powerful and wealthy citizens." These complaints are not a reason to assist in that diversion. This Court should not—now or ever—be a party to degrading a constitutional element of government just because that element's proper operation provokes yawps of complaint from "the more powerful and wealthy citizens" whose "encroachments" it was designed to restrain. To disable an element of our Constitution because it is not working would be a daring task indeed; to disable it because it is working would be anathema.[27]

I dwell on the Roberts Five's fixation with mandatory arbitration because forcing people away from juries is a big deal. The Seventh

Amendment actually gives the American people a constitutional right to those juries that the Court so blithely lets corporations take away. It's bad enough that a majority of the Supreme Court bands with corporate forces to shut the courthouse doors to ordinary citizens; it's worse that they do so with barely an acknowledgment that they are denying Americans a constitutional right. Some "originalists."

One measure of corporations' advantage in the Roberts Supreme Court is how well our old friend the Chamber of Commerce has fared. In the years between 1981 and 1986, when deeply conservative Antonin Scalia became a Supreme Court justice, the Chamber won just under half of its cases before the Court—43 percent.[28] When William Rehnquist served as chief justice, from 1994 to 2005, the Chamber's win rate climbed to 56 percent. With Roberts confirmed as chief justice in 2005 and Alito on in 2006, the Chamber's win rate climbed into the 70s.[29] As the nonpartisan Constitutional Accountability Center reported, for the Supreme Court term from October 2019 to June 2020, "when the Supreme Court reviewed decisions that favored individuals or government over big business, the Chamber and its allies succeed most of the time (though not all of the time) in persuading the Court to reverse those decisions. But when the Supreme Court reviewed decisions favoring big business, not once did individuals or the government persuade the Court to reverse those pro-corporate wins."[30] Not once.

"This was not a fluke," CAC researchers reported. "Amazingly, it has been more than four years since the Supreme Court reversed a lower-court decision favoring corporate interests, although the Court has decided more than 70 Chamber cases during that period."[31] One pro-corporate standout is Justice Gorsuch, who has voted for the Chamber 80 percent of the time, a rate the Constitutional Accountability Center calls "stunning." I say it's evidence—evidence that the Court-stacking "coherent plan," connecting "judicial selection and the deregulatory effort" as the "flip side[s] of the same coin," is working beautifully for the special interests behind the Scheme.

CHAPTER SEVENTEEN

Cases Restricting Civil Rights

The true danger is when liberty is nibbled away, for expedience,
and by parts.

—EDMUND BURKE

ACCORDING TO SEVERAL MEDIA PROFILES, CHIEF JUSTICE ROBERTS likes
to think of himself as "color-blind." Regrettably, much of America's
history has been anything but color-blind. Congress has adopted various remedies to address our nation's troubled history of racist laws and
policies that disenfranchised and denied opportunities to Americans.
But centuries of inequity in jobs, housing, benefits, and voting are
not quickly undone. In 2019, the average white family in America had
seven times the wealth of the average Black family.[1]

As part of the Reagan Revolution, Roberts was, according to a 2019
profile in the *Washington Monthly*, "a key player in the administration's aggressive efforts to roll back affirmative action and other civil
rights protections."[2] Nixon and Reagan were expert in weaponizing
race issues to attract white voters, so there was real political advantage
in those aggressive efforts.

On the Supreme Court, Roberts's decisions have been marked by
animosity toward any racial classification, no matter the purpose or
intent. His theory: "The way to stop discrimination on the basis of race
is to stop discriminating on the basis of race."[3] That's cute phrasing,
but it leaves a big hole for any remedies for past racial injustice. Justice Stevens once recalled Anatole France's observation about nominal

equality in the law: "'[T]he majestic equality of the la[w] forbid[s] rich and poor alike to sleep under bridges, to beg in the streets, and to steal their bread.'"[4] It is simply not racially neutral to strike down laws that remedy historic racial injustice.

Sometimes the majority's work seems worse than deliberately oblivious to our legacy of racial inequity; it seems to send messages on how to structure further inequity. Tucked in the majority opinion in a redistricting case was the observation that "a voter's race sometimes correlates closely with party preference."[5] A few years later, the same five justices announced that courts would not police partisan gerry-mandering, even if that "party preference" blatantly subverted major-ity rule—and even if it had a significant racial impact. The signal to state legislatures: stop saying this is about race and make it about party advantage. The result is the same, and we won't stop you.*

The Roberts Five were no friends to women in gender discrimina-tion cases either. They made it harder to bring a claim of gender dis-crimination,[6] harder to bring a claim of sexual harassment,[7] harder to bring a claim of workplace retaliation,[8] harder to obtain birth control, [9] and harder to get an abortion even when the woman's health is in dan-ger.[10] And this was before the elevation of Amy Coney Barrett presaged the dismantling of *Roe v. Wade.*

It's not just civil rights that have been under attack in the Roberts Court. In civil liberties cases, too, the Roberts Five repeatedly took the side of the government against the little guy. So even as they expanded the First Amendment rights of corporations at seemingly every oppor-tunity, they limited First Amendment speech protections for public employees and students.[11] They made it harder to challenge poten-tially unlawful government surveillance,[12] and they limited the ability of prisoners to seek redress for harm under the Civil Rights Act,[13] the Fourth Amendment,[14] and the Eighth Amendment.[15]

When different individual rights and liberties come into conflict,

---

*A similar signal came in the Court's rulings on Trump administration efforts to pur-sue discriminatory policies through the U.S. Census, to impose a Muslim travel ban, and to dismantle the Deferred Action for Childhood Arrivals (DACA) program: for goodness' sake, don't *say* you're deliberately discriminating, even if everyone under-stands that's what you're doing. Find a palatable pretext, and we'll help you. Or as Dahlia Lithwick and Mark Joseph Stern put it: "Lie better next time."[16]

the rights and liberties prioritized by Republicans predictably come out on top.* The freedom of an individual to own a gun trumps the freedom of our children to be safe from gun violence; the right of an employer to discriminate based on "religious liberty" trumps an employee's right to access contraception; the right of a union employee to avoid subsidizing speech he disagrees with trumps the right of the union to get fair compensation for work it must provide; the right of a private Christian school to access funds from a public voucher program trumps the right of a taxpayer to avoid subsidizing a religion they do not subscribe to (a practice that—originalism alert—Thomas Jefferson called "sinful and tyrannical" [17]). When California regulated "crisis pregnancy centers," which lured women in by purporting to be health care clinics but were in fact unlicensed anti-abortion operations without even a doctor on site, the Roberts Five were more concerned with "free-speech" rights of anti-choice activists running these "centers" than the right of women not to be deceived and denied medically relevant information.[18]

Sometimes it seems the justices are setting things up in one case to move the law in the desired direction in another. You might call these provisions springboards or trampolines for the Court to bounce on in later cases. *Bostock v. Clayton County*, for example, holds that federal civil rights laws protect LGBTQ employees from workplace discrimination. The ruling was welcome and overdue. Observers were quick to note, however, that Justice Gorsuch (the author) seemed to be setting up for a longer game. Harvard professor Jeannie Suk Gerson noted in the *New Yorker*:

> [T]here is reason to think that Bostock's formalist articulations on discrimination will bolster a conservative decision to dismantle race-conscious admissions policies. Gorsuch offers a hint of

---

*There's a nice description by Justice Holmes of these boundary disputes between conflicting rights: "All rights tend to declare themselves absolute to their logical extreme. Yet all in fact are limited by the neighborhood of principles of policy which are other than those on which the particular right is founded, and which become strong enough to hold their own when a certain point is reached." [19] The decision as to when that "certain point is reached" presents abundant opportunity for justices' thumbs to press on judicial scales.

that logic, writing that Title VII protects "individuals rather than groups," and that any scheme that treats individuals differently because of their protected characteristic is unlawful, "even if the scheme promotes equality at the group level" and is "motivated by a wish to achieve classwide equality."[20]

A similar trampoline presaged Chief Justice Roberts's opinion in *Shelby County* striking down key portions of the Voting Rights Act. He had added into an earlier 2009 decision, *Northwest Austin v. Holder,* the odd notion of "equal sovereignty," which had last breathed life as a consideration for new states being allowed into the Union—something that hasn't occurred in a while. "Equal sovereignty" returned in *Shelby* as the central rationale that allowed the Court to get rid of preclearance and open the flood of Republican voter suppression laws targeting minority voters.

CHAPTER EIGHTEEN

Cases Advancing a Far-Right Social Agenda

He feeds his base once a week. He knows this is part of his thing.
—SCOTT REED, POLITICAL DIRECTOR
OF THE U.S. CHAMBER OF COMMERCE, ON TRUMP

THE RIGHT-WING COALITION NEEDS TO SERVE ITS SOCIAL issues base. Their extreme views are opposed by the American public, so again, the right wing turns to the Court. Where they win. Repeatedly. After Kavanaugh's confirmation, right-wing lawyer Hugh Hewitt crowed that this "would raise the curtain on a new age."[1] On social issues, the Roberts Court has sure brought a new age—of unpopular and extreme policies.

The Roberts Five rewrote the separation of church and state. In *Hein*, they let religious groups compete for federal grants and upheld a Faith-Based Initiative promoted with taxpayer dollars.[2] In *Winn*, they upheld a state law that provided tax credits for those who fund religious education, requiring taxpayers to subsidize religion—exactly what our Founding Fathers tried to prevent.[3] Some originalists.

On gun control, the Roberts Five in *Heller* held for the first time in our history that the Constitution provides each individual the right to keep and bear "arms."[4] The Supreme Court had never held that the Second Amendment prevented Congress from regulating non-military use and ownership of firearms. Recall that a previous Chief Justice (and Republican) called that argument a "fraud." (I'm sure Justice Scalia's cozy relationship with gun groups as he wrote that decision was just a remarkable coincidence.) In his dissent in *Heller,* Justice Stevens noted that the Court was throwing out a perfectly reasonable interpretation of law that hundreds of judges—not to mention federal, state, and local governments—had relied on for decades, and without any new evidence to support its ruling. As in *Citizens United,* Stevens's dissent provided the true originalist voice, pointing out that "the drafting history of the Amendment demonstrates that its Framers *rejected* proposals that would have broadened its coverage" to private civilian weapons.[5] It had no effect. A few years later, the Roberts Five extended *Heller* to all state and local gun safety laws.[6] Some originalists.

On privacy, the Federalist Society justices for years whittled away a woman's right to choose whether to have an abortion. For fifty years, this constitutional right allowed women to make their own decisions about what happens to their bodies and provided them freedom to participate more wholly and equally in the workplace and society. During those same years, conservative politicians got political mileage by passing abortion laws that were blatantly unconstitutional and then railing against the courts when the courts struck them down—rinse and repeat. But then the Court began to shift. Again, it was personnel, not principle, that drove the shift—the "man on the Court" factor.

In *Gonzales v. Carhart,* the first abortion case the Court considered after Justice Alito replaced Justice O'Connor, the new Roberts Five reversed recent precedent. The Court had previously rejected a Nebraska law banning all second trimester abortions because the law placed an "undue burden" on women, in part for having no exception when the mother's health was endangered.[7] The federal bill at issue in *Gonzales* also allowed no consideration of the health of the woman seeking an abortion—but this time the Supreme Court, 5–4, upheld the law. What had changed? Not the Constitution, but the Court. In fact, one justice: Alito for O'Connor.

There's an interesting side note in this case. The Court was impressed that Congress had concluded—straying a bit from our area of legislative expertise—that the procedure in question was "never medically necessary."[8] Just a few years later, the same Court rejected Congress's findings in areas where federal lawmakers have real-world practical expertise: campaign finance and voting. Tens of thousands of pages of legislative fact-finding supported the Bipartisan Campaign

Finance Reform Act;[9] 15,000 pages of evidence were amassed to renew the Voting Rights Act.[10] In both cases, the conservative justices supplanted Congress's facts with their own fanciful opinions. Some "balls and strikes": federal lawmakers legislating in an area in which they are expert are disregarded; lawmakers practicing medicine without a license have their findings used to ignore precedent and diminish women's privacy rights.

It got a lot worse, quickly, once Justice Barrett joined the Court. I write this in the wake of an Alito leaked draft opinion that would outright overrule *Roe v. Wade*. That case, *Dobbs v. Jackson Women's Health Organization*, involved a Mississippi law banning all abortions after 15 weeks, nearly two months before the "fetal viability" line established by *Roe*. The Court scheduled two hours of oral argument—twice its usual time—and commentators afterwards almost uniformly predicted that the Federalist Society justices were gunning for *Roe v. Wade*. But the Alito leaked opinion was stunning in its ferocity and reach. This book is going to press mere weeks before the Court releases its final decision in *Dobbs*. Perhaps some sense will prevail and the leaked opinion will become a dissent, but I am not hopeful. Regardless, the damage to the Court—from both the leak and the radical sentiments it revealed—are likely to be profound and lasting.

Alito is known to have made a snide remark about precedent, discussed more later, that *stare decisis* applies "when it suits our purposes." Even so, his draft opinion was remarkable. He said *Roe v. Wade* was wrong from its inception, indeed "egregiously wrong from the start"; a position that he conspicuously failed to disclose in his confirmation hearings (presumably this egregious wrong was evident to him before he sat down to his *Dobbs* draft). What Alito said in his confirmation process was: "*Roe v. Wade* is an important precedent of the Supreme Court."[11] That went out the window; it no longer suited his purposes. In an opinion that relied for authority on an English judge who had prosecuted witches, the signatory justices completely destroyed the precedent of *Roe v. Wade*, belittled all the previous justices who had written or upheld it, and undermined the constitutional right to privacy that gives *Roe* its legal foundation

Not treating likes alike is a regular feature of the captured Court, especially where the difference is political, and it was a feature of the

Alito opinion. The Alito opinion complained that the word "abortion" does not appear in the constitution. Evidently, five Republican justices found that meaningful. Well, here's another word that does not appear in the Constitution: "corporation." That was not so meaningful to those justices and their Republican predecessors, who spent decades determinedly reconstructing America's political system to the point where corporate power is now dominant in Congress. (By the way, "contraception" and "marriage," two other rights founded in the right to privacy, are also not found expressly in the Constitution. Look out.)

An abortion case from Texas also looms.[12] The Texas law bars all abortions, with no exceptions, after about six weeks. The law's oddity is its enforcement mechanism—state lawmakers gave the power to enforce the law to everyone *except* state officials. Why? Typically, to challenge an unconstitutional law, a plaintiff sues the public officials charged with enforcing it and gets the court to enjoin them from doing so. The new law closed off that avenue for women to protect their rights. Instead, Texas gave private busybodies the power to act as abortion bounty hunters, authorized to sue anyone—taxi driver, counselor, friend, family member—who helps a woman obtain an abortion after the law's new cut-off date. The bounty, on top of court fees, is $10,000; those who successfully defend themselves against the bounty-hunter's lawsuit get nothing.

The law is a stunning attempt to, as Justice Sotomayor put it, "nullify federal constitutional rights."[13] ("Nullify" is strong language here; nullification was the theory of Confederate states that they could overrule federal civil rights laws.) "[W]hatever one thinks about the constitutional right to obtain a pre-viability abortion," a constitutional law professor told senators, "allowing this procedural Rube Goldberg device to succeed sets a terrible precedent for the ability of courts to protect all constitutional rights going forward."[14] Even Chief Justice Roberts joined in dissent against his fellow Federalist Society Justices. He saw that the case was not just about "the federal right infringed" by Texas; instead, he wrote, "it is the role of the Supreme Court in our constitutional system that is at stake."[15] The Chief Justice's too-little-too-late realization is cold comfort. As *Slate's* Dahlia Lithwick grimly noted of the Court's abortion docket in 2021, "The real story . . . is that Chief Justice John Roberts has now lost control of his court."[16]

Don't feel too badly for the Chief Justice. Even before Justice Barrett joined the Court, the Roberts Five gave "closely-held" companies—which make up more than 90 percent of all U.S. businesses and employ over half the American workforce—the right to deny women who work for them contraception coverage, insurance that is ordinarily available on the market.[17] Roberts's 5–4 Court let business owners infuse into corporations their own personal religious beliefs, launching the radical notion that a corporation can actually *have* religious beliefs, even second-hand ones. Corporations are not people; they are legal fictions, permitted to organize for economic activity. The notion that corporations, not even mentioned in the constitution, qualify for such a constitutional right is bizarre. In dissent, Justice Ginsburg asked if there were limits to the majority's newly created theory: "Would [it] extend to employers with religiously grounded objections to blood transfusions (Jehovah's Witnesses); antidepressants (Scientologists); medications derived from pigs, including anesthesia, intravenous fluids, and pills coated with gelatin (certain Muslims, Jews, and Hindus); and vaccinations (Christian Scientists, among others)?"[18] It remains to be seen how far the new 6–3 Court will go. Over and over, even before Alito's *Dobbs* torpedo went on display, the Court's 5–4 partisan decisions moved the law to the right—often way to the right—even if that meant treating corporate entities as having human characteristics they don't actually have.

The majority of Americans don't endorse any of this. Step back and you see that by overwhelming majorities, Americans think there is too much money in politics.[19] They think there should be more robust disclosure.[20] They don't approve of partisan gerrymanders.[21] They support voting rights.[22] They want stricter gun measures.[23] They support labor unions and workers' rights.[24] They think that corporations have too much power, and certainly don't think corporations are people.[25] They want the government to tackle climate change.[26] And they support reasonable gun regulation,[27] separation of church from state,[28] and women being the ones who choose when to have children.[29]

At every turn, the Roberts Court has worked against them. And at every turn, the beneficiary has been a right-wing donor elite: the Court's embrace of this far-right social agenda appeases a small, activist fringe of the right-wing coalition, and that helps corporate interests maintain their political power.

PART VIII

Rebuttal

CHAPTER NINETEEN

So-Called Conservative Principles

Few exercises of the judicial power are more likely to undermine public confidence in the neutrality and integrity of the Judiciary than one which casts the Court in the role of a Council of Revision, conferring on itself the power to invalidate laws at the behest of anyone who disagrees with them.
—JUSTICE ANTHONY KENNEDY,
Arizona Christian School Tuition Org. v. Winn

WELL, YOU MAY BE THINKING, NONE OF THIS is particularly surprising. After all, these are conservative justices, so doesn't it make sense that they would favor conservative priorities? Perhaps. But an 80–0 record for right-wing special interests is a heck of a pattern. If I were a lawyer trying to prove bias in a jury trial, I'd like those facts.

I'd be more open to the argument that these are just conservatives being conservatives if the rulings out of the Federalist Society wing of the Court actually reflected conservative legal principles. One of the biggest tells that the Supreme Court has been captured is how often its partisan decisions align with desired outcomes rather than nominal principles. In practice, it turns out these "principles" aren't principles at all.

In my review of the Court's partisan 5–4 decisions, I found that not only did Republicans and big donors win every time, but that in more than half of these cases, the five conservative justices ran over one or more of the following supposedly conservative judicial principles:

respect for precedent (also known as *stare decisis*); judicial restraint (sometimes called "modesty"); a proper aversion to appellate fact-finding; and "originalism" and its siblings "textualism" and "federalism" (often called "states' rights"). The Roberts Court has left its tire tracks across them all.

RESPECT FOR PRECEDENT

In June 1992, the eyes of the nation were on the Supreme Court as it reached the end of its term—the time of the year when, Court-watchers know, decisions in the big cases typically drop. In this term there had been a big case: a challenge to a set of Pennsylvania abortion restrictions that raised the possibility that the Court might overturn *Roe v. Wade*. Much had changed on the Court since *Roe*. Only two justices remained of the original seven who had been in the *Roe* majority in 1973. The new justices—Stevens, O'Connor, Scalia, Kennedy, Souter, and Thomas—had all been appointed by Republican presidents, at least two of whom were vocal in their opposition to abortion. Anti-abortion activists were tasting victory.

They were disappointed. On June 29, 1992, the Supreme Court announced its decision in *Planned Parenthood v. Casey*. Three Republican-appointed justices signed the principal opinion, which concluded: "After considering the fundamental constitutional questions resolved by *Roe*, principles of institutional integrity, and the rule of *stare decisis*, we are led to conclude this: the essential holding of *Roe v. Wade* should be retained and once again reaffirmed."[1] Their ruling, the justices noted, was not based on their personal preference or views. Rather, it was because *stare decisis* was at the heart of the Court's legitimacy:

> [O]nly the most convincing justification under accepted standards of precedent could suffice to demonstrate that a later decision overruling the first was anything but a surrender to political pressure, and an unjustified repudiation of the principle on which the Court staked its authority in the first instance. So to overrule under fire in the absence of the most compelling reason to reexamine a watershed decision would subvert the Court's legitimacy beyond any serious question.[2]

Respect for precedent, they said, is "indispensable" to the "very concept of the rule of law underlying our own Constitution."[3] Justice Lewis Powell—yes, of the Powell Memo—separately argued that "the elimination of constitutional *stare decisis* would represent an explicit endorsement of the idea that the Constitution is nothing more than what five Justices say it is."[4]

For many reasons—reliance, consistency, integrity of the judicial process, separation of powers—courts have long recognized that, as Justice Brandeis wrote, *stare decisis* reflects the reality that it is often "more important that the applicable rule of law be settled than that it be settled right."[5] Justice Cardozo wrote: "One of the most fundamental societal interests is that the law shall be uniform and impartial. There must be nothing in its action that savors of prejudice or favor or even arbitrary whim or fitfulness. Therefore in the main there shall be adherence to precedent."[6] Concern about "arbitrary discretion in the courts" goes back to the Founding; the cure, Alexander Hamilton wrote in Federalist No. 78, is that judges "should be bound down by strict rules and precedents, which serve to define and point out their duty in every particular case that comes before them."

Things have changed.

Justice Alito told the Senate Judiciary Committee during his 2006 confirmation hearing that "courts should only overrule prior precedents if they have a special justification for doing so," a power that should be used "sparingly."[7] Fast-forward the Alito tape. Speaking to the Federalist Society a decade later, Justice Alito said something very different. Justice Alito likes to style himself an "originalist," and our Founders were quite explicit in their view that courts should respect precedent.[8] But that didn't prevent the Justice from joking to a roomful of right-wing lawyers about *stare decisis*: "As I'm sure all of the lawyers in the room know, it is a Latin phrase. It means, to leave things decided when it suits our purposes."[9] Just in case they didn't get the joke, Justice Alito stated it even more baldly: "It not difficult for a judge to make the *stare decisis* inquiry come out however the judge wants it to come out."

Clarence Thomas, too, had assured senators before his confirmation of his view that "you cannot simply, because you have the votes, begin to change rules, to change precedent."[10] Once confirmed to life tenure on the nation's highest court, he sang a different tune: "When faced with a demonstrably erroneous precedent, my rule is simple: We should not follow it."[11] He's not kidding. In 2019, *New York Times* legal reporter Adam Liptak reported research showing that "Justice Thomas has written more than 250 concurring or dissenting opinions seriously questioning precedents, calling for their reconsideration or suggesting that they be overruled."[12] And of course Thomas gets to decide what he thinks is "demonstrably erroneous."

Chief Justice Roberts gave lip service to the importance of precedent during his confirmation, assuring senators that a judge's job was simply to "decide the case according to the rule of law consistent with the precedents; not to take sides in a dispute as a matter of policy, but to decide it according to the law."[13] Just a few years after this confirmation-hearing flummery, the Chief Justice in *Citizens United* announced a new rule: if a precedent is "hotly contested," it has less precedential value and can be replaced.[14] Of course, justices can "hotly contest" any precedent they don't like (just ask Justice Thomas). Coached by the Chief Justice, so can conservative special interests.

Stare decisis also figured in Brett Kavanaugh's confirmation. My colleague Senator Susan Collins was reassured by Brett Kavanaugh that he would not vote to overturn *Roe*, which Senator Collins has always professed to support. In an interview on *60 Minutes* shortly after her vote to confirm Kavanaugh, she related this from her private meeting with him: "What Judge Kavanaugh told me—and he's the first Supreme Court nominee that I've interviewed, out of six, who has told me this—is that he views precedent not just as a legal doctrine, but as rooted in our Constitution."[15] Kavanaugh's stated respect for *Roe* as precedent earned him her vote. But in the case that many believe will overturn *Roe v. Wade*, now-Justice Kavanaugh seemed to pivot away from *stare decisis* "if," as he suggested at oral argument, "we think that the prior precedents are seriously wrong."[16]

Respect for precedent is a recurring confirmation-hearing bromide, but it has an equally recurring evaporative quality when Federalist Society justices are confronted with the interests of big right-wing donors. Of course, precedent fell violently in the Alito leaked opinion, though *Roe v. Wade* had stood—and been reaffirmed—for half a century. Precedent fell to the Roberts Five in gun cases (including *Heller* and *McDonald*); in campaign finance cases (*Citizens United* and others); in voter protection cases (*Shelby County*); and in labor cases (such as the *Friedrichs/Janus* saga), *always* to the benefit of the Republican right. In *Heller* and *McDonald*, the Roberts Five jettisoned a precedent that had stood since 1939. In *Janus*, the conservative majority overturned a case the Court had repeatedly affirmed for forty years and that at least twenty states had relied on in drafting their own labor laws. Justice Kagan noted in her *Janus* dissent that every argument for *stare decisis* counseled against the majority's actions:

> Rarely if ever has the Court overruled a decision—let alone one of this import—with so little regard for the usual principles of stare decisis. There are no special justifications for reversing *Abood*. It has proved workable. No recent developments have eroded its underpinnings. And it is deeply entrenched, in both the law and the real world. . . . Reliance interests do not come any stronger than those surrounding *Abood*. And likewise, judicial disruption does not get any greater than what the Court does today.[17]

It didn't matter.

According to the Washington University Law School's Supreme Court Database, the Roberts Court has a unique distinction: the majority of its cases reversing precedent have been decided by a narrow 5–4 vote.[18] The Court's partisan lineup of 5–4 donor-friendly decisions correlates with overturned precedent. Contrast this with *Brown v. Board of Education*, the 1954 case that got conservative reactionaries screaming about "activist" justices. Chief Justice Earl Warren understood that even in a case where precedent was so deeply wrong, overruling precedent was a big deal. He didn't release the ruling ending "separate but equal" schooling until all nine justices signed off on it. The Roberts Five tend to overturn precedent as soon as they have the votes.

In cases where the Roberts Five avoid reversing precedent outright, they can still accomplish the desired outcome through what Professor Barry Friedman calls "stealth overruling."[19] In these cases, the majority opinion so hollows out an earlier holding that it leaves only a husk. For example, in 2020 the Court was asked to rule on the constitutionality of a Louisiana law targeting abortion providers that was for all intents and purposes identical to a Texas law the Court had rejected just four years earlier.[20] Striking down the new Louisiana law should have been an easy application of that recent precedent. But there was a wrinkle: the Court's composition had changed in the intervening years; Justice Kennedy had been replaced by Justice Kavanaugh, who had auditioned his opposition to *Roe v. Wade*. With Justice Kennedy's departure, the Chief Justice was now the swing vote. No fan of abortion rights, in the Texas case he had voted with those who would have upheld the restrictive law.

But in 2020 he joined the Court's liberals in striking down the Louisiana restrictions. He claimed he switched his vote because he respected precedent, and the Texas case was now precedent.[21] Fine. Except that as New York University professor Melissa Murray explained, the way Chief Justice Roberts wrote his concurrence "preserve[d] the outer shell of the earlier decision while gutting its substance" and "invited states to push the envelope on abortion legislation."[22] Sure enough, just weeks after the decision, the Eighth Circuit cited the Chief Justice's concurrence to lift an injunction on several anti-abortion Arkansas laws, one of which was so extreme as to require a rape victim to notify her rapist before she can obtain an abortion.[23]

The Court, with a new 6–3 conservative majority, is now poised to strike down *Roe v. Wade* altogether. In *Dobbs v. Jackson Women's Health Center*, which remains undecided as this book goes to press, a grim Justice Sotomayor observed at oral argument that the sponsors of the challenged state law introduced it "because we have new Justices."[24] The legislators assumed that a new vote count on the Court meant a new outcome, as if the Court were a political legislative body. "Will this institution survive the stench that this creates in the public perception that the Constitution and its reading are just political acts?" she asked.[25]

I suspect we're about to find out.

JUDICIAL RESTRAINT

The greatest irony of the right-wing activist legal effort, which is out to exert its will on the rest of us through the Court, is that it came masked as a call for "judicial restraint." Movement conservatives invented the term "judicial activism" to criticize court rulings they didn't like, usually rulings that challenged the status quo and demanded our country live up to its values.

Conservatives called the Warren Court of the 1950s and '60s "activist" because, in their view, it struck down too many laws. But, as Adam Liptak of the *New York Times* has noted, the Burger Court of the 1970s and '80s struck down a higher percentage of laws.[26] And it's hard to argue against the bulk of the Warren Court's rulings, even those that were controversial at the time, including *Brown v. Board of Education* and *Loving v. Virginia.* At her confirmation hearing, Amy Coney Barrett said that she regards *Brown*, once a lightning rod for the conservative movement, as a "super-precedent."[27]

The ultimate measure of judicial restraint is not those statistics; it's whether courts respect the rules and practices designed to check the tremendous power the Constitution grants them. Several long-standing canons of judicial interpretation constrain courts from becoming freewheeling unelected policymakers. One, enshrined in the Constitution, is that the court should rule only on an actual live dispute—a "case or controversy." Another is that courts should go only as far in their decisions as is necessary to resolve the case in front of them, and not range off into general policy-making.* A third is that courts should extend reasonable deference to congressional judgments; judges shouldn't substitute their policy views for those of democratically elected officials.† (This isn't because we in Congress are necessarily wiser than jurists; it's because leaving policy-making in the hands of elected officials gives citizens the power to correct errant policies at the ballot box.) Finally, appeals courts should eschew fact-finding and respect process. The Supreme Court's own practice has been to let issues percolate in lower courts and not step in until necessary to resolve a disagreement among them. The Roberts Court

---

* The principle of separation of powers requires that federal courts use their power to declare the law "only in the last resort, and as a necessity in the determination of real, earnest, and vital controversy between individuals."[28]

† Here's how the Supreme Court dispatched that notion in an earlier time: "The theory upon which, apparently, this suit was brought is that parties have an appeal from the legislature to the courts, and that the latter are given an immediate and general supervision of the constitutionality of the acts of the former. Such is not true. . . . It never was the thought that by means of a friendly suit, a party beaten in the legislature could transfer to the courts an inquiry as to the constitutionality of the legislative act."[29]

routinely ignores all of these conservative judicial principles when it serves the interests of the Republican Party and its donor elite.

For example, in a recent anti-union case, *Cedar Point Nursery*, a swarm of right-wing interest groups challenged a long-standing rule that allowed unions limited access to farmworkers housed on the farm property. As in *Friedrichs* and *Janus*, the interest group lawyers tried to lose in the courts below as quickly as possible so that they could get their challenge before a friendly Supreme Court. The so-called public interest lawyers were using *Cedar Point* to push a fringe constitutional theory about what constitutes a "taking" under the Constitution's Takings Clause, a clause requiring the government to compensate a private landowner for "taking" his or her property. This argument hadn't percolated through the lower courts, and it went far beyond what was necessary to resolve the actual dispute (in fact, there was a good argument that the challenged law didn't apply to the underlying facts at all). The Supreme Court practice to "never formulate a rule of constitutional law broader than is required by the precise facts to which it is to be applied" stood no chance here.[30] The Federalist Society justices took the hook the right-wing front group lawyers offered and ran with it, expanding the "takings" doctrine as requested and notching another win for anti-union forces.

This is not a first for the Federalist Society justices. The *Citizens United* question too was a narrow one—whether campaign finance limitations were constitutional "as applied" to the unique circumstances of that case. There had originally been a broader "facial" challenge to the entire law, but the challengers had dropped that part of their case. No party even argued that the law itself should be overturned.

Enter Chief Justice Roberts. *Citizens United* turned into a monster because the Chief Justice rewrote the "questions presented" and resurrected the abandoned challenge to the entire law. Conveniently, he did this at a stage in the case that left the law's defenders no opportunity to develop a record of evidence about what would ensue if the law were struck down, or why the law was justified. Justice Stevens called this out for what it was: "Five Justices were unhappy with the limited nature of the case before us, so they changed the case to give themselves an opportunity to change the law."[31] And change the law they did.

In *Citizens United*, as in *Shelby County*, the Roberts Five blatantly substituted their own policy judgments about elections for Congress's—never mind that the laws they struck down were based on dozens of hearings, scores of witnesses, mountains of evidence, and a multiyear bipartisan lawmaking process, not to mention having been written by lawmakers with actual practical knowledge of elections. The Bipartisan Campaign Reform Act and the Voting Rights Act, both of which Congress had passed with substantial bipartisan majorities, fell to the policy predilections of five justices. It did not matter to the Roberts Five that they did not know what they were talking about; and they deliberately closed off the ordinary process that could have informed them. They had other plans.

The Roberts Five used free-range gallivanting elsewhere to go beyond the question at hand. In *Comcast v. Behrend*, the question before the Court was the admissibility of expert evidence in antitrust class actions. That is what the parties debated with the justices during oral argument. But the 5–4 majority opinion leaped beyond the admissibility question to change the rules of class-action certification and reverse lower court decisions allowing the class to be certified at all. The effect of this was to make it harder for consumers to bring antitrust claims as class actions.

A word on class actions. Litigation is daunting; it takes a considerable injury to make it worthwhile. This creates an opening for massive, low-dollar, multi-victim frauds. Class actions provide the answer: victims can gather in one common lawsuit to seek a common remedy. Corporations loathe class actions. It's hard to believe it's a coincidence that the Roberts Five have consistently undermined the class action. The *Comcast* leap worked this purpose.

The Roberts Five's disdain for the work of lawmakers was again on display in *Heller* and *McDonald*, the cases that rewrote the Second Amendment. Again, Justice Stevens's dissent told the tale. "No one has suggested that the political process is not working exactly as it should in mediating the debate between the advocates and opponents of gun control," he wrote.[32] "What impact the Court's unjustified entry into this thicket will have on that ongoing debate—or indeed on the Court itself—is a matter that future historians will no doubt discuss at length. It is, however, clear to me that adherence to a policy of judicial restraint would be far wiser than the bold decision announced today."

Forget "judicial restraint"; the gun lobby wanted the Court in that "thicket" because it wasn't winning the "ongoing debate." So in the Court went, and changed the law as the gun lobby wished.

And of course, as I described above, in *West Virginia v. EPA* and *Sackett v. EPA* the newly emboldened "reactionary" justices will pass judgment on a rule that no longer exists, apparently to upend the administrative law system that has served this country well for nearly a century but that irritates big polluters. Taking a case when the challenged rule no longer exists ignores the Constitution's requirement that justices can rule only on a "case or controversy" and turns "judges into advice columnists." (That's not my phrasing—it's what Chief Justice Roberts accused his colleagues of doing in another recent case where the challenged law no longer existed.[33])

It is a clear pattern with this Supreme Court that judicial restraint is a "principle" that yields when Republican big-donor interests are on the line. When asked to step in and prevent partisan gerrymanders from entrenching Republican minority rule, the Roberts Five exercised excessive restraint, to the point of allowing redistricting anarchy and empowering REDMAP. When asked to do away with entire legal regimes the far right doesn't like, the Roberts Five go out of their way to issue as broad a ruling as desired, restraint be damned.

APPELLATE FACT-FINDING

The maxim that appellate courts are places of legal judgment, not fact-finding or policy-making, is central to our separation of powers. Fact-finding is reserved to lower courts, for many good reasons. One is to tether appellate courts to fixed facts, so they can't engage in too much policy-making "knight-errantry."

The willingness of today's conservative justices to roam far beyond the judicial record and make up facts in order to reach their desired policy outcome has been eye-popping. Such a departure from the theory and practice of appellate judging is a massive tell. Combined with the reliable rightward direction of the desired policy outcomes, it is a tell of the right-wing agenda that drives the Court's current majority.

A difference between *McConnell v. FEC*, the decision that upheld most of the Bipartisan Campaign Reform Act, and *Citizens United*, the case that overturned *McConnell*, was the existence of a factual record. In *McConnell*, the justices were presented with a record over 100,000 pages long assembled by the district court. This "voluminous" record showed that the political process was threatened by both real and apparent corruption in the form of unregulated "soft money" donations and "issue ads." The majority opinion in *McConnell* cited the factual record dozens of times in its ruling upholding the law.

Chief Justice Roberts made sure that *Citizens United* had no troublesome record. The Roberts Five relied on politically inexperienced intuitions to announce—wrongly—that "[t]he appearance of influence or access . . . will not cause the electorate to lose faith in our democracy" and that "independent expenditures, including those made by corporations, do not give rise to corruption or the appearance of corruption."[34] They just made that up.

Poll after poll today shows the error of the first statement. "Faith in our democracy" has predictably crashed since that decision.[35] And actual real-world experience proved wrong both of the majority's complacent supporting assumptions: that "independent" expenditures would actually be independent, and that "transparency" would actually reveal who was behind political advertising. As John McCain and I wrote to the Court: "Whether independent expenditures pose dangers of corruption or apparent corruption depends on the actual workings of the electoral system; it is a factual question, not a legal syllogism."[36] On appeal, factual questions are usually answered in a factual record. Without a record, there was no pesky evidence for the Court's conservatives to deal with. "[T]he record is not simply incomplete or unsatisfactory; it is nonexistent," warned Justice Stevens in his *Citizens United* dissent.[37] "Congress crafted BCRA in response to a virtual mountain of research on the corruption that previous legislation had failed to avert. The Court now negates Congress' efforts without a shred of evidence on how [the federal law] or its state-law counterparts have been affecting any entity other than Citizens United."

Janus, the anti-union case, was also decided without an evidentiary record after its fast-lane rush to the Court. Constitutional law scholar Garrett Epps observed that oral argument in *Janus* was notable for all the questions raised about basic facts.[38] The justices had no basis to know, for example, that reversing a forty-year-old precedent "would cause no real problems for the states, their employees, or the unions those employees chose to represent them," as petitioners argued, because the record didn't support that assurance. And it didn't support that assurance, as Epps noted, "simply because . . . well, there is no record in this case."[39] Instead, there was simply big donors' desire to change the unwelcome law, and "the unspoken corollary that conservatives now at last have five votes and can get rid of it."

Brianne Gorod, chief counsel at the Constitutional Accountability Center, illustrated why a record matters. At the oral argument in *Janus*, the Chief Justice noted anti-union advocates had argued that "the need to attract voluntary payments will make the unions more efficient, more effective, more attractive to a broader group of their employees" and asked, "What's wrong with that?" As Gorod pointed out, "the Chief Justice was asking an empirical question—he wanted to know how unions and employees respond in the real world if unions cannot charge fair share fees. The answer to that question is incredibly important to the case, which is why how the Court answers it is also so important."[40] In regular litigation, without partisan fast lanes and with evidentiary records developed in lower courts, this would not have been a problem. "If a record had been developed below, both parties could have offered real-world evidence and experts that could have been tested by the other side," Gorod explained. "But that didn't happen. And as a result, there is a real danger that the Justices will rest their legal conclusion in this critically important case not on tested facts, but on untested assumptions."[41]

Which is just what the Roberts Five did.

When there is an issue in an appeal that requires further factual elaboration, principles of proper fact-finding dictate a simple, standard solution: send the case back to the district court to develop those facts. But in *Janus*, *Citizens United*, *Shelby County*, and others, the Court just made up its own facts.* When a court operates without real-world evidence, it's amazing how often it can create "facts" that get the case to come out the way the majority wants. Which is exactly why this free-range appellate "fact-finding" is so wrong.

---

* In another case, Justice Breyer noted in dissent that the argument upon which the Court relied "has sprung full-grown from the Court's own brow, like Athena from the brow of Zeus."[42]

"ORIGINALISM," "TEXTUALISM," AND "FEDERALISM"

As a lawyer in the Reagan administration, Federalist Society founder Steven Calabresi urged Attorney General Ed Meese to turn the Department of Justice into "an agent of counterrevolutionary change."[43] He denounced notions of "judicial restraint," and argued that "the courts and the executive must start using their constitutional powers to hold the Congress within its proper constitutional sphere." So much for judicial modesty.

One tool for this activist "counterrevolutionary change" was "originalism," the notion that the Constitution must be read to preserve the Founders' "original" intentions. As Judge Richard Posner has noted, "The long-dead framers are a convenient group to whom to pass the buck."[44] This "originalism" notion was obviously convenient for big-donor special interests who want as few constraints on corporations as possible, since at the founding there were essentially no corporations and thus no regulation of them. Along with originalism came its bastard cousin, "textualism," which asserts that courts should look only at the words on the page and not stray into interpreting context or intent. In theory, these are touchstones of conservative jurisprudence.

In practice, the right-wing notions of "originalism" and "textualism" have managed never to get in the way of big-donor special interests. The Bill of Rights protects individuals, not corporations, but that didn't stop the Roberts Five from discovering a corporate right to free speech, which became a corporate right to unlimited political spending, which is on its way to becoming a corporate right to anonymous unlimited political spending—none of it with any "originalist" or "textualist" basis. While they were at it, the Roberts Five threw in a corporate right to religious "freedom." And that's just the First Amendment.

Look at how the conservative members of the Supreme Court re-read the Second Amendment in *Heller.* As my Senate colleagues and I reported, from "1888, when law review articles were first indexed, to 1959, not a single academic article argued that the Second Amendment protected an individual's right to bear arms."[45] The theory was so lacking in historical support that former Chief Justice Warren Burger, as I've mentioned, referred to it as "fraud." Judge Posner, a famed conservative jurist, dryly observed that "[t]he true springs of the *Heller* decision must be sought elsewhere than in the majority's declared commitment to originalism."[46]

Heller was neither "textualist" nor "originalist," but it gave the National Rifle Association what it wanted. The NRA funneled millions of dollars to conservative historians and legal scholars to build a historical narrative at odds with history's record, and then flog it incessantly, in ads, in legislatures, and in the press. It channeled millions more to the Federalist Society effort to secure jurists who would agree with that manufactured theory. And in politics, in 2016 alone, the NRA spent nearly $55 million on so-called independent expenditures for conservative candidates.[47] It both spent and received dark money. And its work paid off; the Court that it helped pay to create changed the law to its benefit.

An individual right to bear arms isn't anywhere in the text of the Constitution. But you know what is in the text of the Constitution? A right to jury trial. The right in civil cases is in the Seventh Amendment. Trial by jury predates our nation's founding by centuries. Royal interference with colonial trial by jury was a listed cause of the Revolution. Its absence in the original Constitution was an impetus for the Bill of Rights. That's strong "originalist" stuff. But the Roberts Five have whittled away that jury trial right in case after case—textualism and originalism be damned.

Someone looking for originalism in *Citizens United* would have to look to the Stevens dissent; the dark-money majority's free-range political predilections had no foundation in the text of the Constitution. Nor in history: independence was declared by "We the People"; the Constitution and Bill of Rights were set up as an experiment in popular governance; our greatest president in our worst moment described ours as a government "of the people, by the people, and for the people." Corporations just aren't in it, not if you're an originalist. But from Powell's campaign finance decisions forward, Republican justices have steadily constructed an increasingly powerful, and now increasingly clandestine, role for corporate power in our democracy. They made it up, step by step, out of thin air. Some "originalism." Some "restraint."

Then comes "federalism," which defines the relationship between the federal government and the states, much as "separation of powers" defines the relationship among the branches of the federal government. Federalism is often referred to as "states' rights."

"States' rights" was the rallying cry of the Southern "massive resistance" to integration. Right-wing lawmakers and pundits still love to talk about "states' rights" when they want to buck a federally protected right like abortion or find a way to oppose federal laws that challenge corporations' ability to pollute or discriminate against their employees. But when Republicans want to weaken local regulation of banks, undermine state campaign finance restrictions, or override state standards for pollutants or conditions for worker safety, we hear a lot less about "federalism" and "states' rights." Again, the alignment with the interests of big corporations is quite perfect.

A quick personal story: years ago the Supreme Court decided that regulation of the relationship between banks and consumers would be determined by the home state of the bank, not the home state of the customer.[48] Banks promptly registered headquarters in states with the weakest usury and consumer protection laws—a true "race to the bottom." State laws protecting home-state consumers from bad practices by big, out-of-state banks lost their effect. I tried to change this by law, to restore "states' rights" to protect their citizens. My effort failed, as Republican senators lined up with the big banks against my amendment. (To be fair, so did a bunch of Democrats, from banking states.) My lesson early on: "federalism" is a doctrine of convenience.

"Federalism" empowered conservative justices to strike down a federal law that restricted the possession of guns near school property, yet uphold a federal law that cracked down on homegrown marijuana.[49] Concern for states' rights was nowhere to be found when Florida tried to recount its ballots during the Bush v. Gore debacle, nor when states tried to adjust their voting rules in the face of a historic pandemic.[50] And forget about deferring to state laws when they conflict with a big-donor special interest. The Roberts Five overturned an Illinois state law that designated home health care workers "full-fledged" government employees for purposes of the state's labor law,[51] overturned state law designed to protect consumers against corporate fraud,[52] overturned decisions of democratically elected local school boards,[53] and upended a state law that had barred corporations and special interests from interfering in state political races.[54]

The conservative jurists on today's Supreme Court would gladly line up to tell a ballroom of Federal Society donors that they believe in states' rights, small government, a strong executive, and a weak Congress. And every big donor in the room would understand that when these principles come up against their interests, exceptions will be made.

"BALLS AND STRIKES"

During a now-notorious exchange during his confirmation hearing, Chief Justice Roberts assured senators that his past partisan political activities would be left at the courthouse door. A judge does nothing more than "call balls and strikes," he said.[55] A sitting federal judge recently called this statement a "masterpiece of disingenuousness."[56] As *Slate*'s Dahlia Lithwick has observed, "a conservative supermajority has changed the strike zone, corked the bats, and set the whole infield on fire—all while telling us that the game remains the same."[57]

The law shouldn't be interpreted differently depending on who the plaintiff is. If employees can opt out of paying union dues, why are lawyers required to be paying members of their state bar associations?[58] And why can't shareholders disassociate from corporate political spending? There's a different rule for "compelled subsidy of speech" depending on whether you are a covered union employee, a member of the bar, or a corporate shareholder.[59]

Balls and strikes, indeed.

A state law allows a Christian chaplain to be present with a prisoner in an execution chamber, yet Justices Kavanaugh, Alito, and Roberts refused to extend it to other religions, denying a Black Muslim the opportunity to have an imam present for his final moments.[60] Six weeks later, a white Buddhist made a "strikingly similar" request, which was granted by the Court.[61] The reversal was so stunning that a full month after the decision Justice Kavanaugh took the "highly unusual move" of releasing a public statement to explain his vote.[62] (I wonder if CRC Advisors helped with that.)*

---

* Justice Kavanaugh claimed that he reached the apparently contrary results because he did not understand the Black prisoner's claim to be about equal treatment and because the petition had been filed late. Murphy v. Collier, 139 S. Ct. 1475 (2019) (mem.). But Justice Kagan's dissent from the order barring the imam from the execution had blasted

Sometimes the Roberts Five obstinately refuse to recognize differences obvious to anyone else. Recall *AFPF*, the case where dark-money groups obtained a new constitutional right to keep their donors a secret. There, the conservative justices perceived no difference between right-wing oligarchs fueling the dark-money influence machine and NAACP members at risk of violence in the Jim Crow South.

The Supreme Court's behavior has become so egregious that jurists themselves are speaking out. In the *Harvard Law & Policy Review*, sitting U.S. District Court judge Lynn Adelman wrote an article titled "The Roberts Court's Assault on Democracy."* He warned that "the Court's hard right majority is actively participating in undermining American democracy. Indeed, the Roberts Court has contributed to ensuring that the political system in the United States pays little attention to ordinary Americans and responds only to the wishes of a relatively small number of powerful corporations and individuals."[63] That's tough talk from a sitting federal judge. Recall too retired federal judge Nancy Gertner's similar warning, with Professor Tribe, quoted on page 156.

In 2020, a retired state judge, who had been a lawyer for more than

---

the Court's conservative members for violating "the Establishment Clause's core principle of denominational neutrality"; Justice Kavanaugh could hardly have missed the issue. And as for the complaint that the petition was filed too late? That was because the prisoner wasn't told about the prison's policy until just before his execution—as Justice Kagan also highlighted in her dissent. In fact, the prisoner had filed his complaint within days of learning about the protocols.[64] As *Slate*'s Dahlia Lithwick wrote at the time, "bad timing" is a particularly poor argument in a case like this:

> This is a court that has staked its moral legitimacy on the proposition that religion, above all, is at the very core of humanity, to be elevated in all instances no matter the competing interests. In so many faiths, there is no more sacred moment than entry and departure from this life. But never mind. For a court that cannot bear the thought of a religious baker forced to frost a cake in violation of his spiritual convictions to be wholly unaffected at the prospect of a man given last rites by a member of another faith borders on staggering.[65]

* When a draft of Judge Adelman's article was made public, the right-wing response was straight out of the playbook I described earlier, prompting *Slate*'s Dahlia Lithwick and Mark Joseph Stern to call out the "long-standing trick" of the conservative outrage machine: insisting "that conservative judges demonstrate deeply felt passion when they delve into such issues, while everyone else just demonstrates 'bias' if they decide to weigh in."[66]

fifty years, sat down and wrote the following letter to the Chief Justice.[67] It's worth reading in its entirety:

Dear Chief Justice Roberts:

I hereby resign my membership in the Supreme Court Bar.

This was not an easy decision. I have been a member of the Supreme Court Bar since 1972, far longer than you have, and appeared before the Court, both in person and on briefs, on several occasions as Deputy and First Deputy Attorney General of Hawaii before being appointed as a Hawaii District Court judge in 1986. I have a high regard for the work of the Federal Judiciary and taught the Federal Courts course at the University of Hawaii Richardson School of Law for a decade in the 1980s and 1990s. This due regard spanned the tenures of Chief Justices Warren, Burger, and Rehnquist before your appointment and confirmation in 2005. I have not always agreed with the Court's decisions, but until recently I have generally seen them as products of mainstream legal reasoning, whether liberal or conservative. The legal conservatism I have respected—that of, for example, Justice Lewis Powell, Alexander Bickel or Paul Bator—at a minimum enshrined the idea of stare decisis and eschewed the idea of radical change in legal doctrine for political ends.

I can no longer say that with any confidence. You are doing far more—and far worse—than "calling balls and strikes." You are allowing the Court to become an "errand boy" for an administration that has little respect for the rule of law.

The Court, under your leadership and with your votes, has wantonly flouted established precedent. Your "conservative" majority has cynically undermined basic freedoms by hypocritically weaponizing others. The ideas of free speech and religious liberty have been transmogrified to allow officially sanctioned bigotry and discrimination, as well as to elevate the grossest forms of political bribery beyond the ability of the federal government or states to rationally regulate it. More than a score of decisions during your tenure have overturned established precedents—some more than forty years old—and you voted with the majority in most. There is nothing "conservative" about this trend. This is radical "legal activism" at its worst.

Without trying to write a law review article, I believe that the Court majority, under your leadership, has become little more than a result-oriented extension of the right wing of the Republican Party, as vetted by the Federalist Society. Yes, politics has always been a factor in the Court's history, but not to today's extent. Even routine rules of statutory construction get subverted or ignored to achieve transparently political goals. The rationales of "textualism" and "originalism" are mere fig leaves masking right wing political goals; sheer casuistry.

Your public pronouncements suggest that you seem concerned about the legitimacy of the Court in today's polarized environment. We all should be. Yet your actions, despite a few bromides about objectivity, say otherwise.

It is clear to me that your Court is willfully hurtling back to the cruel days of *Lochner* and even *Plessy*. The only constitutional freedoms ultimately recognized may soon be limited to those useful to wealthy, Republican, White, straight, Christian, and armed males—and the corporations they control. This is wrong. Period. This is not America.

I predict that your legacy will ultimately be as diminished as that of Chief Justice Melville Fuller, who presided over both *Plessy* and *Lochner*. It still could become that of his revered fellow Justice John Harlan the elder, an honest conservative, but I doubt that it will. Feel free to prove me wrong.

The Supreme Court of the United States is respected when it wields authority and not mere power. As has often been said, you are infallible because you are final, but not the other way around.

I no longer have respect for you or your majority, and I have little hope for change. I can't vote you out of office because you have life tenure, but I can withdraw whatever insignificant support my Bar membership might seem to provide.

Please remove my name from the rolls.

With deepest regret,
James Dannenberg

Stare decisis, judicial restraint, originalism and textualism, federalism, and a proper aversion to appellate fact-finding—in the hands of the Court's conservative bloc, these are doctrines of convenience. Two conservative justices of a different era once wrote, "the Court's legitimacy depends on making legally principled decisions under circumstances in which their principled character is sufficiently plausible to be accepted by the Nation." [68] The Dark Money Justices on this Court seem more to be following the Groucho Marx rule: "Those are my principles, and if you don't like them . . . well, I have others."

CHAPTER TWENTY

The Shadow Docket

Sunlight is the best disinfectant.
—LOUIS BRANDEIS

INCREASINGLY, THE ROBERTS COURT HAS EMBRACED IN ITS own behavior the stealth favored by right-wing special interests. Nothing better illustrates this than the Roberts Court's ramped-up use of the "shadow docket." This refers to cases that the Court decides without full briefing and oral argument, often in a single sentence without even explaining its reasoning. "Shadow docket" matters often take the form of unsigned "emergency orders" of questionable precedential value. Traditionally, these were mostly for judicial housekeeping—an extension to file a brief, divvying up oral argument time, declining to grant certiorari in noncontroversial cases—and attracted attention only when used for emergency appeal of a criminal execution.

The first partisan and politically mischievous use of the shadow docket I could find was the 2016 decision by the Roberts Five to undo President Obama's EPA climate regulation, the Clean Power Plan—making the fossil fuel industry very happy but damaging America's response to the climate emergency. The five, all Republican appointees, without hearing oral argument or issuing a formal opinion, granted an emergency stay pending appeal of the district court's judgment, stopping the regulation in its tracks. Ordinarily, a properly promulgated regulation would remain presumptively valid pending appeal. Ordinarily, a decision of that importance would result from a formal opinion, following a grant of certiorari, with full merits briefing and oral argument.

But as University of Texas professor Steve Vladeck explained in separate appearances before the House and Senate Judiciary Committees in 2021, the Court's "shadow docket" has dramatically expanded since 2017.[1] In the sixteen years between 2001 and 2017, the U.S. government sought an emergency order from the Court—allowing it to sidestep a full merits review and standard judicial process—a total of eight times, and only one of those instances provoked a dissent.[2] During the four years combining a Trump presidency with a Federalist Society Court, forty-one emergency applications were filed.[3] That's about twenty times the frequency. In response, the Court issued thirty-six orders.[4] Twenty-seven of those orders provoked a dissent, suggesting that these were far from the routine, "nothing to see here" cases that the Court typically deals with outside its merits docket.*

The Trump-era Court repeatedly waded into politically charged waters in its shadow docket, acting by fiat to resolve disputes about the border wall,[5] COVID-19 restrictions,[6] access to the polls,[7] and the first federal executions in seventeen years.[8] Many of these orders were issued in the middle of the night—one came after 10 p.m. the Wednesday of Thanksgiving week. As Professor Vladeck noted to my committee, in one instance "the Court used a shadow docket ruling to resolve major First Amendment questions about a policy that wasn't even in effect—and did so before the litigation had a chance to make its way through the courts on the merits."[9]

The Roberts Court's rulings using the shadow docket have blown through procedural guardrails designed to maintain judicial

---

* "By waiting for most cases to go through multiple layers of review by lower courts," Professor Vladeck explained in the *Harvard Law Review*, "the Court gives itself the benefit of multiple rounds of briefing and argument." So to now

abandon this norm only in cases in which the federal government is the complaining party is to invite serious objections grounded in fairness and equity—and to necessarily tilt the Court's limited resources toward an undoubtedly important, but importantly narrow, class of disputes. Worse still, such a shift gives at least the appearance that the Court is showing favoritism not only for the federal government as a party, but for a specific political party when it's in control of the federal government.[10]

restraint—guardrails that preserve judicial legitimacy. Some rulings decided cases on the merits rather than deciding the narrow procedural question presented, allowing parties to skip the normal judicial review process.[11] Some blocked laws that were no longer in effect (which in my book hardly constitutes an "emergency"),[12] and others sat at the Court for so long that if the justices had wished, they could have had the merits briefed and argued rather than issuing an unsigned, unreasoned opinion—again, hard to see the "emergency" there.[13]

In at least one instance, the Court announced a new interpretation of the law through its shadow docket—something it's actually barred by law from doing.[14] Even more eyebrow-raising, it has instructed lower courts that at least some of its shadow docket rulings—rulings made with no reasoned analysis to explain its decision—should have the force of precedent. What the heck is a lower court judge—or a lawmaker who wants to legislate within the bounds of what the Supreme Court deems acceptable—supposed to do with that? As Professor Vladeck told my committee,

> It is no longer possible for any reasonable observer to dispute that there has been a dramatic uptick in significant, broad-impact rulings on the shadow docket in the past few years; that these rulings have been unusually divisive; that they are leading to novel forms of procedural relief from the Court; and that their substantive effects are causing significant uncertainty both in lower courts and among those government officers, lawyers, and court-watchers left to parse what, exactly, these rulings portend both for the specific policies at issue and for the broader contours of the relevant legal doctrines.[15]

All of this came to a head in September 2021, when the Supreme Court used its shadow docket to allow Texas's draconian abortion law to go into effect—the one that bars all abortions in that state after about six weeks (before many women know they are pregnant).[16] Abortion providers sought to block the clearly unconstitutional law while the litigation proceeded. The district court agreed, but the Fifth Circuit reversed, and the question came to the Supreme Court. In such cases, the Court would ordinarily suspend implementation of the challenged

law, based on its plain violation of multiple previous precedents upholding a right to abortion pre-viability.

But that's not what happened. In an unsigned single paragraph,
the Supreme Court conservatives used the shadow docket to let the
challenged law stand. Justice Kagan dissented on both substance and
procedure, noting that "the majority's decision is emblematic of too
much of this Court's shadow-docket decision-making—which every
day becomes more unreasoned, inconsistent, and impossible to defend."[17] *Slate*'s Mark Joseph Stern said: "The Supreme Court overturned *Roe v. Wade* in the most cowardly manner imaginable"—in the
middle of the night, with no reasoning, on a procedural point.[18] Even
the Chief Justice publicly noted his dissent. When the new Federalist
Society bloc on the Court goes too far for John Roberts, it's a worrying
sign that Frankenstein's monster is unchained and smashing about our
constitutional landscape.*

---

* Of course, worse was to come. First, the five conservative justices allowed the Texas
law to stay in place, signaling its likely fate when the lawsuit is ultimately decided and
perpetuating a dystopian, neighbor-spying-on-neighbor legal regime that states could
use to impede a variety of constitutional rights. Then came the Alito draft opinion
bomb, prefiguring complete destruction of the underlying *Roe v. Wade* precedent, and
with it the first judicial termination of a recognized constitutional right.

PART IX

Closing Argument

CHAPTER TWENTY-ONE

The Scheme

The stairway . . . leads to a dark gulf. It is a fine, broad stairway at the beginning, but after a bit, the carpet ends. A little further on there are only flagstones, and a little further on still these break beneath your feet.

—WINSTON CHURCHILL

SO THERE IT IS. IT'S NOW TIME TO deliver what a lawyer at the end of a trial would call the closing argument.

Our evidence has a big gap in it: we don't know exactly who is behind the Scheme to capture the Court, because, like Fight Club, Scheme Rule Number One is not to talk about who is behind the Scheme. But that gap itself is evidence. We can't see what's hidden, but we can sure see the effort to obscure it. Enormous effort has been applied, and massive sums have been spent, to create avenues for unlimited hidden money to flow, to set up dozens of phony front groups for it to flow through, and to co-opt existing lobbying and advocacy groups into its anonymous service. And while the methods are hidden, the results are all too evident: partisan, unprincipled judicial rulings that are deeply out of step with mainstream America, that supplant our democratic processes, that privilege the powerful over ordinary citizens, and that have real and tragic consequences for our lives and for our country.

In World Wars I and II, it was common for naval vessels to burn oil and create thick clouds of smoke they could hide behind. The smoke threw off the gunnery of their adversaries. Those gunners may not have been able to target the smoke-screened ships with precision, but they sure as hell knew there were battleships in the smoke. Here too there are battleships in the smoke.

While there are specifics we do not know about the Scheme because of its dark-money smokescreen, there is a lot that we do know, and all of it points to the same conclusion. Let's review the evidence.

We know first that there has been enormous effort to keep the Scheme secret. Organizations with multiple "fictitious names" are not ordinary; neither are massive hidden donors; nor is dark money. It's weird. That smoke is a clue in and of itself.

We know that front groups by the dozen were co-opted or created to facilitate the Scheme and that over half a billion dollars was run through them. People don't spend more than half a billion dollars for no reason.

We know that never before in history have judicial selections to the Court been turned over to a partisan private organization, let alone one simultaneously receiving massive anonymous donations. We know this happened, because the President, and his counsel, and the organization receiving the funds all admitted it. We know too that the selected justices show up for pep-rally Washington, DC, galas thrown to raise yet more money for the donee organization.

We know that massive checks were written by unknown donors for advertising campaigns to pressure senators to vote for the chosen nominees. We know that big donors behind the Scheme are also big Republican political donors. We know from the Court's own decisions that there are constitutional concerns with donors spending big money to influence judicial selection and Court outcomes, yet the Court maintains a studied obliviousness to big donors prowling its own halls. It's the dog that won't bark.

We know that the selected Supreme Court nominees went out of their way to signal their adherence to Federalist Society dogma before their selection. That tells you that the insiders themselves knew there was an audience, a group that could cast them on the Court. We know their judicial colleagues saw this behavior, even named it: "auditioning."

We know that controlling appointments to agencies and commissions is the core technique of agency capture (also known as "regulatory capture"), and it mirrors the way the Scheme controlled appointments to the Court. We know that corporate America's administrative mercenaries, the right wing's oddball fringe groups, and tobacco's denial operation gave the Scheme resources ready to deploy and to expand. We know that repeated far-right failures in the political realm created a motive. We know that Powell created a plan. We know that the group for which Powell created the plan became the biggest "gorilla" in my political jungle, a gorilla with a big interest—and big wins—in the Court.

We know that a very similar play, with many of the same front groups, was run to produce climate denial and destroy the American government's ability to address climate change. To our shame, it succeeded. (But then, so has Court capture.)

We know that a pattern at the Court of blown precedents and violated doctrines aligns with a pattern at the Court of partisan 5–4 decisions, and that those decisions produced for big Republican donor interests a win record of at least 80 to zero. We know that the Court created a fast lane for right-wing front groups to rush political cases up to the Court, and we know that justices have both invited those cases and rewarded that effort. We know that big money orchestrates flotillas of right-wing dark-money amici and litigation groups to appear before the Court, and that when they do they have an improbably high win rate.

We know that both the dark-money front groups and the Dark Money Justices plan ahead, creating springboard doctrines that drive results in future cases.

We know that there has been a vicious cycle of pro-corporate and politically naive justices who get on the Court and pave the way for political dark money, which then allows more dark-money influence, and produces more Dark Money Justices on the Court. We know that the Court ignores its own ethics rules, or indulges ridiculous readings of them, in ways that foment special-interest misuse.

We know that a Court that is not supposed to meddle at all in factfinding not only does so, but invents false facts that allow it to reach the desired outcome, and then conspicuously fails to correct the error even after the facts' falsity is indisputably proven by subsequent events.

We know that the same organizations fund an overlapping amicus armada of front groups over and over and over, and that they have political goals. We know that they also fund political mischief, including climate denial and voter suppression. Indeed, it appears they fund Mitch McConnell's own PAC and super PAC.

We know that when you threaten to expose this operation or put the endeavor at risk, a scripted eruption of "faux outrage" from right-wing outlets (and essentially only right-wing outlets) ensues, all parroting the same talking points pushing a false narrative.

We know that Senate Republicans gave up precious Senate prerogatives, while smashing a path through Senate norms, rules, and traditions—even FBI background procedures—to turn the institution into a coldly efficient conveyor belt for processing big donors' unqualified and extreme nominees. Let me assure you, senators are ordinarily loath to give up our long-standing prerogatives. Only tremendous pressure could make that happen.

When we know all that, it's pretty easy to do the math and conclude that there is a secretive, private Scheme, contrived and perpetrated by very wealthy interests, to create a Court willing to do its bidding. All the pieces line up. No other conclusion makes sense.

It is also evident that the Court has done the Scheme's bidding with unerring aim. No other explanation for its pattern of decisions makes statistical sense.

And it's horrible.

The reason for all the deception is simple: the radical right long ago realized that it could not achieve its objectives openly. Goldwater lost in a rout. David Koch's libertarian campaign won just 1 percent of the vote. The far-right "Reagan Revolution" attack ended with a whimper, and the far-right nominee Bork got a bipartisan rejection in the Senate. Even after all of the Federalist Society's years of work and recruitment—and the avenue to high judicial office it provides—its membership encompasses not even 6 percent of American lawyers. How do oligarchs push their rejected agenda in the face of the reality that the majority of Americans simply don't share their worldview? Appoint judges who do, and drive change clandestinely through the undemocratic courts.

The Roberts Court embodies as well as imposes minority rule. A full third of the Court's members today were appointed by a president who lost the popular vote by 3 million, and then confirmed by senators who received fewer votes and represented fewer Americans than senators who opposed their confirmations. This had never happened before in our nation's history, much less three times in rapid succession. (Justices Thomas and Alito were confirmed by senators who had received fewer votes than the senators in opposition, but at least they were nominated by presidents who had won a majority of the popular vote.)

This leaves the Court, as Michael Tomasky wrote in the *New York Times* during the Kavanaugh confirmation debacle, in a legitimacy crisis of historic proportions. Our highest court, he explained,

> was never to stray far from the mainstream of American political life. The fact that justices represented that mainstream and were normally confirmed by lopsided votes gave the court's decisions their legitimacy. It's also why past chief justices worked to avoid 5-4 decisions on controversial matters: They wanted Americans to see that the court was unified when it laid down a major new precedent. But now, in an age of 5-4 partisan decisions, we're on the verge of having a five-member majority who figure to radically rewrite our nation's laws. And four of them will have been narrowly approved by senators representing minority will.[1]

With Justice Barrett, that four is now five. A decisive majority of our Supreme Court—the ultimate arbiters of law, shielded from voter feedback, appointed for life—was confirmed by senators representing less than half of the electorate.

Three justices of the Supreme Court observed not long ago, "The Court's power lies . . . in its legitimacy, a product of substance and perception that shows itself in the people's acceptance of the Judiciary as fit to determine what the Nation's law means and to declare what it demands."[2] That is why it is such a dangerous and cynical act for powerful interests to pursue capture of the Supreme Court, as if it were some ordinary regulatory agency to be brought under industry's thumb. And worse yet for justices to yield to it.

A court that is willing to do the bidding of others is not a court any longer. All the high benches, all the "your Honors," all the black robes, and all the "Oyez, oyez, oyez" in the world can't make it a court. We have to address the terrible fact that on the issues important to the big donors, The Court That Dark Money Built is a mere simulacrum of a court, like a judicial Potemkin village. All of the pomp and ceremony is still there. But the justice is gone. And without justice, kingdoms are just great bands of robbers.

It kills me to say this. It truly does. But even through the fog of secrecy shrouding the Scheme, all the evidence points to the same, terrible conclusion: the Court is captured. We've seen the motive, the plan, the means, the method, and the prizes of the Scheme, as well as some pretty telling admissions by word and deed. While we don't know all the donors, and the specific secret deals that were made with them, I expect history will dig out those sordid details. Maybe whistle-blowers will come forward. But even without those final details, what we see is bad enough.

It is also heartbreaking. Courts were, for a long time, more impervious than other branches to the corrosive influence of money; courts were thus the safe refuge of the little guy, the place where everyone truly could aspire to be equal in the eyes of the law. The capture Scheme has broken that.

There are times when we need the courts to stand firm against the tyranny of the majority, but there are also times when the Court needs to protect the public from the schemes of big influencers. This latter role is one the Court has undertaken in the past, but now it's a role to which Court Republicans seem completely oblivious. The Roberts Court—now controlled by justices hand-picked by right-wing groups backed with millions from shadowy funders—is embracing raw judicial activism to enact fringe political theories that are deeply out of step with mainstream America but that benefit the big influencers.

According to his public pronouncements, Chief Justice Roberts is concerned about judicial legitimacy. He took the unusual step of issuing a public rebuke to Donald Trump when the president criticized a ruling as coming from "an Obama judge." "We do not have Obama judges or Trump judges, Bush judges or Clinton judges," the Chief Justice wrote. "What we have is an extraordinary group of dedicated judges doing their level best to do equal right to those appearing before them."[3] Look behind public pablum like that. Dark Money Justices are cannibalizing the integrity and reputation of their own branch to appease big donors. The corporations and special interests behind the Scheme, motivated by short-term goals and disinterested in democracy, couldn't care less. Loss of public confidence in the Supreme Court is simply not a problem for them. Justice Stevens cautioned when the Court began down this road in *Bush v. Gore*: "It is confidence in the men and women who administer the judicial system that is the true backbone of the rule of law."[4]

I had some hope for President Biden's Presidential Commission on the Supreme Court, but the reports it produced completely missed the danger. Thank goodness for Judge Gertner and Professor Tribe's dissenting voices. We are way past a time for academic rumination on the history of court reform and the pros and cons of judicial codes of conduct. We are in a crisis of judicial legitimacy, a five-alarm fire fueled and stoked by anti-government billionaires whose anti-democratic, anti-consumer, anti-worker, anti-women agenda is becoming increasingly hard to hide—but now that they have six justices, they really don't need to hide much.

The most important responsibility, as the Court's standing falls, is on the Court itself. But if the Court is a willing victim of its degradation, linked to and loyal to the dark-money apparatus that is the instrument of its degradation, then reliance on the Court to save itself may be misplaced. In that case, Congress will have to step in. When we do, the dark arts of the dark-money apparatus behind the Scheme will be brought to bear with maximum political force to protect and defend its captured Court. It will be a battle for the ages, as well as a battle for the Court.

As we battle for the soul of the Court, no reform will be meaningful if we do not disrupt the flow of undisclosed dark money into all stages of the pipeline: the pseudo-academic hothouses that make it worth someone's while to manufacture reverse-engineered theories; the organizations that indoctrinate, groom, and audition judicial candidates; a Senate that has abandoned its own institutional processes and prerogatives to install reliable policy agents on the courts; and a Supreme Court whose "ethics" program has neither binding rules nor referees. Nor will it be meaningful if we do not grapple with the damage already done, procured through unprincipled decisions that rewarded unprincipled special interests. The worst of the damage is the damage done to American democracy.

I don't relish calling out this cherished American institution. But the only thing worse than calling out a captured Court would be a captured Court that no one calls out.

The restoration of the Court should not be a Republican or Democratic project. It should be an American project, to restore democracy's City on a Hill. If we care about our constitutional system—a system of, by, and for the people, not corporations and secret billionaires—something must be done, and soon. As a certain Virginia attorney and soon-to-be justice once wrote, we are in deep trouble. And the hour is late.

Acknowledgments

I am grateful to The New Press for asking me for another book after *Captured*, and for patiently guiding me through the process again
and dealing with my inveterate editing. In particular, I thank Diane
Wachtell, Rachel Vega-DeCesario, and Emily Albarillo for facilitating
that editing process. This book would not have been possible without
Jen Mueller. She assembled into order masses of material from my
Senate speeches and articles, added her own excellent work and editor's eye, filled in gaps and suggested ideas and phrasing, and was in
every way a helpful colleague. Rich Davidson from my staff managed
the task of helping gather official materials for me from years of Senate work, and I am grateful for his always able and cheerful assistance.

I have spoken about the crisis in our courts in dozens of speeches,
including remarks on the Senate Floor and talks at New York University and the National Press Club. I have also written about this issue
in multiple op-eds, my report for the American Constitution Society,
and articles in the *Harvard Journal on Legislation* and the *Yale Law
Journal*. Copies of all of these, including transcripts of my speeches,
can be found at my website, and edited versions of some have been
incorporated into this book at places.

While my work is my own, I know it is infinitely better for the work
of the many Senate staffers, researchers, and editors who have helped
me analyze this issue and bring it to the public's attention. I am grateful for their dedicated and careful work, especially Niko Paladino, Je-
nae Longenecker, Owen Flomberg, Meghan Lovett, and Julia Rose
Aguilera, who provided valuable research assistance on this book.

As ever, I'm grateful to Sandra, who puts up with a lot as a senator's spouse in today's noxious political environment, with a husband who is regularly the subject of dark-money hostilities. For me, it's a fight worth having; for her, it's a lot of stress and unpleasantness. Her support means the world to me, as I know the price she pays.

—S.W.

I am deeply grateful to Sheldon Whitehouse for trusting me to help him bring this important story to light, and I appreciate the good humor, intellect, and courtesy he brought to the endeavor. My sincere thanks, too, to Diane Wachtell and the staff at The New Press, especially Emily Albarillo and Rachel Vega-DeCesario, and to Rich Davidson and Leah Seigle on Senator Whitehouse's staff. Significant parts of early drafts were written from the homes of family and friends who charitably withheld the title worst houseguest ever; my thanks to Debbie Matties and Russ Hanser, Tom and Gretchen Toles, Kathy and Blazer Catzen, and Barb and Bruce Mueller. My friend and former colleague Stacy Beck provided exceptional headshots on short notice. I was fortunate to receive support from more family and friends than I can name here, but special thanks are due to Amanda, Lisa, Leena, Megan, and Aimee. Last, I would not have gotten involved in this project were it not for the kind words of Robert Raben, and I would never have met Robert were it not for Mark Glaze.

—J.M.

Appendix A

"The 80": Decisions by the Roberts Five, 2005–2019

THE FOLLOWING CHART EXPANDS UPON THE ANALYSIS FIRST presented in Senator Whitehouse's April 2019 article for the American Constitution Society, "A Right-Wing Rout: What the 'Roberts Five' Decisions Tell Us About the Integrity of Today's Supreme Court." It has been updated to reflect eighty cases that were decided by a 5–4 opinion by the Roberts Five (Justices Roberts, Alito, Kennedy, Thomas, and Scalia or Gorsuch), each of which served one of the following conservative interests: (1) controlling the political process to benefit conservative candidates and policies; (2) protecting corporations from liability and letting polluters pollute; (3) restricting civil rights and condoning discrimination; and (4) advancing a far-right social agenda. The final five cases are decisions by the Roberts Five in which no clear donor interests are presently identified.

Where appropriate, the appendix also identifies the judicial principles these conservative justice generally espouse, but which they arguably disregarded in these cases to achieve a desired outcome, including: (1) stare decisis; (2) judicial restraint; (3) originalism; (4) textualism; and (5) aversion to fact finding.

Case Name	Citation	Holding	Conservative Interest	Judicial Principle Disregarded
League of Latin American Citizens v. Perry	548 U.S. 399 (2006)	Upheld racial and partisan gerrymandering that burdened the rights of minority voters in Texas.	Controlling the Political Process: Voter Suppression	**Stare Decisis**, *see* 548 U.S. at 462-63, 474-75 (Stevens, J., concurring and dissenting in part); *see also, id.* at 483 (Souter, J., concurring and dissenting in part)
Garcetti v. Ceballos	547 U.S. 410 (2006)	Narrowed speech protections for public employees, holding that statements made pursuant to official duties are not shielded for purposes of employer discipline.	Restricting Civil Rights & Condoning Discrimination	**Stare Decisis**, *see* 547 U.S. at 427 (citing *Pickering v. Board of Ed. of Township High School Dist. 205, Will Cty. and Givhan v. Western* (Souter, J. dissenting)
FEC v. Wisconsin Right to Life	551 U.S. 449 (2007)	Struck down the ban on issue ads during the 60 days before elections.	Controlling the Political Process: Dark Money	**Judicial Restraint**, *see* 551 U.S. at 504 (Souter, J., dissenting) **Stare Decisis**, *see id.* at 522, 534-35 (citing *McConnell v. FEC*)
Leegin Creative Leather Products v. PSKS	551 U.S. 877 (2007)	Limited Section 1 of the Sherman Act to allow manufacturers to set mandatory minimum prices for their products, replacing the bright-line rule that resale price fixing agreements are per se illegal with a rule that vertical price restraints should be judged according to the "rule of reason."	Protecting Corporations from Liability	**Stare Decisis**, *see* 551 U.S. at 908 (citing *Dr. Miles Medical Co. v. John D. Park & Sons Co.*) (Breyer, J., dissenting)
National Association of Home Builders v. Defenders of Wildlife	551 U.S. 644 (2007)	Limited the reach of the Endangered Species Act and eliminated a major regulatory hurdle for developers.	Protecting Corporations from Liability: Letting Polluters Pollute	
Ledbetter v. Goodyear Tire	550 U.S. 618 (2007)	Made it more difficult for employees to bring Title VII claims and ignored the realities around proving wage discrimination.	Restricting Civil Rights & Condoning Discrimination	
Morse v. Frederick	551 U.S. 393 (2007)	Limited both the speech rights of high school students.	Restricting Civil Rights & Condoning Discrimination	

Case Name	Citation	Holding	Conservative Interest	Judicial Principle Disregarded
Parents Involved in Community Schools v. Seattle School District No. 1	551 U.S. 701 (2007)	Limited the ability of primary and secondary public schools to use affirmative action programs that promote diversity.	Restricting Civil Rights & Condoning Discrimination	**Stare Decisis**, *see* 551 U.S. at 799 (citing misapplication of *Brown v. Board of Ed.*) (Stevens, J., dissenting); *see also id.* at 803 (alleging majority "distorts precedent") (Breyer, J., dissenting) **Federalism**, *see* 551 U.S. at 866
Hein v. Freedom From Religion Foundation	551 U.S. 587 (2007)	Restricted the ability of citizens to sue the government under the First Amendment for entangling church and state.	Advancing a Far-Right Social Agenda	**Stare Decisis**, *see* 551 U.S. at 637-38 (citing *Flast v. Cohen*) (Stevens, J., dissenting)
Gonzalez v. Carhart	550 U.S. 124 (2007)	Made it harder for women to exercise their reproductive rights by holding Congress's ban on partial-birth abortion was not unconstitutionally vague and did not impose an undue burden on the right to an abortion.	Advancing a Far-Right Social Agenda	**Stare Decisis**, *see* 550 U.S. at 170-71, 173-175 (citing *Casey* and *Stenberg v. Carhart* and noting *Stenberg v. Carhart* was decided only 7 years prior) (Ginsburg, J., dissenting)
Davis v. FEC	554 U.S. 724 (2008)	Eliminated the "Millionaire's Amendment" to the Bipartisan Campaign Reform Act, increasing the influence of wealth as a criterion for public office.	Controlling the Political Process: Dark Money	**Originalism**, *see* 554 U.S. at 751 (Stevens, J., dissenting)
Stoneridge Inv. Partners, LLC v. Scientific-Atlanta 5-3 (Breyer Recused)	552 U.S. 148 (2008)	Limited the ability of shareholders alleging securities fraud to sue, holding that they must be able to show that they had relied, in making their decisions to acquire or hold stock, on the deceptive behind-the-scenes behavior of financial institutions (and their lawyers and accountants).	Protecting Corporations from Liability	

Case Name	Citation	Holding	Conservative Interest	Judicial Principle Disregarded
Winter v. Natural Resources Defense Council	555 U.S. 7 (2008)	Invalidated an injunction to halt a naval training exercise despite its projected irreparable harm to marine life.	Protecting Corporations from Liability: Letting Polluters Pollute	
Plains Commerce Bank v. Long Family Land and Cattle Co.	554 U.S. 316 (2008)	Made it more difficult for Native American plaintiffs to challenge discriminatory conduct by banks.	Restricting Civil Rights & Condoning Discrimination	
District of Columbia v. Heller	554 U.S. 570 (2008)	Drastically expanded the scope of the Second Amendment and limited commonsense gun regulation.	Advancing a Far-Right Social Agenda	**Originalism & Stare Decisis**, *see* 554 U.S. at 637 (Stevens, J., dissenting) **Judicial Restraint**, *see* 554 U.S. at 680 (Stevens, J., dissenting)
Bartlett v. Strickland	556 U.S. 1 (2009)	Held that the Voting Rights Act does not require state officials in certain circumstances to redraw election district lines to help allow racial minority groups elect a candidate of their choice.	Controlling the Political Process: Voter Suppression	
14 Penn Plaza v. Pyett	556 U.S. 247 (2009)	Diminished employees' access to the federal courts and skewed employment agreements in favor of employers through mandatory arbitration.	Protecting Corporations from Liability: Restricting Individual's Access to Courts	**Stare Decisis**, *see* 556 U.S. at 274 (Stevens, J., dissenting); *see also id.* at 281 (Souter, J., dissenting) **Judicial Restraint**, *see* 556 U.S. at 277 (Stevens, J., dissenting)
Ashcroft v. Iqbal	556 U.S. 662 (2009)	Heightened the civil pleading standard, making it more difficult for plaintiffs to sue in federal court.	Protecting Corporations from Liability: Restricting Individual's Access to Courts	
Summers v. Earth Island Institute	555 U.S. 488 (2009)	Restricted the right of environmental groups to sue over environmental violations.	Protecting Corporations from Liability: Letting Polluters Pollute	

Case Name	Citation	Holding	Conservative Interest	Judicial Principle Disregarded
Entergy v. Riverkeeper	556 U.S. 208 (2009)	Ignored the Clean Water Act's mandate that power plants use the "Best Technology Available" to protect fish and aquatic life, allowing them to use less-costly, less-effective devices.	Protecting Corporations from Liability: Letting Polluters Pollute	
Gross v. FBL Financial Services	557 U.S. 167 (2009)	Heightened the standard for age discrimination claims and made it more difficult for victims to obtain relief.	Restricting Civil Rights & Condoning Discrimination	**Judicial Restraint,** *see* 557 U.S. at 190 (Stevens, J., dissenting)
District Attorney's Office for the Third Judicial District v. Osborne	557 U.S. 52 (2009)	Held that the Due Process Clause does not require states to turn over DNA evidence to a plaintiff post-conviction.	Restricting Civil Rights & Condoning Discrimination	
Horne v. Flores	557 U.S. 433 (2009)	Diminished minority students' access to English as a Second Language programs.	Restricting Civil Rights & Condoning Discrimination	**Aversion to Fact Finding,** *see* 557 U.S. at 513-14 (Breyer, J., dissenting)
Ricci v. Destefano	557 U.S. 557 (2009)	Distorted federal civil rights law to promote the disproportionate exclusion of minority groups from career advancement.	Restricting Civil Rights & Condoning Discrimination	
Citizens United v. FEC	558 U.S. 310 (2010)	Opened the door to special interests and lobbyists influencing American politics through unlimited corporate spending.	Controlling the Political Process: Dark Money	**Originalism, Textualism, & Judicial Restraint** 558 U.S. at 948 (Stevens, J., dissenting)
Conkright v. Frommert 5–3 (Sotomayor Recused)	559 U.S. 506 (2010)	Held that courts are required to defer to a trust administrator's exercise of discretion even when the trustee's previous construction of the same terms was found to violate ERISA.	Protecting Corporations from Liability	

Case Name	Citation	Holding	Conservative Interest	Judicial Principle Disregarded
Stolt-Nielsen S.A. v. AnimalFeeds International Corp. 5–3 (Sotomayor Recused)	559 U.S. 662 (2010)	Restricted plaintiffs from using class arbitration (similar to a class action lawsuit) unless all parties specifically agree to it.	Protecting Corporations from Liability: Restricting Individual's Access to Courts	
Rent-A-Center, West, Inc. v. Jackson	561 U.S. 63 (2010)	Diminished employees' access to the federal courts and skewed arbitration agreements in favor of employers over employees.	Protecting Corporations from Liability: Restricting Individual's Access to Courts	
Perdue v. Kenny A.	559 U.S. 542 (2010)	Heightened the standards for civil rights plaintiffs' attorneys to receive compensation for their services.	Protecting Corporations from Liability: Restricting Individual's Access to Courts	**Aversion to Fact Finding**, *see* 559 U.S. at 572 (Breyer, J., dissenting)
McDonald v. Chicago	561 U.S. 742 (2010)	Continued the expansion of Second Amendment rights and made it more difficult for states to implement gun regulations.	Advancing a Far-Right Social Agenda	**Originalism**, *see* 561 U.S. at 912 (Breyer, J., dissenting)
Salazar v. Buono	559 U.S. 700 (2010)	Allowed a cross to stay on federal property, chipping away at the separation of church and state.	Advancing a Far-Right Social Agenda	
Arizona Free Enterprise Club's Freedom Club PAC v. Bennett	564 U.S. 721 (2011)	Struck down Arizona law restricting PACs and dark money sources from funding political candidates without limit.	Controlling the Political Process: Dark Money	**Originalism**, *see* 564 U.S. at 757, 784 (Kagan, J., dissenting) **Stare Decisis**, *see* 564 U.S. at 776–77 (Kagan, J., dissenting)
Schindler Elevator Corp. v. U.S. ex rel. Kirk 5–3 (Kagan Recused)	563 U.S. 401 (2011)	Limited the ability of plaintiffs to bring suit as whistleblowers on behalf of the government.	Protecting Corporations from Liability: Restricting Individual's Access to Courts	
AT&T Mobility v. Concepcion	563 U.S. 333 (2011)	Reduced consumers' ability to bring class-action claims against corporations for low-dollar, high-volume frauds.	Protecting Corporations from Liability: Restricting Individual's Access to Courts	**Federalism**, *see* 564 U.S. at 357, 367 (Breyer, J., dissenting)

Case Name	Citation	Holding	Conservative Interest	Judicial Principle Disregarded
Janus Capital Group v. First Derivative Traders	564 U.S. 135 (2011)	Heightened the pleading bar in private securities fraud cases seeking to hold defendants liable for the misstatements of their companies or others. Held that SEC liability was limited to individuals or entities with "ultimate authority" over the misstatements, regardless of who contributed to those statements.	Protecting Corporations from Liability: Restricting Individual's Access to Courts	Textualism, *see* 564 U.S. at 150-51 (Breyer, J., dissenting)
Wal-Mart Stores v. Dukes	564 U.S. 338 (2011)	Limited the ability of individuals to bring class-action lawsuits.	Protecting Corporations from Liability: Restricting Individual's Access to Courts	
Pliva v. Mensing	564 U.S. 604 (2011)	Preempted state law tort claims against generic drug makers who failed to warn consumers about dangerous side effects.	Protecting Corporations from Liability	Federalism, *see* 564 U.S. at 627 (Sotomayor, J., dissenting)
Chamber of Commerce of U.S. v. Whiting 5–3 (Kagan Recused)	563 U.S. 582 (2011)	Allowed states to pass laws that target immigrant workers.	Restricting Civil Rights & Condoning Discrimination	
Connick v. Thompson	563 U.S. 51 (2011)	Made it harder to hold prosecutors' offices liable for the illegal misconduct of individual prosecutors.	Restricting Civil Rights & Condoning Discrimination	Aversion to Fact Finding, *see* 563 U.S. at 94 (Ginsburg, J., dissenting)
Arizona Christian School Tuition Organization v. Winn	563 U.S. 125 (2011)	Made it harder for plaintiffs to challenge Establishment Clause violations in court, chipping away at the separation of church and state.	Advancing a Far-Right Social Agenda	Stare Decisis, *see* 563 U.S. at 147-48 (citing *Flast v. Cohen*) (Kagan, J., dissenting) Originalism, *see* 563 U.S. at 168-69 (Kagan, J., dissenting)

Case Name	Citation	Holding	Conservative Interest	Judicial Principle Disregarded
American Tradition Partnership v. Bullock	567 U.S. 516 (2012)	Struck down Montana statute regulating independent corporate expenditures on behalf of candidates, allowing special interests and lobbyists to influence American politics through money.	Controlling the Political Process: Dark Money	Federalism, see 567 U.S. at 517 (Breyer, J., dissenting)
F.A.A. v. Cooper 5–3 (Kagan Recused)	566 U.S. 284 (2012)	Made it more difficult for plaintiffs to recover for intangible harms caused by government privacy violations.	Protecting Corporations from Liability: Restricting Individual's Access to Courts	Textualism, see 566 U.S. at 306-07 (Sotomayor, J., dissenting)
Coleman v. Court of Appeals of Maryland	566 U.S. 30 (2012)	Limited plaintiffs from bringing suits against states for denying them sick leave under the Family Medical Leave Act.	Protecting Corporations from Liability: Restricting Individual's Access to Courts	
Christopher v. SmithKline Beecham	567 U.S. 142 (2012)	Expanded fair wage exemptions under the Fair Labor Standards Act, depriving certain categories of workers of statutory fair pay protections.	Protecting Corporations from Liability	
Florence v. Board of Chosen Freeholders of County of Burlington	566 U.S. 318 (2012)	Allowed strip searches of inmates without reasonable suspicion, reducing the Fourth Amendment protections of arrestees.	Restricting Civil Rights & Condoning Discrimination	
Shelby County v. Holder	570 U.S. 529 (2013)	Invalidated sections of the Voting Rights Act, making it easier for states with a history of racial discrimination to pass discriminatory voting laws.	Controlling the Political Process: Voter Suppression	Originalism, see 570 U.S. at 567 (Ginsburg, J., dissenting) Aversion to Fact Finding, Id. at 576
American Exp. Co. v. Italian Colors Restaurant 5–3 (Sotomayor Recused)	570 U.S. 228 (2013)s	Diminished employees' access to the federal courts and skewed employment agreements in favor of employers.	Protecting Corporations from Liability: Restricting Individual's Access to Courts	Stare Decisis, see 570 U.S. at 240, 247 (Kagan, J., dissenting)

Case Name	Citation	Holding	Conservative Interest	Judicial Principle Disregarded
Comcast v. Behrend	569 U.S. 27 (2013)	Made class action certification more difficult and limited suits against corporations for low-dollar, high-volume antitrust violations.	Protecting Corporations from Liability: Restricting Individual's Access to Courts	Aversion to Fact Finding, *see* 569 U.S. at 46 (Ginsburg & Breyer, Js., dissenting)
Genesis Healthcare v. Symczk	569 U.S. 66 (2013)	Limited plaintiffs' ability to bring collective action claims under the Fair Labor Standards Act.	Protecting Corporations from Liability: Restricting Individual's Access to Courts	Judicial Restraint, *see* 569 U.S. at 79 (Kagan, J., dissenting)
Mutual Pharmaceutical v. Bartlett	133 S. Ct. 2466 (2013)	Limited plaintiffs' ability to sue generic drug manufactures under state law for failure to adequately label medication.	Protecting Corporations from Liability	Federalism, *see* 133 S. Ct. at 2482 (Breyer, J., dissenting)
Koontz v. St. Johns River Water Management District	570 U.S. 595 (2013)	Deprived local and state governments of the flexibility to ensure environmentally sound and economically productive development.	Protecting Corporations from Liability: Letting Polluters Pollute	Federalism, *see* 570 U.S. at 635-36 (Kagan, J., dissenting)
Vance v. Ball State University	570 U.S. 421 (2013)	Made it harder for plaintiffs to bring workplace harassment claims.	Restricting Civil Rights & Condoning Discrimination	
University of Texas Southwestern Medical Center v. Nassar	570 U.S. 338 (2013)	Increased the standard of proof for employer retaliation claims, making these claims more difficult to bring.	Restricting Civil Rights & Condoning Discrimination	
Clapper v. Amnesty International	568 U.S. 398 (2013)	Blocked plaintiffs' access to the courtroom even if they claim a reasonable likelihood that their communications will be illegally intercepted by the government under FISA surveillance.	Restricting Civil Rights & Condoning Discrimination	
McCutcheon v. FEC	572 U.S. 185 (2014)	Created a loophole that allows a single individual to donate millions of dollars to a political party or campaign.	Controlling the Political Process: Dark Money	Originalism, Textualism, Stare Decisis, & Judicial Restraint, *see* 572 U.S. at 232 (Breyer, J., dissenting)

Case Name	Citation	Holding	Conservative Interest	Judicial Principle Disregarded
Harris v. Quinn	134 S. Ct. 2618 (2014)	Weakened public sector unions and took a major step toward overturning public sector fee collection from all non-union members in another 5-4 decision, Janus v. AFSCME.	Controlling the Political Process: Union Busting	**Invitation to Challenge Precedent,** *see* 134 S. Ct. at 669 (citing *Abood v. Detroit Board of Education*) (Kagan, J., dissenting)
Town of Greece v. Galloway	572 U.S. 565 (2014)	Allowed legislative prayer even when a town fails to represent a variety of religions in its meetings.	Advancing a Far-Right Social Agenda	**Originalism,** *see* 572 U.S. at 619-21 (Kagan, J., dissenting)
Burwell v. Hobby Lobby Stores	573 U.S. 682 (2014)	Permitted corporations to deny contraception based on objections to facially neutral, non-discriminatory laws.	Advancing a Far-Right Social Agenda	**Originalism,** *see* 573 U.S. at 740 (Ginsburg, J., dissenting) **Stare Decisis,** *Id.* at 744 (citing *Employment Div., Dept. of Human Resources of Ore. v. Smith*) **Judicial Restraint,** *Id.* at 746
Michigan v. EPA	135 S. Ct. 2699 (2015)	Limited EPA's ability to regulate power plants by requiring it to consider cost at every stage of the regulatory process, impeding the agency's ability to pursue aggressive public health and environmental priorities.	Protecting Corporations from Liability: Letting Polluters Pollute	
Glossip v. Gross 5–3 (Vacancy)	135 S. Ct. 2726 (2015)	Made challenging execution methods more difficult and thus limited prisoners' Eighth Amendment rights.	Restricting Civil Rights & Condoning Discrimination	
California Public Employees' Retirement System v. Anz Securities	137 S. Ct. 2042 (2017)	Made it harder for individual investors to protect their rights via class action.	Protecting Corporations from Liability: Restricting Individual's Access to Courts	
Abbott v. Perez	138 S. Ct. 2305 (2018)	Allowed the use of electoral maps that a lower court determined had been drawn with discriminatory intent.	Controlling the Political Process: Voter Suppression	**Stare Decisis & Aversion to Fact Finding,** *see* 138 S. Ct. at 2235-36 (Sotomayor, J., dissenting)

Case Name	Citation	Holding	Conservative Interest	Judicial Principle Disregarded
Husted v. A. Phillip Randolph Institute	138 S. Ct. 1833 (2018)	Allowed Ohio to purge voter rolls in a way that disproportionately affects minority voters.	Controlling the Political Process: Voter Suppression	
Janus v. AFSCME	138 S. Ct. 2448 (2018)	Overturned a 40-year-old precedent allowing public sector unions to collect fair share fees.	Controlling the Political Process: Union Busting	**Stare Decisis & Judicial Restraint,** *see* 138 S. Ct. at 2487 (citing *Abood v. Detroit Board of Education*) (Kagan, J., dissenting)
Epic Systems v. Lewis	138 S. Ct. 1612 (2018)	Prohibited workers from banding together to redress workplace violations including sexual harassment, racial discrimination, and wage theft.	Protecting Corporations from Liability: Restricting Individual's Access to Courts	**Judicial Restraint,** *see* Garrett Epps, *An Epic Supreme Court Decision on Employment,* ATLANTIC (May 22, 2018) (noting "[t]his is a judge-made policy invention, reflecting conservative justices' empathy for corporations. . .")
Jesner v. Arab Bank	138 S. Ct. 1386 (2018)	Held that foreign corporations may not be sued under the Alien Tort Statute, protecting them from liability for human rights abuses.	Protecting Corporations from Liability: Restricting Individual's Access to Courts	
Encino Motorcars v. Navarro	138 S. Ct. 1134 (2018)	Expanded exemptions from the Fair Labor Standards Act and deprived certain categories of workers of statutory fair pay protections.	Protecting Corporations from Liability	
Wisconsin Central Ltd. v. United States	138 S. Ct. 2067 (2018)	Ruled that railroad executives are exempt from federal employment taxes on stock-based compensation.	Protecting Corporations from Liability	
Ohio v. American Express	138 S. Ct. 2274 (2018)	Held that federal antitrust laws do not prohibit corporate "anti-steering" provisions, allowing credit cards to prevent merchants from steering customers toward alternative payment methods.	Protecting Corporations from Liability	**Aversion to Fact-Finding,** *see* 138 S. Ct. at 2303-05 (Breyer, J., dissenting)

Case Name	Citation	Holding	Conservative Interest	Judicial Principle Disregarded
Jennings v. Rodriguez 5–3 (Kagan Recused)	138 S. Ct. 830 (2018)	Allowed immigrants to be detained for prolonged periods of time without a bail hearing.	Restricting Civil Rights & Condoning Discrimination	Originalism, *see* 138 S. Ct. at 863, 866, 869 (Breyer, J., dissenting)
Murphy v. Smith	138 S. Ct. 784 (2018)	Reduced compensation for prisoners when government officials violate their constitutional rights.	Restricting Civil Rights & Condoning Discrimination	
Trump v. Hawaii	138 S. Ct. 2392 (2018)	Allowed the discriminatory Muslim ban to go into effect and restricted immigration from eight, mostly Muslim-majority, countries.	Restricting Civil Rights & Condoning Discrimination	Originalism & Stare Decisis, *see* 138 S. Ct. at 2433 (Sotomayor, J., dissenting)
NIFLA v. Becerra	138 S. Ct. 2361 (2018)	Struck down a California law mandating disclosure related to available medical services for pregnant women, potentially deceiving women into believing that anti-abortion pregnancy centers are medical clinics.	Advancing a Far-Right Social Agenda	
Nielsen v. Preap	139 S. Ct. 954 (2019)	Expanded executive branch powers to detain aliens without hearing on flight risk or dangerousness. Advanced Republican anti-immigrant agenda through contorted and atextual statutory analysis.	Restricting Civil Rights & Condoning Discrimination	
Bucklew v. Precythe	139 S. Ct. 1112 (2019)	Further extending Glossip v. Gross, above, making civil challenges of execution methods more difficult and thus limiting prisoners' Eighth Amendment rights.	Restricting Civil Rights & Condoning Discrimination	
Lamps Plus Inc. v. Varela	139 S. Ct. 1407 (2019)	Pro-corporate arbitration ruling, raising the standard for plaintiffs to show a defendant consented to class arbitration.	Protecting Corporations from Liability: Restricting Individual's Access to Courts	

Case Name	Citation	Holding	Conservative Interest	Judicial Principle Disregarded
Franchise Tax Board of California v. Hyatt	139 S. Ct. 1485 (2019)	Overruled long-standing pro-plaintiff precedent Nevada v. Hall and limited the ability of injured plaintiffs to sue states.	Protecting Corporations from Liability: Restricting Individual's Access to Courts	
Manhattan Community Access Corp. v. Halleck	139 S. Ct. 1921 (2019)	Held that a public access station was not considered a state actor for purposes of evaluating free speech claims. Limited relief for plaintiffs, expounding a property-interest-focused view of state action that advances the libertarian project to elevate property rights.	Protecting Corporations from Liability: Restricting Individual's Access to Courts	
Knick v. Township of Scott, Pennsylvania	139 S. Ct. 2162 (2019)	Denied states and local courts the first say in disputes over "just compensation" for landowners.	Protecting Corporations from Liability: Restricting Individual's Access to Courts	
Rucho v. Common Cause	139 S. Ct. 2484 (2019)	Greenlit partisan gerrymandering through selective invocation of the political question doctrine.	Controlling the Political Process: Voter Suppression	
F.C.C. v. Fox Television Stations, Inc.	556 U.S. 502 (2009)	Upheld a Federal Communications Commission regulation that bans "fleeting expletives" on television broadcast.	No Presently Identified Donor Interest	
Free Enterprise Fund v. Public Co. Accounting Oversight Board	561 U.S. 477 (2010)	Struck down the dual layer of "for cause" protection against presidential removal for PCAOB members.	No Presently Identified Donor Interest	
Stern v. Marshall	564 U.S. 462 (2011)	Held that bankruptcy courts lack the constitutional authority under Article III to enter a final judgment on a state law counterclaim.	No Presently Identified Donor Interest	

Case Name	Citation	Holding	Conservative Interest	Judicial Principle Disregarded
Kerry v. Din	135 S. Ct. 2128 (2015)	Held that the government is not required to give an explanation for denying an alien's visa based on terrorism-related grounds under the Immigration and Nationality Act.	No Presently Identified Donor Interest	
SAS Institute v. Iancu	138 S. Ct. 1348 (2018)	Held that when the United States Patent and Trademark Office institutes a review to reconsider an already-issued patent, it must rule on the patentability of all claims the petitioner challenges.	No Presently Identified Donor Interest	

Appendix B

Amicus Briefs filed by Senator Sheldon Whitehouse

UNLIKE MANY OF THE DONORS DISCUSSED IN THIS book, when I make an argument to the Court, I put my name on it. This list shows every "friend of the court" brief I have filed in the Supreme Court and in other cases discussed in this book. They are available to read in full at whitehouse.senate.gov or at scotusblog.com.

Case	Date Filed	Submitters	Counsel of Record	Decision
American Tradition Partnership v. Bullock	May 2012	Sheldon Whitehouse John McCain	Neal Kumar Katyal	567 U.S. 516 (2012)
Bank Markazi v. Peterson	December 2015	United States Senate	Patricia Mack Bryan	136 S. Ct. 1310 (2016)
U.S. v. Texas	March 2016	Sheldon Whitehouse and 186 Members of the U.S. House and 38 Members of the U.S. Senate	Seth P. Waxman	136 S. Ct. 2271 (2016)
Jesner v. Arab Bank PLC	Nov. 14, 2016	Sheldon Whitehouse	Peter Margulies	138 S.Ct. 1386 (2018)
Gill v. Whitford	September 2017	Sheldon Whitehouse John McCain	Mark W. Mosier	138 S. Ct. 1916 (2018)
Janus v. AFSCME	January 2018	Sheldon Whitehouse Jon Tester Richard Blumenthal	Peter Karanjia	138 S. Ct. 2448 (2018)
New Prime v. Oliveira	July 25, 2018	Sheldon Whitehouse	Sheldon Whitehouse	139 S. Ct. 532 (2019)

Case	Date Filed	Submitters	Counsel of Record	Decision
Kisor v. Wilke	March 4, 2019	Sheldon Whitehouse	Sheldon Whitehouse	139 S. Ct. 2400 (2019)
Rucho v. Common Cause	March 2019	Sheldon Whitehouse	Mark W. Mosier	139 S. Ct. 2484 (2019)
CREW v. FEC	April 24, 2019	Sheldon Whitehouse Jon Tester Richard Blumenthal	Jennifer R. Cowan	971 F.3d 340, 351 (D.C. Cir. 2020)
Lieu v. FEC	June 28, 2019	Sheldon Whitehouse Richard Blumenthal Mazie Hirono	Jennifer R. Cowan	370 F. Supp. 3d 175 (D.D.C. 2019)
N.Y. State Rifle & Pistol Assoc. v. City of N.Y.	Aug. 12, 2019	Sheldon Whitehouse Mazie Hirono Richard Blumenthal Richard Durbin Kirsten Gillibrand	Sheldon Whitehouse	140 S. Ct. 1525 (2020)
Kelly v. U.S.	Nov. 27, 2019	Sheldon Whitehouse	Michael Dominic Meuti	140 S. Ct. 1565 (2020)
Seila Law v. CFPB	Jan. 22, 2020	Sheldon Whitehouse Richard Blumenthal Mazie Hirono	Stephen D. Susman	140 S. Ct. 2183 (2020)
Lieu v. FEC	July 22, 2020	Sheldon Whitehouse Patrick Leahy Tom Udall Richard Blumenthal Mazie Hirono Chris Van Hollen	David A. O'Neil	141 S. Ct. 814 (2020)
BP P.L.C. v. Mayor and City Council of Baltimore	Dec. 23, 2020	Sheldon Whitehouse Ben Cardin Richard Blumenthal Elizabeth Warren Edward J. Markey Chris Van Hollen	Gerson H. Smoger	141 S. Ct. 1532 (2021)
Cedar Point Nursery v. Hassid	Jan. 24, 2021	Sheldon Whitehouse Jeff Merkley Richard Blumenthal Cory Booker Alex Padilla	Glenn Rothner	141 S. Ct. 2063 (2021)

Case	Date Filed	Submitters	Counsel of Record	Decision
Americans for Prosperity Foundation v. Bonta	March 31, 2021	Sheldon Whitehouse Patrick Leahy Ron Wyden Richard J. Durbin Amy Klobuchar Jeffrey A. Merkley Christopher A. Coons Richard Blumenthal Tammy Baldwin Mazie K. Hirono Elizabeth Warren Edward J. Markey Cory A. Booker Chris Van Hollen Tammy Duckworth	Daniel P. Chiplock	141 S. Ct. 2373 (2021)
West Virginia v. EPA	Jan 24, 2022	Sheldon Whitehouse Richard Blumenthal Bernie Sanders Elizabeth Warren	Erwin Chemerinsky	

Appendix C

Whitehouse Brief Appendix: Overlapping Amici Funders in Seila Law

WE TRIED TO ALERT THE COURT TO HOW some donors were abusing its amicus system in this appendix to our 2020 brief in *Seila Law v. CFPB*.

We told the Court, "These amicus briefs may appear to be a broad outpouring of support for a legal position, but publicly available information gleaned elsewhere suggests them to be an echo chamber funded by a small and powerful cabal of self-interested entities."

	DonorsTrust	Lynde and Harry Bradley Foundation	Sarah Scaife Foundation	Searle Freedom Trust	Charles Koch Foundation	F.M. Kirby Foundation	William Donner Foundation
Center for Constitutional Jurisprudence (Claremount Institute)	X	X	X	X			X
Pacific Legal Foundation	X		X	X			
Southeastern Legal Foundation	X	X	X				
National Federation of Independent Business Small Business Legal Center	X	X					
Washington Legal Foundation	X	X				X	

	DonorsTrust	Lynde and Harry Bradley Foundation	Sarah Scaife Foundation	Searle Freedom Trust	Charles Koch Foundation	F.M. Kirby Foundation	William Donner Foundation
Cato Institute	X	X			X		
Landmark Legal Foundation	X	X	X			X	
New Civil Liberties Alliance	X	X	X	X	X		
Buckeye Institute	X			X			
Competitive Enterprise Institute (CEI)	X	X	X	X	X		X
60 Plus Association	X						

Appendix D

Wharton Analysis of Corporate Funding Disclosure

DESPITE MORE THAN A DECADE OF SHAREHOLDER EFFORTS to find out how their money is being spent, more than half the companies in the S&P 500 Index still do not disclose their donations to 501(c)(4) groups. This chart is based on research reported in November 2021 by the Center for Political Accountability and the Zicklin Center for Business Ethics Research at the University of Pennsylvania's Wharton School of Business.

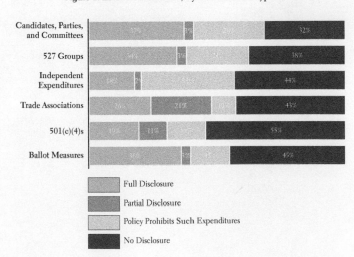

Figure 1: Levels of Disclosure, by Contribution Type

Notes

Introduction

1. Robert O'Harrow Jr. and Shawn Boburg, "A Conservative Activist's Behind-the-Scenes Campaign to Remake the Nation's Courts," *Washington Post*, May 21, 2019; "What's Wrong with the Supreme Court: The Big-Money Assault on Our Judiciary," Hearing Before the United States Senate Committee on the Judiciary Subcommittee on Federal Courts, Oversight, Agency Action and Federal Rights, 117th Cong. 6 (March 10, 2021) (testimony of Lisa Graves, president of the Center for Media and Democracy); True North Research, "Leonard Leo's Court Capture Web Raised Nearly $600 Million Before Biden Won; Now It's Spending Untold Millions from Secret Sources to Attack Judge Ketanji Brown Jackson," March 22, 2022, truenorthresearch.org/2022/03/leonard-leos-court-capture-web-raised-nearly-600-million-before-biden-won-now-its-spending-untold-millions-from-secret-sources-to-attack-judge-ketanji-brown-jackson/.

2. Ruth Marcus, "Opinion: The Rule of Six: A Newly Radicalized Supreme Court Is Poised to Reshape the Nation," *Wash. Post* (Nov. 28, 2021).

3. *See, e.g.*, The Committee on Federal Criminal Jury Instructions for the Seventh Circuit, *Pattern Criminal Federal Jury Instructions for the Seventh Circuit* 6 (1998).

4. Brief of Senators Sheldon Whitehouse, Richard Blumenthal, Bernie Sanders, and Elizabeth Warren as Amici Curiae in Support of Respondents, Cedar Point Nursery v. Hassid, No. 20-107, 141 S. Ct. 2063 (2021).

5. Martin Gilens and Benjamin Page, "Testing Theories of American Politics: Elites, Interest Groups, and Average Citizens," *Perspectives on Politics*, Vol. 12, Is. 3, 564-581 (Sept. 2014).

6. AP-NORC Center, "Views on Power and Influence in Washington" (June 2017).

7. Mark Mellman, *Winning Messages: On Judges, Guns and Owning the Constitution's Text, History & Values*, Constitutional Accountability Ctr. 9 (Feb. 29, 2020), https://www.theusconstitution.org/wp-content/uploads/2018/03/PUBLIC-Mellman-CAC-Poll-Presentation.pdf [https://perma.cc/BA53-DNAE].

Chapter One: Climate Denial, Regulatory Capture, and Covert Ops

1. *See* Edward Fitzpatrick, "Senator Whitehouse Delivers 279th and Final 'Time to Wake Up' Climate Change Speech," *Boston Globe* (Jan. 27, 2009).

2. "Total Outside Spending by Election Cycle, Excluding Party Committees," *OpenSecrets*, https://www.opensecrets.org/outsidespending/cycle_tots.php (last visited Feb. 3, 2022).

3. Ian Parry et al., *Still Not Getting Energy Prices Right: A Global and Country Update of Fossil Fuel Subsidies* 26 (International Monetary Fund, Working Paper 21/236, 2021).

4. "What's Wrong with the Supreme Court: The Big-Money Assault on Our Judiciary," Hearing Before the United States Senate Committee on the Judiciary Subcommittee on Federal Courts, Oversight, Agency Action and Federal Rights, 117th Cong. 6 (2021) (testimony of Lisa Graves, president of the Center for Media and Democracy).

5. *See, e.g.*, J. Jonas Anderson, "Court Capture," 59 *B.C. L. Rev.* 1543, 1555 (2018).

6. "CIA Chief Historian David Robarge on Pivotal Global Events— 'Intelligence Matters,'" *CBS News*, Oct. 13, 2021.

Chapter Two: Of Courts and Corporations

1. Benjamin N. Cardozo, *The Nature of the Judicial Process* 8 (1921).

2. *The Federalist* No. 51 (James Madison).

3. *The Federalist* No. 27 (Alexander Hamilton), Nos. 10, 57 (James Madison).

4. Ruth Marcus, "Opinion: The Rule of Six: A Newly Radicalized Supreme Court Is Poised to Reshape the Nation," *Wash. Post* (Nov. 28, 2021).

5. "Supreme Court Cases, October Term 2019–2020," *Ballotpedia* (reporting an average of seventy-six cases a year between 2007 and 2019).

6. Planned Parenthood of Southeastern Pa. v. Casey, 505 U.S. 833 (1992).

7. "Nomination of the Honorable Amy Coney Barrett to Be an Associate Justice of the Supreme Court of the United States (Day 2)," Hearing Before the S. Comm. on the Judiciary, 116th Cong. (Oct. 13, 2020) (statement of nominee Amy Coney Barrett).

8. Benjamin N. Cardozo, *The Nature of the Judicial Process* 141 (1921).

9. *The Federalist* No. 78 (Alexander Hamilton).

10. Benjamin N. Cardozo, *The Nature of the Judicial Process* 9 (1921).

11. James Madison, *I Annals of Cong.* 454 (June 8, 1789).

12. 4 William Blackstone, *Commentaries* *350; 3 William Blackstone, *Commentaries* *380.

13. 3 William Blackstone, *Commentaries* *380.

14. *The Federalist* No. 83 (Alexander Hamilton).

15. Theodore Roosevelt, U.S. President, State of the Union Address (Dec. 3, 1907).

16. Marshall v. Baltimore & Ohio Railroad Co., 57 U.S. 314 (1853).

17. 3 William Blackstone, *Commentaries* *380.

18. Grover Cleveland, President of the U.S., State of the Union Address (Dec. 3, 1888).

19. Theodore Roosevelt, President of the U.S., Fifth Annual Message (Dec. 5, 1905).

20. Theodore Roosevelt, "The New Nationalist," Speech at John Brown Memorial Park (Aug. 31, 1910).

21. Standard Oil Co. of NJ v. US, 221 US 1, 83 (1901) (Harlan, J., concurring in part and dissenting in part).

22. Louis K. Liggett Co. v. Lee, 288 US 517, 549 (1933) (Brandeis, J., dissenting).

Chapter Three: Of Social Gains and Election Losses

1. Heart of Atlanta Motel, Inc. v. United States, 379 U.S. 241 (1964).

2. Reynolds v. Sims, 377 U.S. 522 (1964).

3. Harper v. Virginia State Bd. of Elections, 383 U.S. 663 (1966).

4. Mapp v. Ohio, 367 U.S. 643 (1961).

5. Brady v. Maryland, 373 U.S. 83 (1963).

6. Gideon v. Wainwright, 372 U.S. 335 (1963).

7. *Ibid.* at 799.

8. Nancy MacLean, *Democracy in Chains* 176 (2017).

9. *See* William Greider, "The Education of David Stockman," *The Atlantic,* Editor's Note (Dec. 1, 1981); David Stockman, *The Triumph of Politics: Why the Reagan Revolution Failed* (1986), *quoted in* MacLean, *Democracy in Chains,* 176.

10. MacLean, *Democracy in Chains* at 175.

11. *Ibid.* at 177.

12. *Ibid.*

13. Jack Nelson, "Conservatives' Goals Tied to Judicial Appointments," *LA Times* (Mar. 18, 1986).

14. Linda Greenhouse, "Playing the Long Game for the Supreme Court," *N.Y. Times* (Oct. 25, 2018).

Chapter Four: The Plan: The Powell Memo

1. Jim Newton, "'Influence Machine' Reveals How U.S. Chamber of Commerce Oils the Engine of Politics," *LA Times* (July 2, 2015).

2. Confidential Memorandum from Lewis F. Powell Jr. to Eugene D. Sydor Jr., Chairman of the Educ. Comm., U.S. Chamber of Com. (Aug. 23, 1971), *available at* https://scholarlycommons.law.wlu.edu/powellmemo/1 ("Powell Memo").

3. Joan Biskupic and Fred Barbash, "Retired Justice Powell Dies at 90," *Wash. Post* (Aug. 26, 1998).

4. Powell Memo at 1.

5. *Ibid.*

6. *Ibid.* at 6–8.

7. *Ibid.* at 10.

8. *Ibid.* at 2–3.
9. *Ibid.* at 4–6.
10. *Ibid.* at 8.
11. *Ibid.* at 9.
12. *Ibid.*
13. *Ibid.* at 24.
14. *Ibid.* at 25.
15. *Ibid.* at 16–17.
16. *Ibid.* at 18.
17. *Ibid.* at 18–19.
18. *Ibid.* at 21.
19. *Ibid.* at 24.
20. *Ibid.* at 30.
21. *Ibid.* at 25.
22. *Ibid.* at 26.
23. *Ibid.*
24. *Ibid.* at 26–27.
25. *Ibid.*
26. *Ibid.* at 11.
27. *Ibid.*
28. *Ibid.* at 19.
29. *Ibid.* at 24.
30. *Ibid.* at 34.

Chapter Five: Building the Influence Machine: Campaign Finance Cases

1. Roe v. Wade, 410 U.S. 113 (1973); Regents of Univ. of Cal. v. Bakke, 438 U.S. 265 (1978); United States v. Nixon, 418 U.S. 683 (1974).

2. McConnell v. FEC, 540 U.S. 93, 224 (2003).

3. Gaspee Project v. Mederos, 13 F.4th 79, 88 (2021) (1st Cir. 2021) (internal quotes omitted).

4. Brief of Senators Sheldon Whitehouse, Richard Blumenthal, and Mazie Hirono as *Amici Curiae* in Support of Petitioners at 21, Top of Form Lieu v. FEC, 370 F. Supp. 3d 175 (D.D.C. 2019), *cert denied* 141 S. Ct. at 814.

5. Maurice Cunningham, "Koch Connections and Sham Grassroots of Parents Defending Education," *MassPoliticsProfs* (Apr. 12, 2021).

6. Maurice Cunningham, "Phony Parent Groups Lead Attacks on Critical Race Theory," *DianeRavitch.net* (July 31, 2021).

7. Joe Hagan, "The Coming Tsunami of Slime," *N.Y. Mag.* (Jan. 20, 2012).

8. Karl Evers-Hillstrom, "Most Expensive Ever: 2020 Election Cost $14.4 Billion," *OpenSecrets* (Feb. 11, 2021).

9. Richard L. Hasen, "The Untold Drafting History of Buckley v. Valeo." 2 *Election L. J.* 241, 241 (2004).

10. Lawrence Lessig, Republic, *Lost: How Money Corrupts Congress—and a Plan to Stop It* 99–100 (2011).

11. Powell Memo at 2.

12. Conor M. Dowling and Amber Wichowsky, "Attacks Without Consequence? Candidates, Parties, Groups, and the Changing Face of Negative Advertising," 59 *Am. J. Pol. Sci.* 19, 24–35 (2015); *see also* McConnell v. FEC, 540 U.S. 93 (2003).

13. Powell Memo at 30.

14. Sheldon Whitehouse, U.S. Senator for Rhode Island, "The Scheme 1: The Powell Memo," Speech to the U.S. Senate (May 27, 2021).

15. Austin v. Mich. State Chamber of Commerce, 494 U.S. 652, 660 (1990).

16. *See* McConnell v. FEC, 540 U.S. 93, 124 (2003).

17. Timothy P. O'Neill, "'The Stepford Justices': The Need for Experiential Diversity on the Roberts Court," 60 *Okla. L. Rev.* 701, 702 (2007).

18. *See* FEC v. Wis. Right to Life, Inc., 551 U.S. 449 (2007); "The Impact of FEC v. Wisconsin Right to Life, Inc. on State Regulation of 'Electioneering Communications' in Candidate Elections, Including Campaigns for the Bench," Brennan Ctr. for Justice (Feb. 2008).

19. John Schwarz, "Farewell to Anthony Kennedy, Author of Some of the Most Ludicrous Pronouncements in Supreme Court History," *The Intercept* (June 28, 2018).

20. Trevor Potter, "The Failed Promise of Unlimited 'Independent' Spending in Elections," *ABA Hum. Rts. Mag.* (June 25, 2020).

21. *Ibid.*

22. Dave Wasserman, "2012 National House Popular Vote Tracker," *Cook Pol. Rep.* (Nov. 2012); Karl Rove, "The GOP Targets State Legislatures," *Wall St. J.* (Mar. 4, 2010) ("He who controls redistricting controls Congress").

23. SpeechNow.org v. FEC, 599 F.3d 686 (D.C. Cir. 2010) (en banc), *cert. denied*, 562 U.S. 1003 (2010); Am. Tradition P'ship, Inc. v. Bullock, 567 U.S. 516 (2012); Lieu v. FEC, 370 F. Supp. 3d 175 (D.D.C. 2019), *cert. denied*, 141 S. Ct. 814 (2020).

Chapter Six: Mercenaries, Fringe Groups, and Lobbyists

1. "The History of Business Roundtable," *Bus. Roundtable*, https://www.busi nessroundtable.org/about-us-timeline (last visited Jan. 19, 2022).

2. Jacob S. Hacker and Paul Pierson, *Winner-Take-All Politics: How Washington Made the Rich Richer, and Turned Its Back on the Middle Class* (2010), excerpted in "The Powell Memo: A Call-to-Arms for Corporations," BillMoyers .com (Sept. 14, 2012).

3. *Lobbying Data Summary*, OpenSecrets, https://www.opensecrets.org/federal -lobbying (last visited Jan. 17, 2022).

4. Hacker and Pierson, *Winner-Take-All Politics*.

5. "Reagan and Heritage: A Unique Partnership," *Heritage Found.* (June 7, 2004); "Trump Administration Embraces Heritage Foundation Policy Recommendations," *Heritage Found.* (Jan. 23, 2018).

6. *Business-Labor-Ideology Split in PAC & Individual Donations to Candidates, Parties, Super PACs and Outside Spending Groups*, OpenSecrets, https://

www.opensecrets.org/elections-overview/business-labor-ideology-split (last visited Jan. 17, 2022).

7. Jerry Taylor, "What Changed My Mind About Climate Change?," *Bulwark* (May 21, 2019).

8. Marc Gunther, "Climate Converts: The Conservatives Who Are Switching Sides on Warming," *Yale Environment 360* (Mar. 30, 2017).

Chapter Seven: The Front Group Archipelago

1. U.S. v. Philip Morris, 449 Fed. Supp. 2d 1, 2006 WL 2380650 *934 (D.D.C. 2006).

2. U.S. v. Philip Morris, 449 Fed Supp. 2d 1, 2006 WL 2380650 at *852.

3. Wallace Ravven, "Internal Documents Reveal Tobacco Industry Strategy to Undermine Unwelcome Research," U. Cal. S.F. (Dec. 30, 2001).

4. Amanda Fallin et al., " 'To Quarterback Behind the Scenes, Third-Party Efforts': The Tobacco Industry and the Tea Party," 23 *Tobacco Control* 322, 322 (2014).

5. Robert J. Brulle, "Institutionalizing Delay: Foundation Funding and the Creation of U.S. Climate Change Counter-movement Organizations," 122 *Climatic Change* 681 (2014).

6. *Ibid.*

7. Hiroko Tabuchi, "How One Firm Drove Influence Campaigns Nationwide for Big Oil," *N.Y. Times* (Nov. 11, 2020).

8. *Ibid.*

9. *Ibid.*

10. *Ibid.*

11. Ian Parry et al., *Still Not Getting Energy Prices Right: A Global and Country Update of Fossil Fuel Subsidies* 26 (International Monetary Fund, Working Paper 21/236, 2021).

12. "Statistical Summary of 24-Month Campaign Activity of the 2019–2020 Election Cycle," U.S. Federal Election Commission (Apr. 2, 2021).

13. Jessica Rendall, "99% of Covid Deaths Are Now of Unvaccinated People, Experts Say," *CNET* (July 29, 2021).

14. Sheldon Whitehouse, U.S. Senator for Rhode Island, 98th Weekly "Time to Wake Up" Speech on Climate Change, Speech to the U.S. Senate (May 6, 2015).

15. Brief of Senator Sheldon Whitehouse, Mazie Hirono, Richard Blumenthal, Richard Durbin, and Kirsten Gillibrand as Amici Curiae in Support of Respondents, N.Y. State Rifle & Pistol Ass'n v. City of N.Y., 140 S. Ct. 1525 (2020).

16. N.Y. State Rifle & Pistol Ass'n v. City of N.Y., 140 S. Ct. 1525 (2020) (Alito, J., dissenting).

17. Todd Ruger, "Justice Alito Speech Leads to Rare Court-Congress Dialogue," *Roll Call* (Nov. 13, 2020).

18. *See* "Editorial: Senators File an Enemy-of-the-Court Brief," *Wall St. J.* (Aug. 15, 2019); Roger Parloff, "Senator Sheldon Whitehouse Sounds Off on Impeachment, Court-Packing and 'Getting to 67 Votes,' " *Newsweek* (Oct. 21, 2019).

19. Josh Barro, "Fact-Free Conservative Media Is a Symptom of GOP Troubles, Not a Cause," *Bus. Insider* (Oct. 24, 2016).

20. *Ibid.*

21. Brief of Sen. Sheldon Whitehouse as Amicus Curiae in Support of Respondent, Kisor v. Wilkie, 139 S. Ct. 2400 (2019).

22. Jackie Calmes, *Dissent: The Radicalization of the Republican Party and Its Capture of the Court* 25 (2021).

23. "Examining the Impact from This Week's Revelations from the Capitol Attack," NPR (Dec. 16, 2021).

Chapter Eight: Super PACs, 501(c)s, and Corporate Shareholders

1. Michelle Ye Hee Lee, "Eleven Donors Have Plowed $1 Billion into Super PACs Since They Were Created," *Wash. Post* (Oct. 26, 2018).

2. Rev. Proc. 2018-38, 2018-31 IRB 280.

3. Dan Carroll et al., "2021 CPA-Zicklin Index of Corporate Political Disclosure and Accountability," *Ctr. for Pol. Accountability* (Nov. 29, 2021).

4. Letter from Public Citizen to Securities and Exchange Chair and Commissioners (June 14, 2021).

Chapter Nine: The Federalist Society Turnstile

1. Jackie Calmes, *Dissent: The Radicalization of the Republican Party and Its Capture of the Court* 138 (2021).

2. Michael Kruse, "The Weekend at Yale That Changed Politics," *Politico* (Sept./Oct. 2018).

3. *Ibid.* (quoting Ambassador Grover Joseph Rees III).

4. David Montgomery, "Conquerors of the Courts," *Wash. Post Mag.* (Jan. 2, 2019).

5. Evan Mandery, "Why There's No Liberal Federalist Society," *Politico* (Jan. 23, 2019).

6. Kruse, "The Weekend at Yale."

7. Noah Feldman, "Takeover: How a Conservative Student Club Captured the Supreme Court," *Pushkin* (Feb. 23, 2021), https://www.pushkin.fm/audiobook/takeover-noah-feldman/.

8. Kruse, "The Weekend at Yale."

9. *See* Matthew Sheffield, "The Koch Brothers Are Now Happily Aboard the Trump Train," *Salon* (Jan. 29, 2018).

10. Feldman, "Takeover" at 132.

11. Dahlia Lithwick, "Most Americans Think the Supreme Court Is Politically Motivated," *Slate* (Nov. 22, 2021).

12. Ruth Marcus, "The Rule of Six," *Wash. Post* (Dec. 2, 2021).

13. Debbie Stabenow, Chuck Schumer, and Sheldon Whitehouse, Democratic Pol'y & Commc'ns Comm., *Captured Courts: The GOP's Big Money Assault on the Constitution, Our Independent Judiciary, and the Rule of Law* 31 (May 2020) ("*Captured Courts*").

14. Anna Massoglia and Andrew Perez, "Secretive Conservative Legal Group Funded by $17 Million Mystery Donor Before Kavanaugh Fight," *OpenSecrets* (May 17, 2019); Margaret Sessa-Hawkins and Andrew Perez, "Dark Money Group Received Massive Donation in Fight Against Obama's Supreme Court Nominee," *Maplight* (Oct. 24, 2017).

15. *Captured Courts* at 28.

16. Calmes, *Dissent* at 173.

17. Env't Protection Agency, "Fact Sheet: The Clean Power Plan" (2015).

18. *Captured Courts* at 32.

19. *Ibid.* (quoting Judicial Crisis Network, Press Release, "Multi-Million Dollar Campaign Targets Vulnerable Democrat Senators" [Jan. 9, 2017]).

20. Eric Lipton, "Energy Firms in Secret Alliance with Attorneys General," *N.Y. Times* (Dec. 6, 2014).

21. DISCLOSE Act of 2021, S.443, 117th Congress (2021).

22. Anna Massoglia and Sam Levine, "Conservative 'Dark Money' Network Rebranded to Push Voting Restrictions Before 2020 Election," *OpenSecrets* (May 27, 2020).

23. Alyce McFadden, "Secretive 'Dark Money' Network Launches Anti-Critical Race Theory Campaign," *OpenSecrets* (June 30, 2021).

24. Sam Levine and Anna Massoglia, "Revealed: Conservative Group Fighting to Restrict Voting Tied to Powerful Dark Money Network," *The Guardian* (May 27, 2020),

25. "What's Wrong with the Supreme Court: The Big-Money Assault on Our Judiciary," Hearing Before the United States Senate Committee on the Judiciary Subcommittee on Federal Courts, Oversight, Agency Action and Federal Rights, 117th Cong. 6 (2021) (testimony of Lisa Graves, president of the Center for Media and Democracy) ("Graves Testimony").

26. Eliana Johnson, "PR Firm Helped Whelan Stoke Half-Baked Kavanaugh Alibi," *Politico* (Sept. 21, 2018).

27. Robert O'Harrow Jr. and Shawn Boburg, "A Conservative Activist's Behind-the-Scenes Campaign to Remake the Nation's Courts," *Wash. Post* (May 21, 2019).

28. Jackie Calmes, *Dissent* 377 (2021).

29. O'Harrow and Boburg, "A Conservative Activist."

30. *Ibid.*

31. Michael Scherer, Josh Dawsey, Caroline Kitchener and Rachel Roubein, "A 49-Year Crusade: Inside the Movement to Overturn Roe v. Wade," *Washington Post*, May 7, 2022.

32. O'Harrow and Boburg, "A Conservative Activist."

33. *Ibid.*

34. Heather Higgins, "Moving the Needle," *Frontpage Mag.* (Nov. 30, 2015) (transcribing a speech that took place at the David Horowitz Freedom Center's 2015 Restoration Weekend).

35. O'Harrow and Boburg, "A Conservative Activist."

36. Graves Testimony.

37. O'Harrow and Boburg, "A Conservative Activist."

38. Jonathan Swan and Alayna Treene, "Leonard Leo to Shape New Conservative Network," *Axios* (Jan. 7, 2020).

39. *Ibid.*

40. "Voter Suppression Watch: Honest Elections Project Exposed," *FairFight*, https://fairfight.com/honest-elections-project-exposed/ (last visited Feb. 3, 2022).

41. Swan and Treene, "Leonard Leo."

42. "Total Outside Spending by Election Cycle, Excluding Party Committees," *OpenSecrets*, https://www.opensecrets.org/outsidespending/cycle_tots.php (last visited Feb. 3, 2022).

43. *Ibid.*

44. *Ibid.*

45. *Ibid.*

46. "Races in Which Outside Spending Exceeds Candidate Spending, 2020 Election Cycle," *OpenSecrets*, https://www.opensecrets.org/outsidespending/out vscand.php?cycle=2020 (last visited Feb. 3, 2022).

47. Karl Evers-Hillstrom, "More Money, Less Transparency: A Decade Under *Citizens United*," *OpenSecrets* (Jan. 14, 2020).

Chapter Ten: The Doctrine Factory and Casting Call

1. Nancy McLean, *Democracy in Chains* 12 (2017).

2. *Ibid.* at xxi.

3. *Ibid.*

4. Steve Eder, "Neomi Rao, the Scholar Who Will Help Lead Trump's Regulatory Overhaul," *N.Y. Times* (July 9, 2017).

5. Anemona Hartocollis, "Revelations over Koch Gifts Prompt Inquiry at George Mason University," *N.Y. Times* (May 1, 2018).

6. Erica L. Green and Stephanie Saul, "What Charles Koch and Other Donors to George Mason University Got for Their Money," *N.Y. Times* (May 5, 2018).

7. Allison Pienta, update to "Report on the Federalist Society's Takeover of George Mason University's Public Law School," *UnKoch My Campus* (Dec. 20, 2018).

8. Zoe Tillman, "After Eight Years on the Sidelines, This Conservative Group Is Primed to Reshape the Courts Under Trump," *BuzzFeed* (Nov. 20, 2017).

9. Mark Joseph Stern, "What the Koch Brothers' Money Buys," *Slate* (May 2, 2018).

10. Eder, "Neomi Rao."

11. Mark Joseph Stern, "Neomi Rao's Flynn Opinion Is Dangerous and Anti-Democratic," *Slate* (June 24, 2020); Elie Mystal, "Trump Appointee Lays out Whackadoodle, Undemocratic Dissent . . . That Will Be Coming to a Supreme Court Majority near You," *AboveTheLaw* (Oct. 11, 2019); Julian Davis Mortenson (@jdmortenson), "The Rao dissent in Mazars might be the most shocking judicial opinion I've read since becoming a lawyer" (Mar. 7, 2020 1:48 p.m., Tweet, https://twitter.com/jdmortenson/status/1236362982587760641).

12. "Interview with Warren Burger," *The News Hour with Jim Lehrer* (PBS television broadcast Dec. 16, 1991).

13. *See* "Questionnaire for Nominee to the Supreme Court," U.S. S. Comm. on the Judiciary, Public Responses of Nom. Brett Kavanaugh, *available at* https://www.judiciary.senate.gov/imo/media/doc/Brett%20M.%20Kavanaugh%20 SJQ%20(PUBLIC).pdf.

14. Garza v. Hargan, No. 17-5236, 2017 U.S. App. LEXIS 20711 (D.C. Cir. Oct. 20, 2017).

15. Heller v. District of Columbia, 670 F.3d 1244 (2011) (Kavanaugh, J., dissenting).

16. Heller v. District of Columbia, 554 U.S. 570 (2008).

17. PHH v. Consumer Fin. Prot. Bureau, 839 F.3d 1, 6 (D.C. Cir. 2016).

18. Emily's List v. FEC, 581 F.3d 1, 9 (D.C. Cir. 2009).

19. Geoffrey R. Stone, "The Many Ambitions That Propelled Kavanaugh to the Supreme Court," *Wash. Post* (Nov. 27, 2019) (review of Ruth Marcus, *Supreme Ambition: Brett Kavanaugh and the Conservative Takeover* [2019]).

20. Gutierrez-Brizuela v. Lynch, 834 F.3d 1142 (2016); Chevron U.S.A. Inc. v. Nat. Res. Def. Council, Inc., 467 U.S. 837 (1984).

21. Margaret Talbot, "Amy Coney Barrett's Long Game," *The New Yorker* (Feb. 7, 2022).

22. Mary Ramsey, "Justice Amy Coney Barrett Argues US Supreme Court Isn't 'a Bunch of Partisan Hacks,'" *Louisville Courier-Journal* (Sept. 12, 2021).

23. Jackie Calmes, *Dissent* 373 (2021).

24. "2017 National Lawyers Convention, White House Counsel McGahn," *C-SPAN* (television broadcast Nov. 17, 2017, at 41:00).

25. Andy Kroll, "Exposed: The Dark-Money ATM of the Conservative Movement," *Mother Jones* (Feb. 5, 2013).

26. David Armiak, "DonorsTrust and Donors Capital Pumped at Least $90 Million into Right-Wing Causes in 2019," *Ctr. for Media & Democracy* (Dec. 3, 2020).

27. Adam N. Glynn and Maya Sen, "Identifying Judicial Empathy: Does Having Daughters Cause Judges to Rule for Women's Issues?" *American Journal of Political Science*, Vol. 59, No. 1, 37–54 (January 2015).

28. Jeffrey Toobin, "The Conservative Pipeline to the Supreme Court," *New Yorker* (Apr. 17, 2017).

29. *Ibid.*

30. Rebecca R. Ruiz, Robert Gebeloff, Steve Eder, and Ben Protess, "A Conservative Agenda Unleashed on the Federal Courts," *N.Y. Times* (Mar. 14, 2020).

Chapter Eleven: The Senate Conveyor Belt

1. "Ohio Senate 2016 Race," *OpenSecrets* (last visited Feb. 3, 2022); "Wisconsin Senate 2016 Race," *OpenSecrets* (last visited Feb. 3, 2022); "Indiana Senate 2016 Race," *OpenSecrets* (last visited Feb. 3, 2022).

2. Minority Members, S. Judiciary Comm., 115th Cong., *Review of Republican Efforts to Stack Federal Courts* (Comm. Print 2018) (*"Dem. Judges Report"*).

3. Barry J. McMillion, *Cong. Research Serv.*, R45622, "Judicial Nomination Statistics and Analysis: U.S. Circuit and District Courts, 1977–2020," at 25 (May 18, 2021), https://sgp.fas.org/crs/misc/R45622.pdf.

4. *Dem. Judges Report* at 10.

5. *Ibid.* at 9.

6. *Ibid.*

7. *Ibid.* at 13.

8. *Ibid.* at 26.

9. *Ibid.* at 11.

10. *Ibid.* at 11.

11. *Ibid.* at 6.

12. Sen. Chuck Grassley, "Working to Secure Iowa's Judicial Legacy," *Des Moines Register* (Apr. 14, 2015).

13. "About the ABA," Am. Bar Ass'n, https://www.americanbar.org/about_the_aba/.

14. Barry J. McMillion, *Cong. Rsch. Serv.*, IN10814, "U.S. Circuit and District Court Nominees Who Received a Rating of 'Not Qualified' from the American Bar Association: Background and Historical Analysis" (Nov. 13, 2017).

15. Lydia Wheeler, "Meet the Powerful Group Behind Trump's Judicial Nominations," *The Hill* (Nov. 16, 2017).

16. Letter from Donald F. McGahn II, White House Counsel, to Linda Klein, President, Am. Bar Ass'n (Mar. 17, 2017).

17. Lexington, "Conservative Lawyers Are Among the President's Biggest Enablers," *The Economist* (Nov. 25, 2017).

18. Senator Dianne Feinstein, "Republicans Keep Confirming Unqualified Judicial Nominees," *Law360* (June 24, 2020).

19. *Dem. Judges Report* at 19.

20. *See* Letter from William C. Hubbard, Standing Comm. on the Fed. Judiciary, Am. Bar Ass'n, to Lindsey Graham, Chairman, Comm. on the Jud., U.S. Senate, and Dianne Feinstein, Ranking Member, Comm. on the Jud., U.S. Senate (Sept. 24, 2019) ("Hubbard Letter").

21. "ABA Ratings During the Trump Administration," *Ballotpedia*, https://ballotpedia.org/ABA_ratings_during_the_Trump_administration (last visited Feb. 3, 2022).

22. *Dem Judges Report* at 14.

23. "Diversity of the Federal Courts," *Am. Const. Soc'y; see also* Debbie Stabenow, Chuck Schumer, and Sheldon Whitehouse, Democratic Pol'y & Commc'ns Comm., *Captured Courts: The GOP's Big Money Assault on the Constitution, Our Independent Judiciary, and the Rule of Law* 31 (May 2020) (*"Captured Courts"*).

24. Micah Schwartzman and David Fontana, "Trump Picked the Youngest Judges to Sit on the Federal Bench. Your Move, Biden," *Wash. Post* (Feb. 16, 2021).

25. *Ibid.; see also* Hubbard Letter.

26. "Attorney General Explains Decision to Defend Former President Trump in Defamation Case," *C-SPAN* (television broadcast June 9, 2021).

27. Lamar Alexander, U.S. Senate Committee on Health, Education, Labor & Pensions, "Alexander Statement on Texas Obamacare Court Case" (June 12, 2018), *Senate.gov*.

28. California v. Texas, 141 S. Ct. 2104 (2021).

29. Rebecca R. Ruiz, Robert Gebeloff, Steve Eder, and Ben Protess, "A Conservative Agenda Unleashed on the Federal Courts," *N.Y. Times* (Mar. 14, 2020).

30. Madlin Mekelburg, "Fact-Check: How Many Bipartisan Bills Has Congress Passed?," *Austin American-Statesman* (Feb. 13, 2020), putting the number between 251 and 275; James Crowley, "'Grim Reaper' Mitch McConnell Admits There Are 395 House Bills Sitting in the Senate: 'We're Not Going to Pass Those,'" *Newsweek* (Feb. 14, 2020).

31. *See Captured Courts.*

32. Eliana Johnson, "Kavanaugh's Friends Promoted Him. Now They Have to Rescue Him," *Politico* (Sept. 25, 2018).

33. "Supreme Court Nominee Brett Kavanaugh Sexual Assault Hearing, Judge Kavanaugh Testimony," *C-SPAN* (Sep. 28, 2017).

34. Jackie Calmes, *Dissent* 346 (2021); *see also* Matt Ferner, "Here Are the People the FBI Didn't Ask About Brett Kavanaugh," *HuffPost* (Oct. 4, 2018); Jane Mayer and Ronan Farrow, "The F.B.I. Probe Ignored Testimonies from Former Classmates of Kavanaugh," *New Yorker* (Oct. 3, 2018).

35. Jordan Carney, "Ford Attorneys Slam FBI's Kavanaugh Investigation for Not Interviewing Ford, Witnesses," *The Hill* (Oct. 3, 2018).

36. Materials provided to the office of Sen. Sheldon Whitehouse.

37. Letter from Jill C. Tyson, Assistant Director of the FBI, to the Senators Sheldon Whitehouse and Christopher A. Coons (June 30, 2021).

38. Videotape: "Inside the FBI's Internet Tip Line," FBI (2012) (https://www.youtube.com/watch?v=KJlDZ4OMIMM).

39. Matthew S. Schwartz, "'Use My Words Against Me': Lindsey Graham's Shifting Position on Court Vacancies," *NPR* (Sept. 19, 2020).

40. *Ibid.*

Chapter Twelve: Plaintiffs of Convenience and Friends of the Court

1. Anemona Hartocollis, "He Took on the Voting Rights Act and Won," *N.Y. Times* (Nov. 19, 2017).

2. Shelby Cnty. v. Holder, 570 U.S. 529, 590 (2013).

3. N.C. State Conf. of the NAACP v. McRory, 831 F.3d 204, 214 (2017).

4. Ruth Marcus, "Opinion: The Rule of Six: A Newly Radicalized Supreme Court Is Poised to Reshape the Nation," *Wash. Post* (Nov. 28, 2021).

5. *See* Mary Bottari, "Behind *Janus*: Documents Reveal Decade-Long Plot to Kill Public-Sector Unions," *In These Times* (Feb. 22, 2018/March); Celine McNicholas and Zane Mokhiber, "Who's Behind the Janus Lawsuit?," *American Prospect* (Feb. 26, 2018).

6. Brendan Greeley, "ALEC's Secrets Revealed; Corporations Flee," *Business-week* (May 3, 2012).

7. Tarini Parti, "'Dark Money': ALEC Wants an Image Makeover," *Politico* (July 30, 2015).

8. "Nomination of the Honorable Amy Coney Barrett to Be an Associate Justice of the Supreme Court of the United States (Day 2)," Hearing Before the S. Comm. on the Judiciary, 116th Cong. (Oct. 13, 2020) (statement of Sen. Sheldon Whitehouse), citing Email from Michael Hartmann, Rep., Bradley Found., to Leonard Leo, Exec. Vice President, Federalist Soc'y (Dec. 16, 2014); *see also* Sheldon Whitehouse, "A Flood of Judicial Lobbying: Amicus Influence and Funding Transparency," *Yale L. J. Forum* (Oct. 24, 2021).

9. Email from Leonard Leo, Exec. Vice President, Federalist Soc'y, to Michael Hartmann, Rep., Bradley Found. (Dec. 16, 2014).

10. *See* "Client Profile: US Chamber of Commerce," *OpenSecrets* (last visited Feb. 3, 2022) (analysis of US Chamber Institute for Legal Reform).

11. *See* "Client Profile: US Chamber of Commerce," *OpenSecrets* (last visited Feb. 3, 2022) (analysis of total Chamber lobbying).

12. Sen. Elizabeth Warren, Debbie Stabenow, Sheldon Whitehouse et al., "Captured Courts: What's at Stake," *Economic Justice* 10 (Sept. 2020) (citing Dan Dudis, "The Chamber of Litigation," *Public Citizen* [Oct. 26, 2016]).

13. Allison Orr Larsen and Neal Devins, "Legal Scholarship Highlight: The Amicus Machine," *SCOTUSblog* (Nov. 15, 2016).

14. Allison Orr Larsen, "The Trouble with Amicus Facts," 100 *Va. L. Rev.* 1757, 1778 (2014).

15. 2 U.S.C. §§1601–14. Senator Elizabeth Warren and I are actually challenging the Chamber of Commerce for failing to report its funders properly to the Senate.

16. N.Y. State Rifle & Pistol Association Inc. v. City of New York, Pet'rs' Reply at 2 ("The project this Court began in *Heller* and *McDonald* cannot end with those precedents").

17. Jackie Calmes, *Dissent* at 2, 372.

18. Warren, Stabenow, Whitehouse, et al., "Captured Courts" at 37.

19. Myers v. U.S., 272 U.S. 52 (1926); Morrison v. Olson, 487 U.S. 654 (1988).

20. John Dean, *Broken Government: How Republican Rule Destroyed the Legislative, Executive, and Judicial Branches* 102 (2008).

21. Brief of U.S. Senators Sheldon Whitehouse, Richard Blumenthal, Bernie Sanders, and Elizabeth Warren as *Amici Curiae* Supporting Respondents, Seila Law LLC v. CFPB, 140 S. Ct. 2183 (2020) (No. 19-7).

22. Peter Overby, "Koch Brothers Put Price Tag on 2016: $889 Million," *NPR: It's All Politics* (Jan. 27, 2015).

23. Alex Kotch, "Conservative Foundations Finance Push to Kill the CFPB," *PRWatch* (Feb. 13, 2020).

24. Bottari, "Behind *Janus*."

25. *See, e.g.*, Isaac Arnsdorf, "Trump Spawned a New Group of Mega-Donors Who Now Hold Sway of the GOP's Future," *ProPublica* (May 6, 2021) (highlighting twenty-nine individuals and couples); Heather Timmons, "The Three Ultra-Rich

Families Battling for Control of the Republican Party," *Quartz* (Nov. 16, 2018); Shane Goldmacher, "Dozen Megadonors Gave $3.4 Billion, One in Every 13 Dollars, Since 2009," *N.Y. Times* (Apr. 20, 2021); Nicholas Confessore, Sarah Cohen, and Karen Yourish, "Buying Power: Interactive," *N.Y. Times* (Oct. 10, 2015) (reporting that out of approximately 120 million households in the United States, "just 158 families have provided nearly half of the early money for efforts to capture the White House").

26. Kotch, "Conservative Foundations."

27. Brian Mahoney, "Conservative Group Nears Big Payoff in Supreme Court Case," *Politico* (Jan. 11, 2016).

28. Bottori, "Behind *Janus*."

29. Elizabeth Warren, "The Supreme Court Has an Ethics Problem," *Politico* (Nov. 1, 2017).

30. "Editorial: Bombed by the Beeb," *Wall St. Journal* (Sept. 2, 1999) ("The issue in this case is global warming, a topic dear to our hearts because it's such an easy target for lampooning. For even if we were to concede the alarmists' claim that the earth's temperature might rise one degree Fahrenheit in the next 100 years, we can see nothing terrible about having more palm trees in Scotland").

31. "Past Winners," Bradley Prizes, https://www.bradleyfdn.org/prizes/winners /paul-a.-gigot (last visited Jan. 23, 2022). *See also* William D. Cohan, " 'Seems like They Are Obsessed with Senator Whitehouse': Is the Wall Street Journal Editorial Board Too Cozy with the Bradley Foundation?," *Vanity Fair* (Oct. 27, 2020).

Chapter Thirteen: Ripe for Capture

1. Caperton v. A. T. Massey Coal Co., 556 U.S. 868, 873 (2009).

2. Williams-Yulee v. Fla. Bar, 575 U.S. 433 (2015).

3. Williams-Yulee v. Fla. Bar, 575 U.S. 433, 445–46 (2015).

4. Williams-Yulee v. Fla. Bar, 575 U.S. 433, 447 (2015) (internal cites and quotations omitted).

5. *See* Kevin M. Lewis, *Cong. Research Serv.*, LSB10255, "A Code of Conduct for the Supreme Court? Legal Questions and Considerations" (2019); "Closing the Gap in Judicial Ethics," Hearing Before the H. Comm. on the Judiciary, 116th Cong. (Jan. 29, 2019) (Statement of Sarah Turberville, Dir. of the Constitution Project at the Project on Government Oversight).

6. *See Guide to Judiciary Policy, Vol. 2: Ethics and Judicial Conduct*, ch. 2: "Code of Conduct for United States Judges"; Lewis, "A Code of Conduct."

7. John G. Roberts Jr., *2011 Year-End Report on the Federal Judiciary* 5 (Dec. 31, 2011).

8. *Ibid.* at 9.

9. Letter to Justice John Roberts from Sheldon Whitehouse, U.S. Senator, and Lindsey Graham, U.S. Senator, Feb. 17, 2021.

10. Sheldon Whitehouse, "Senator Whitehouse Remarks on Day 3 of Judge Barrett's Confirmation Hearing," *Sheldon Whitehouse, United States Senator for Rhode Island* (Oct. 14, 2020).

11. Naomi Nix and Joe Light, "Oracle Reveals Funding of Dark Money Group Fighting Big Tech," *Bloomberg* (Feb. 25, 2020).

12. Whitehouse, "Senator Whitehouse Remarks."

13. 5 U.S.C. App §109(14).

14. Memorandum from the AMICUS Act Subcomm. to the Advisory Comm. on the Fed. Rules of App. Proc. 7 (Mar. 12, 2021).

15. Stephen R. Bruce, "'Any Good Hunting?': When a Justice's Impartiality Might Reasonably be Questioned" (Oct. 5, 2016).

16. *Ibid.* at 30.

17. *Ibid.* at 10.

18. Letter from Ethan V. Torrey, Legal Counsel, to Sheldon Whitehouse, U.S. Senator, and Lindsey Graham, U.S. Senator (July 12, 2021).

19. Bruce, "'Any Good Hunting?,'" at 12–13.

20. Eva Ruth Moravec, Sari Horwitz, and Jerry Markon, "The Death of Antonin Scalia: Chaos, Confusion, and Conflicting Reports," *Wash. Post* (Feb. 14, 2016).

21. Bruce, "'Any Good Hunting?,'" at 43.

22. Kathleen Wells, "Bill Nelson: Keeping Florida (and Planet Earth) Safe from Big Oil," *HuffPost* (May 25, 2011).

23. Department of the Interior, Office of Inspector General, Report No. PI-GA-09-0102-1 (May 25, 2010).

24. Letter from Ethan V. Torrey, Legal Counsel, to Senators Sheldon Whitehouse and Lindsey Graham (July 12, 2021).

25. Mike McIntyre, "Friendship of Justice and Magnate Puts Focus on Ethics," *N.Y. Times* (June 19, 2011).

26. McIntyere, "Friendship of Justice and Magnate."

27. J. Jonas Anderson, "Court Capture," 59 *B.C. L. Rev.* 1543, 1563 (2018).

28. "Exposure Draft: Judges' Involvement with the American Constitution Society, the Federalist Society, and the American Bar Association," *Ethics & Pub. Pol'y Ctr.* 7 (Jan. 2020).

29. *Ibid.* at 2, 7.

30. 28 U.S.C. § 455(a).

31. Roberts, *2011 Year-End Report on the Federal Judiciary* 8.

32. *Ibid.*

33. *Ibid.* at 8–9.

34. Sheldon Whitehouse, *Captured* (2017).

Chapter Fourteen: The 80 (aka The Prize)

1. Robert Bolt, *A Man for All Seasons* 66 (1960).

2. Norm Ornstein, "Why the Supreme Court Needs Term Limits," *The Atlantic* (May 22, 2014).

3. Linda Greenhouse, "Polar Vision," *N.Y. Times* (May 28, 2014) ("[T]he Republican-appointed majority is committed to harnessing the Supreme Court to an ideological agenda").

4. Eve Peyser, "For Politics to Get Less Tribal, the Republicans Have to Lose," *Vice* (Oct. 9, 2018) (interview with Norm Ornstein); Ornstein, "Why the Supreme Court Needs Term Limits."

5. E.J. Dionne Jr., "Opinion: The Supreme Court's Anti-democratic Actions Extend Far Beyond Roe," *Washington Post*, May 8, 2022; Jennifer Rubin, "The Right-Wing Justices Think They Are Unaccountable. Wrong," *Washington Post*, May 5, 2022; Dahlia Lithwick, "The Supreme Court's Legitimacy Is Already Lost," *Slate*, May 2, 2022; Charles M. Blow, "'The Supreme Court as an Instrument of Oppression," *New York Times*, May 8, 2022; Star-Ledger Editorial Board, "The Stench at the Supreme Court," *The Star-Ledger*, May 8, 2022.

6. Nancy Gerner and Laurence Tribe, "The Supreme Court Isn't Well. The Only Hope for a Cure Is More Justices," *Wash. Post* (Dec. 9, 2021).

7. Sheldon Whitehouse, "A Right-Wing Rout: What the 'Roberts Five' Decisions Tell Us About the Integrity of Today's Supreme Court," *Am. Const. Soc'y: Issue Brief* 13 (Apr. 2019). By the May preceding the Amy Coney Barrett hearings, when my presentation about this went viral, the number was up past eighty. *See* Debbie Stabenow, Chuck Schumer, and Sheldon Whitehouse, Democratic Pol'y & Commc'ns Comm., *Captured Courts: The GOP's Big Money Assault on the Constitution, Our Independent Judiciary, and the Rule of Law* 31 (May 2020) ("*Captured Courts*") at 48 n.6. See also Appendix A.

8. Richard L. Hasen, "Polarization and the Judiciary," 22 *Ann. Rev. Pol. Sci.* 261, 267–68 and fig.2 (2019).

9. Sheldon Whitehouse, "Dark Money and U.S. Courts: The Problem and Solutions," 57 *Harv. J. Legis.* 273, 290 (2020).

Chapter Fifteen: Cases Controlling the Political Process

1. *See, e.g.*, SpeechNow.org v. FEC, 599 F.3d 686 (D.C. Cir. 2010) (en banc), *cert. denied*, 562 U.S. 1003 (2010); Am. Tradition P'ship, Inc. v. Bullock, 567 U.S. 516 (2012); Lieu v. FEC, 370 F. Supp. 3d 175 (D.D.C. 2019), *cert. denied*, 141 S. Ct. 814 (2020).

2. Brief of U.S. Senators Sheldon Whitehouse and John McCain as Amici Curiae in Support of Respondents at 2, *Am. Tradition P'Ship*, 567 U.S. 516 (No. 11-1179).

3. "Senate Leadership Fund Outside Spending, 2020," *OpenSecrets* (last visited Feb. 4, 2022).

4. "American Crossroads Outside Spending, 2020," *OpenSecrets* (last visited Feb. 4, 2022).

5. Brief of Senators John McCain and Sheldon Whitehouse in Support of Appellees at 2, Gill v. Whitford, 138 S. Ct. 1916 (2018) (No. 16-1161).

6. Alex Tausanovitch and Danielle Root, "How Partisan Gerrymandering Limits Voting Rights," *Ctr. for Am. Progress* (July 8, 2020).

7. Rucho v. Common Cause, 139 S. Ct. 2484, 2494 (2019).

8. German Lopez, "How the Voting Rights Act Transformed Black Voting Rights in the South, in One Chart," *Vox* (Aug. 6, 2015).

9. N.C. State Conf. of the NAACP v. McRory, 831 F.3d 204, 214 (2017).

10. Hearing on Dept. of Justice Oversight, S. Comm. on the Judiciary 117th Cong. (Oct. 27, 2021) (statement of Attorney General Merrick Garland).

11. Nina Totenberg, "The Supreme Court Deals a New Blow to Voting Rights, Upholding Arizona Restrictions," *NPR* (July 1, 2021).

12. Ari Berman and Nick Surgey, "Leaked Video: Dark Money Group Brags About Writing GOP Voter Suppression Bills Across the Country," *Mother Jones* (May 13, 2021).

13. Editorial Board, "Opinion: Two of Biden's Top DOJ Nominees Are Subjected to Baseless Smear Campaigns," *Wash. Post* (Feb. 28, 2021).

14. Rucho v. Common Cause, 139 S. Ct. 2484, 2525 (2019) (Kagan, J., dissenting).

15. See NAACP v. Alabama *ex rel.* Patterson, 357 U.S. 449, 466 (1958).

16. "AFP Launches Mail and Digital Campaign Ahead of Kavanaugh Hearings," *Ams. for Prosperity* (Sept. 4, 2018).

17. "AFP Leads the Way in Grassroots Efforts to Confirm Next Supreme Court Justice," *Ams. for Prosperity* (July 26, 2018).

18. Gaspee Project v. Mederos, 13 F.4th 79, 94 (1st Cir. 2021).

Chapter Sixteen: Cases Protecting Corporate Interests

1. Robert Barnes and Steven Mufson, "White House Counts on Kavanaugh in Battle Against 'Administrative State,'" *Wash. Post* (Aug. 12, 2018).

2. See Nat'l Ass'n of Home Builders v. Defs. of Wildlife, 551 U.S. 644, 671 (2007).

3. See Winter v. Nat. Res. Def. Council, Inc., 555 U.S. 7, 33 (2008).

4. See Michigan v. EPA, 576 U.S. 743, 759 (2015).

5. See Summers v. Earth Island Inst., 555 U.S. 488, 500–01 (2009).

6. See Koontz v. St. Johns River Water Mgmt. Dist., 570 U.S. 595, 619 (2013).

7. See West Virginia v. EPA, 577 U.S. 1126 (2016).

8. 42 U.S.C. § 7521(a)(1).

9. See Massachusetts v. EPA, 549 U.S. 497, 532 (2007).

10. See West Virginia v. EPA, 142 S. Ct. 420 (2021) (mem.).

11. Adam Liptak, "Supreme Court to Hear Case on E.P.A.'s Power to Limit Carbon Emissions," *N.Y. Times* (Oct. 29, 2021).

12. Ian Millhiser, "A New Supreme Court Case Could Gut the Government's Power to Fight Climate Change," *Vox* (Nov. 3, 2021).

13. *Ibid.*

14. See Leegin Creative Leather Products, Inc. v. PSKS, Inc., 551 U.S. 887, 907 (2007); Ohio v. Am. Express Co., 138 S. Ct. 2274, 2289–90 (2018).

15. See Stoneridge Inv. Partners, LLC v. Scientific-Atlanta, Inc., 552 U.S. 148, 166–67 (2008).

16. See PLIVA, Inc. v. Mensing, 564 U.S. 604, 625–26 (2011); Mut. Pharm. Co. v. Bartlett, 570 U.S. 472, 493 (2013).

17. See Christopher v. SmithKline Beecham Corp., 567 U.S. 142, 165–67 (2012); Encino Motorcars v. Navarro, 579 U.S. 211, 224 (2016).

18. See Wal-Mart Stores v. Dukes, 564 U.S. 338, 358 (2011); Genesis Healthcare

Corp. v. Symczk, 569 U.S. 66, 78 (2013); Comcast v. Behrend, 569 U.S. 27, 38 (2013); Cal. Pub. Emps.' Ret. Sys. V. Anz Sec., Inc., 137 S. Ct. 2042, 2055 (2017).

19. *See* Perdue v. Kenny A, 559 U.S. 542, 559 (2010).

20. Hugh Baran and Elisabeth Campbell, "Forced Arbitration Helped Employers Who Committed Wage Theft Pocket $9.2 Billion in 2019 from Workers in Low-Paid Jobs," Nat'l Emp. L. Project (June 7, 2021).

21. Christopher Ingraham, "There's a Little-Known Employment Contract Provision Enabling Billions of Dollars in Wage Theft Each Year," *Wash. Post* (Feb. 13, 2020).

22. Sen. Elizabeth Warren, Debbie Stabenow, Sheldon Whitehouse et al., "Captured Courts: What's at Stake," *Economic Justice* 10 (Sept. 2020).

23. 561 U.S. 63, 76 (2010) (Stevens, J., dissenting) ("Neither petitioner nor respondent has urged us to adopt the rule the Court does today").

24. Epic Systems Corp., 138 S. Ct. at 1648–49 (Ginsburg, J., dissenting).

25. Parklane Hosiery Co., Inc. v. Shore, 439 U.S. 322, 343 (1979) (Rehnquist, J., dissenting).

26. Lochner v. New York, 198 U.S. 45, 75–76 (1905) (Holmes, J., dissenting).

27. Brief of *Amicus Curiae* Senator Sheldon Whitehouse in Support of Respondent at 6–7, New Prime, Inc. v. Oliveira, 139 S. Ct. 532 (2019) (No. 17-340).

28. Brian R. Frazelle, "Big Business Powers Ahead with Another Successful Term at the Roberts Court: 2019–2020 Term," *Const'l Accountability Ctr.*

29. *Ibid.*

30. *Ibid.*

31. *Ibid.*

Chapter Seventeen: Cases Restricting Civil Rights

1. Emily Moss et al., "The Black-White Wealth Gap Left Black Households More Vulnerable," Brookings (Dec. 8, 2020).

2. Stephanie Mencimer, "John Roberts: Boy in the Bubble," *Wash. Monthly* (Apr. 7, 2019).

3. Parents Involved in Cmty. Schs. v. Seattle Sch. Dist. No. 1, 551 U.S. 701, 748 (2007).

4. *Ibid.* at 799 (Stevens, J., dissenting) (quoting Le Lys Rouge, *The Red Lily* 95, Winifred Stephens trans., 6th ed. 1922).

5. Cooper v. Harris, 137 S. Ct. 1455, 1480 (2017).

6. Wal-Mart Stores, Inc. v. Dukes, 564 U.S. 338, 367 (2011); Ledbetter v. Goodyear Tire & Rubber Co., Inc., 550 U.S. 618, 642–43 (2007).

7. Vance v. Ball State Univ., 570 U.S. 421, 450 (2013).

8. Univ. of Tex. Sw. Med. Ctr. v. Nassar, 570 U.S. 338, 362–63 (2013).

9. Burwell v. Hobby Lobby Stores, Inc., 573 U.S. 682, 736 (2014); Little Sisters of the Poor v. Penn., 140 S. Ct. 2367 (2020).

10. Gonzales v. Carhart, 550 U.S. 124, 168 (2007).

11. *See* Garcetti v. Ceballos, 547 U.S. 410 (2006); Jennings v. Rodriguez, 138 S. Ct. 830 (2018).

12. *See* Clapper v. Amnesty Int'l USA, 568 U.S. 398 (2013).

13. *See* Dist. Attorney's Office for the Third Judicial Dist. v. Osborne, 557 U.S. 52 (2009); Connick v. Thompson, 563 U.S. 51 (2011); Murphy v. Smith, 138 S. Ct. 784 (2018).

14. *See* Florence v. Bd. of Chosen Freeholders of Cty. of Burlington, 566 U.S. 318 (2012).

15. *See* Glossip v. Gross, 135 S. Ct. 2726 (2015).

16. Dahlia Lithwick and Mark Joseph Stern, "John Roberts Played This Supreme Court Term Perfectly," *Slate* (June 28, 2019).

17. "A Bill for Establishing Religious Freedom," in *2 Papers of Thomas Jefferson* 545 (Julian P. Boyd ed. 1950).

18. *See* Nat'l Inst. of Fam. & Life Advocs. v. Becerra, 138 S. Ct. 2361, 2378 (2018).

19. Hudson Cnty. Water Co. v. McCarter, 209 U.S. 349, 355 (1908).

20. Jeannie Suk Gersen, "Could the Supreme Court's Landmark L.G.B.T.-Rights Decision Help Lead to the Dismantling of Affirmative Action?," *New Yorker* (June 27, 2020).

Chapter Eighteen: Cases Advancing a Far-Right Social Agenda

1. Hugh Hewitt, "Opinion: The Supreme Court's 30 Years War Is Finally Over," *Washington Post* (Oct. 22, 2018).

2. Hein v. Freedom from Religion Foundation, Inc., 551 U.S. 587, 614–15 (2007).

3. Ariz. Christian Sch. Tuition Org. v. Winn, 563 U.S. 125, 145–46 (2011).

4. District of Columbia v. Heller, 554 U.S. 570, 636 (2008).

5. *Ibid.* at 639 (Stevens, J., dissenting).

6. McDonald v. City of Chicago, 561 U.S. 742, 791 (2010).

7. Stenberg v. Carhart, 530 U.S. 914, 945–46 (2000).

8. Gonzales, 550 U.S. at 124.

9. Citizens United v. FEC, 558 U.S. 310, 360 (2010).

10. Shelby County v. Holder, 570 U.S. 529, 553 (2013).

11. Becky Sullivan, "What Conservative Justices Said—and Didn't Say—About Roe at Their Confirmations," *NPR* (May 3, 2022).

12. *See* Whole Woman's Health v. Jackson, 142 S. Ct. 522 (2021).

13. Whole Woman's Health, 142 S. Ct. at 550 (Sotomayor, J., concurring in the judgment in part and dissenting in part).

14. "Texas's Unconstitutional Abortion Ban and the Role of the Shadow Docket," Hearing Before the S. Comm. on the Judiciary, 117th Cong. 30 (2021) (testimony of Professor Steve Vladeck).

15. Whole Woman's Health, 142 S. Ct. at 545 (Roberts, C.J., concurring in the judgment in part and dissenting in part).

16. Dahlia Lithwick, "John Roberts Has Lost Control," *Slate* (Dec. 10, 2021).

17. Burwell v. Hobby Lobby Stores, Inc., 573 U.S. 682, 736 (2014).

18. *Ibid.* at 770–71 (Ginsburg, J., dissenting).

19. Bradley Jones, "Most Americans Want to Limit Campaign Spending, Say Big Donors Have Greater Political Influence," *Pew Rsch. Ctr.* (May 8, 2018).

20. Grace Sparks, "Very Few Americans Are Satisfied with Campaign Finance Laws, but Most Don't Know a Lot About Them," *CNN* (Apr. 4, 2019).

21. John Kruzel, "American Voters Largely United Against Partisan Gerrymandering, Polling Shows," *The Hill* (Aug. 4, 2021).

22. Nathaniel Rakich, "Americans Mostly Support Voting by Mail," *FiveThirtyEight* (July 24, 2020).

23. John Bowden, "2 in 3 Support Stricter Gun Control Laws: Poll," *The Hill* (Apr. 14, 2021).

24. Megan Brenan, "Approval of Labor Unions at Highest Point Since 1965," *Gallup* (Sept. 2, 2021).

25. Lydia Saad, "In U.S., Majority Still Wants Less Corporate Influence," *Gallup* (Feb. 1, 2011).

26. Frank Newport, "Americans Want Government to Do More on Environment," *Gallup* (Mar. 29, 2018).

27. Rani Molla, "Polling Is Clear: Americans Want Gun Control," *Vox* (Jun. 1, 2011).

28. "In U.S., Far More Support Than Oppose Separation of Church and State," *Pew Research Center* (Oct. 28, 2021).

29. Ariel Edwards-Levy, "CNN Poll: As Supreme Court Ruling on Roe Looms, Most Americans Oppose Overturning It," *CNN*, Jan. 21, 2022.

Chapter Nineteen: So-Called Conservative Principles

1. Planned Parenthood of Se. Pa. v. Casey, 505 U.S. 833, 845–46 (1992).

2. *Ibid.* at 867.

3. *Ibid.* at 854.

4. Lewis F. Powell Jr., "Stare Decisis and Judicial Restraint," 47 *Wash. & Lee L. Rev.* 281, 288 (1990).

5. Burnet v. Coronado Oil & Gas Co., 285 U.S. 393, 406 (1932) (Brandeis, J., dissenting).

6. Benjamin N. Cardozo, *The Nature of the Judicial Process* 112 (1921).

7. "Confirmation Hearing on the Nomination of Samuel A. Alito, Jr. to Be an Associate Justice of the Supreme Court of the United States," Hearing Before the S. Comm. on the Judiciary, 109th Cong. 319, 342 (2006).

8. *The Federalist* No. 78, at 470 (Alexander Hamilton) (Clinton Rossiter ed., 1961) ("To avoid an arbitrary discretion in the courts, it is indispensable that they should be bound down by strict rules and precedents, which serve to define and point out their duty in every particular case that comes before them").

9. Josh Blackman, "Justice Alito Reflects on His Tenth Anniversary on #SCOTUS," *JoshBlackman.com* (Sept. 21, 2015).

10. "Nomination of Judge Clarence Thomas to Be Associate Justice of the Supreme Court of the United States," Hearings Before the S. Comm. on the Judiciary, 102d Cong. 470 (1991).

11. Gamble v. United States, 139 S. Ct. 1960, 1984 (2019) (Thomas, J., concurring).

12. Adam Liptak, "Precedent, Meet Clarence Thomas. You May Not Get Along," *N.Y. Times* (Mar. 4, 2019).

13. "Confirmation Hearing on the Nomination of John G. Roberts, Jr. to Be Chief Justice of the United States," Hearing Before the S. Comm. on the Judiciary, 109th Cong. 393 (2005).

14. Citizens United v. FEC, 558 U.S. 310, 379 (2010) (Roberts, C.J., concurring).

15. Brit McCandless Farmer, "Why Sen. Susan Collins Voted 'Yes' on Brett Kavanaugh," *CBS News* (Oct. 7, 2018).

16. Transcript of Oral Argument at 80, Dobbs v. Jackson Women's Health Org., 141 S. Ct. 2619 (mem.) (No. 19-1392).

17. Janus v. Am. Fed'n of State, Cnty., and Mun. Emps., Council 31, 138 S. Ct. 2448, 2487–88 (2018) (Kagan, J., dissenting).

18. *See* "Analysis Specifications—Modern Data (1946–2018)," *Sup. Ct. Database*, http://scdb.wustl.edu/analysis.php.

19. Barry Friedman, "The Wages of Stealth Overruling (with Particular Attention to *Miranda v. Arizona*)," 99 *Geo. L.J.* 1, 15–16 (2010).

20. June Med. Servs. L.L.C. v. Russo, 140 S. Ct. 2103, 2112 (2020).

21. *Ibid.* at 2141–42 (Roberts, C.J., concurring in the judgment).

22. Melissa Murray, "Opinion: The Supreme Court's Abortion Decision Seems Pulled from the 'Casey' Playbook," *N.Y. Times* (June 29, 2020).

23. Dahlia Lithwick and Mark Joseph Stern, "John Roberts' Stealth Attack on Abortion Rights Just Paid Off," *Slate* (Aug. 7, 2020).

24. Transcript of Oral Argument at 14, Dobbs v. Jackson Women's Health Org., 141 S. Ct. 2619 (mem.) (No. 19-1392).

25. *Ibid.* at 15.

26. Adam Liptak, "How Activist Is the Supreme Court?," *N.Y. Times* (Oct. 12, 2013).

27. "Nomination of the Honorable Amy Coney Barrett to Be an Associate Justice of the Supreme Court of the United States (Day 2)," Hearing Before the S. Comm. On the Judiciary, 116th Cong. (Oct. 13, 2020) (statement of nominee Amy Coney Barrett).

28. Ashwander v. Tenn. Valley Auth., 297 U.S. 288, 346 (1936) (Brandeis, J., concurring).

29. Chicago & Grand Trunk Ry. Co. v. Wellman, 143 U.S. 339, 344–45 (1892).

30. United States v. Raines, 362 U.S. 17, 21 (1960) (quoting Liverpool, N.Y. & Phila. S.S. Co. v. Comm'rs of Emigration, 113 U.S. 33, 39 [1885]).

31. Citizens United v. FEC, 558 U.S. 310, 398 (2010) (Stevens, J., concurring in part and dissenting in part).

32. District of Columbia v. Heller, 554 U.S. 570, 680 n.39 (2008) (Stevens, J., dissenting).

33. Uzuegbunam v. Preczewski, 141 S. Ct. 792, 804 (2021) (Roberts, C.J., dissenting).

34. *Citizens United*, 558 U.S. at 357, 360.

35. *See* Michael Dimock, "How Americans View Trust, Facts, and Democracy Today," *Pew Rsch. Ctr.* (Feb. 19, 2020).

36. Brief of U.S. Senators Sheldon Whitehouse and John McCain as Amici Curiae in Support of Respondents at 5, Am. Tradition P'ship v. Bullock, 567 U.S. 516 (2012) (No. 11-1179).

37. *Citizens United*, 558 U.S. at 400.

38. Garrett Epps, "When the Supreme Court Doesn't Care About Facts," *The Atlantic* (Feb. 27, 2018).

39. *Ibid.*

40. Brianne J. Gorod, "Where Are the Facts?," *Take Care Blog* (Mar. 1, 2018).

41. *Ibid.*

42. Horne v. Flores, 557 U.S. 433, 498 (2009) (Breyer, J., dissenting).

43. Calvin TerBeek, "The Kavanaugh Nomination and Originalism as 'Counterrevolutionary,'" *A House Divided* (Sept. 26, 2018).

44. Richard A. Posner, *Overcoming Law* 245 (1995).

45. Sheldon Whitehouse et al., "What's at Stake: Gun Safety" 5 (2020) (quoting Michael Waldman, "How the NRA Rewrote the Second Amendment," *Brennan Ctr.* [May 20, 2014]).

46. Richard A. Posner, "In Defense of Looseness," *New Republic* (Aug. 27, 2008).

47. "National Rifle Ass'n," *OpenSecrets* (last visited Feb. 5, 2022).

48. Marquette Nat'l Bank of Minneapolis v. First of Omaha Serv. Corp., 439 U.S. 299, 314 (1978).

49. *See* United States v. Lopez, 514 U.S. 549, 567–68 (1995); Gonzales v. Raich, 545 U.S. 1, 33 (2005) (Scalia, J., concurring in the judgment).

50. *See* Bush v. Gore, 531 U.S. 98 (2000); Democratic Nat'l Comm. v. Wis. State Legislature, 141 S. Ct. 28, 28–30 (2020) (mem.) (Gorsuch, J., concurring in denial of application to vacate stay).

51. Harris v. Quinn, 573 U.S. 616, 656–57 (2014).

52. AT&T Mobility LLC v. Concepcion, 563 U.S. 333, 352 (2011).

53. Parents Involved in Cmty. Schs. v. Seattle Sch. Dist. No. 1, 551 U.S. 701, 745–78 (2007).

54. Am. Tradition P'ship, Inc. v. Bullock, 567 U.S. 516, 516–17 (2012) (per curiam).

55. "Confirmation Hearing on the Nomination of John G. Roberts, Jr. to Be Chief Justice of the United States," Hearing Before the S. Comm. on the Judiciary, 109th Cong. 56 (2005).

56. Lynn Adelman, "The Roberts Court's Assault on Democracy," 14 *Harv. L. & Pol'y Rev.* 131, 131 (2019).

57. Dahlia Lithwick, "John Roberts Has Lost Control," *Slate* (Dec. 10, 2021).

58. *See* Ocol v. Chi. Tchrs. Union, 142 S. Ct. 423 (2021) (mem.) (denying certiorari to party seeking to extend *Janus* to bar dues).

59. *See* Jennifer Mueller, *The Paycheck Problem*, 20 *U. Penn. J. of Const. L.* 561 (2018) (reporting how the Court treats "compelled subsidy of speech" payments differently if they are going to a union or a corporation).

60. Dunn v. Ray, 139 S. Ct. 661 (2019) (mem.).

61. Murphy v. Collier, 139 S. Ct. 1475 (2019) (mem.).

62. Devin Dwyer, "Conservative Supreme Court Justices Spar over Execution of Muslim, Buddhist Inmates," *ABC News* (May 13, 2019). In another highly unusual move, Justice Alito, joined by Justices Gorsuch and Thomas, "released a lengthy rebuttal, criticizing Kavanaugh's rationale." *Ibid.*

63. Lynn Adelman, "The Roberts Court's Assault" at 131, 131.

64. Dunn v. Ray, 139 S. Ct. 661 (2019) (mem.) (Kagan, J., dissenting).

65. Dahlia Lithwick, "An Execution Without an Imam," *Slate* (Feb. 8, 2019).

66. Dahlia Lithwick and Mark Joseph Stern, "A Federal Judge Condemned the 'Roberts Court's Assault on Democracy.' It's About Time," *Slate* (Mar. 10, 2020).

67. Dahlia Lithwick, "Former Judge Resigns from the Supreme Court Bar," *Slate* (Mar. 13, 2020).

68. Planned Parenthood of Se. Pa. v. Casey, 505 U.S. 833, 866 (1992).

Chapter Twenty: The Shadow Docket

1. "The Supreme Court's Shadow Docket," Hearing Before the Subcomm. on Courts, Intellectual Property, and the Internet of the H. Comm. on the Judiciary, 117th Cong. (Feb. 18, 2021) (testimony of Professor Steve Vladeck); "Texas's Unconstitutional Abortion Ban and the Role of the Shadow Docket," Hearing Before the S. Comm. on the Judiciary, 117th Cong. 5 (Sept. 29, 2021) (testimony of Professor Steve Vladeck).

2. *Ibid.* at 4.

3. *Ibid.* at 7.

4. *Ibid.*

5. *See, e.g.,* Trump v. Sierra Club, 140 S. Ct. 2620 (2020) (mem.).

6. Roman Catholic Diocese v. Cuomo, 141 S. Ct. 63 (2020) (per curiam); Agudath Israel of Am. v. Cuomo, 141 S. Ct. 889 (2020) (mem.); Tandon v. Newsom, 141 S. Ct. 1294 (2021) (mem.).

7. *See* Merrill v. People First of Ala., 141 S. Ct. 25 (2020) (mem.); Andino v. Middleton, 141 S. Ct. 9 (2020) (mem.).

8. *See* Barr v. Lee, 140 S. Ct. 2590 (2020) (per curiam).

9. Vladeck Senate Testimony at 19.

10. Stephen I. Vladeck, "The Solicitor General and the Supreme Court," 133 *Harv. L. Rev.* 123, 126–27 (2019).

11. *See* S. Bay United Pentecostal Church v. Newsom, 141 S. Ct. 716 (2021) (mem.); United States v. Higgs, 141 S. Ct. 645 (2021) (mem.).

12. Roman Catholic Diocese of Brooklyn v. Cuomo, 141 S. Ct. 63, 68 (2020) (per curiam).

13. *See* Food & Drug Admin. v. Am. Coll. of Obstetricians & Gynecologists, 141 S. Ct. 578 (2021) (mem.); *see also* Vladeck Senate Testimony at 12 (explaining the procedural history of the case: "The Court sat on the application for months (complicated, perhaps, by Justice Ginsburg's death while the application was pending). Finally, over three public dissents, the Court granted the government's

application on January 12, 2021—four-and-a-half months after it was filed. During that same time period, the Court: (1) added to its merits docket a challenge to President Trump's proposal to exclude undocumented immigrants from the post-Census reapportionment; (2) received full merits and amicus briefings; (3) heard oral argument; and (4) handed down a lengthy merits opinion. In other words, the Court clearly had time to elevate the dispute to its merits docket if it wanted to; it just didn't want to").

14. Tandon v. Newsom, 141 S. Ct. 1294 (2021) (per curiam) (making new law under the Constitution's Free Exercise Clause).

15. Vladeck Senate Testimony at 10.

16. Whole Woman's Health v. Jackson, 141 S. Ct. 2494, 2500 (2021).

17. *Ibid.* at 2500 (Kagan, J., dissenting).

18. Mark Joseph Stern, "The Supreme Court Overturned *Roe v. Wade* in the Most Cowardly Manner Imaginable," *Slate* (Sept. 2, 2021).

Chapter Twenty-One: The Scheme

1. Michael Tomasky, "The Supreme Court's Legitimacy Crisis," N.Y. *Times* (Oct. 5, 2018).

2. Planned Parenthood of Se. Pa. v. Casey, 505 U.S. 833, 865 (1992).

3. Mark Sherman, "Roberts, Trump Spar in Extraordinary Scrap over Judges," *Associated Press* (Nov. 21, 2018).

4. Bush v. Gore, 531 U.S. 98, 128-29 (Stevens, J., dissenting).

Index

Nader, Ralph, 30, 40
National Association for the
   Advancement of Colored People
   (NAACP), 169–70, 209
National Association of Manufacturers,
   62, 67
National Employment Law Project, 176
National Environmental Policy Act, 31,
   173
National Public Radio (NPR), 73n, 166
National Review, 71
National Rifle Association (NRA), 86,
   89–90; and *District of Columbia v.
   Heller,* 98, 145–46, 206; and *N.Y. State
   Rifle & Pistol Assoc. v. City of N.Y.,*
   129
National Traffic and Motor Vehicle
   Safety Act, 30–31
Nelson, Bill, 146
*Nevada Department of Human Resources
   v. Hibbs,* 101n
The New Climate War (Mann), 69n
New Mexicans for Economic Prosperity,
   68
*New York State Rifle & Pistol Assoc. v.
   City of N.Y.,* 70, 129
New York Times, 67–68, 85n, 95, 102,
   112–13, 147, 196, 199, 223
New York Times v. Sullivan, 32
New York Times v. U.S., 32
New Yorker, 101–2, 183–84
Nixon, Richard, 31, 32, 44, 47–48, 51, 101,
   110, 113, 181
No Left Turn in Education, 46n
"non-delegation doctrine," 174
Norquist, Grover, 72, 97
Northwest Austin v. Holder, 184
"nuclear option," 109

Obama, Barack: and climate change
   issue, 13–14; EPA Clean Power
   Plan, 85, 173–74, 213–14; and
   501(c) organizations, 76; Garland's
   blockaded Court seat, 2, 84, 104,
   108, 119–20; judicial nominees, 2, 84,
   103–4, 107–9, 110, 111, 119–20, 124
O'Connor, Sandra Day, 45, 53, 56,
   144–45, 160, 194
Olson, Ted, 82
one person, one vote, 31
OpenSecrets, 62n, 63n
Oracle v. Google, 141
Oreskes, Naomi, 132

originalism, 96, 183, 205–8; Alito and,
   195; Second Amendment cases, 205–6;
   "textualism," 205–6, 211. *See also*
   "federalism" ("states' rights")
Ornstein, Norm, 156
Orwell, George, 93

Pacific Legal Foundation, 63
PACs. *See* political action committees
   (PACs); super PACs
"The Paranoid Style in American
   Politics" (Hofstadter), 33
Parents Defending Education (PDE),
   46n
Pelosi, Nancy, 13–14
Philip Morris, 39, 66–67
Pienta, Allison, 143
Pitlyk, Sarah, 111–12
Planned Parenthood v. Casey, 194–95
Plessy v. Ferguson, 211
Poindexter, John, 143
Point of Order (documentary), 143
political action committees (PACs),
   45–47, 50–51, 55, 62–63, 74–77; and
   campaign finance rulings, 45–48,
   50–51, 55, 74–77, 163; corporate/
   business, 45–46, 50–51, 62–63, 74–77;
   donor disclosure requirements, 45–48,
   74–77; McConnell's leadership PAC,
   163, 222; super PACs, 45–47, 50–51, 55,
   74–77, 163; union/labor PACs, 62–63.
   See also super PACs
political process, Roberts Court cases
   controlling, 160–71; campaign finance
   cases, 53–56, 160–64; dark money
   cases, 167–71; gerrymandering cases,
   56, 164–65, 182, 202; voting rights
   cases, 165–67, 184, 196–97
Politico, 82, 114
poll taxes, 31
Posner, Richard, 205–6
Potter, Trevor, 54–55
Powell, Lewis, 39–43, 82, 210; career
   and corporate background, 39–40;
   landmark campaign finance rulings,
   44, 47–51, 56; on *stare decisis,* 195;
   Supreme Court confirmation, 42–43.
   See also Powell Memo
Powell Memo (1971 memo to the
   Chamber of Commerce), 39–43, 50,
   51, 56, 62, 81, 82, 221; recommended
   corporate political strategies and
   legislation, 41–42; recommended

About the Authors

Sheldon Whitehouse represents Rhode Island in the U.S. Senate where he is chair of the Judiciary Committee's sub-committee on the federal courts. He has served as his state's United States Attorney and as the state Attorney General, as well as its top business regulator. The author of *Captured*, he lives in Newport, Rhode Island.

Jennifer Mueller is a writer based in Washington, DC. She has worked on issues related to campaign finance and political participation as an attorney, academic, and consultant for more than twenty years.

Publishing in the Public Interest

Thank you for reading this book published by The New Press. The New Press is a nonprofit, public interest publisher. New Press books and authors play a crucial role in sparking conversations about the key political and social issues of our day.

We hope you enjoyed this book and that you will stay in touch with The New Press. Here are a few ways to stay up to date with our books, events, and the issues we cover:

- Sign up at www.thenewpress.com/subscribe to receive updates on New Press authors and issues and to be notified about local events
- www.facebook.com/newpressbooks
- www.twitter.com/thenewpress
- www.instagram.com/thenewpress

Please consider buying New Press books for yourself; for friends and family; or to donate to schools, libraries, community centers, prison libraries, and other organizations involved with the issues our authors write about.

The New Press is a 501(c)(3) nonprofit organization. You can also support our work with a tax-deductible gift by visiting www.thenewpress.com/donate.